National Socialism
and Gypsies in Austria

Gypsy memorial in Salzburg, erected in
1985 (courtesy of Hubert Winklbauer,
Salzburg).

National Socialism
and
Gypsies in Austria

ERIKA THURNER

Edited and Translated by Gilya Gerda Schmidt

With a Foreword by Michael Berenbaum

THE UNIVERSITY OF ALABAMA PRESS

TUSCALOOSA AND LONDON

∞

The paper on which this book is printed meets the minimum requirements of American National Standard for Information Science-Permanence of Paper for Printed Library Materials, ANSI Z39.48-1984.

This book was originally published in German as *Nationalsozialismus und Zigeuner in Österreich* by Erika Thurner, volume 2 in series *Veröffentlichungen zur Zeitgeschichte*, Erika Weinzierl, Ernst Hanisch, and Karl Stuhlpfarrer, eds., Geyer Edition, Wien, 1983. The addition in chapter 3 was originally published in German as "Die Verfolgung der Zigeuner," in *Widerstand und Verfolgung in Salzburg 1934–1945*, Vienna, 1991. Reprinted by permission.

Library of Congress Cataloging-in-Publication Data

Thurner, Erika.
[Nationalsozialismus und Zigeuner in Osterreich. English]
National Socialism and Gypsies in Austria / Erika Thurner ;
edited and translated by Gilya Gerda Schmidt ;
with a foreword by Michael Berenbaum
p.   cm.
Includes bibliographical references (p.) and index.
ISBN 0-8173-0924-1 (paper meets minimum requirements)
1. Gypsies—Nazi persecution—Austria.   2.   World War,
1939–1945—Concentration camps—Austria.   3.   World War,
1939–1945—Atrocities.   4.   National socialism.   I. Title.
D810.G9T4813   1998   940.54'7243'094363—dc21
98-8880

British Library Cataloguing-in-Publication Data available

Jacket cover: Roma survivor with concentration camp number tattoo (courtesy of DÖW, Vienna).

Frontispiece: Gypsy memorial in Salzburg, erected in 1985 (courtesy of Hubert Winklbauer, Salzburg).

Contents

Foreword

Historians must be grateful for Erika Thurner's detailed and meticulous work on the fate of Gypsies [Roma and Sinti] in Austria. So little is known of the Roma and Sinti, and so much needs to be learned, that this volume is a most welcome contribution. Indeed, similar studies should be conducted for each of the German-occupied territories where Roma and Sinti were persecuted.

If Jews were at the center of the Nazi inferno, Roma and Sinti were their neighbors. Their fate closely parallels what happened to the Jews. We must understand the parallels—and also the divergences.

Throughout Nazi rule, Jews were the major Nazi target, but not the only one. Political dissidents—communists, socialists and liberals alike—and trade unionists were persecuted because of their politics. Dissenting clergy were arrested when they spoke out against the regime. German (and later Austrian) male homosexuals were arrested and their institutions destroyed because of their sexual practices; there is no evidence that lesbians were *systematically* persecuted. Jehovah's Witnesses were repressed and incarcerated because they would not register for the draft or utter the words "Heil Hitler"; they were offered the choice to convert and thus go free or to remain in the camps. Most remained faithful.

Beginning in 1939, mentally retarded, physically handicapped, and emotionally disturbed Germans were deemed unsuitable raw material for breeding the "master race"; they too were gassed by the Nazis.

Thus, some groups were victimized for what they did, others for what they refused to do, and still others for who they were. In the Nazi mind-set, the world was divided into a series of lesser races by color, ethnicity, culture, and national identity. Blacks and Slavs were special objects of Nazi contempt.

Three groups were subject to gassing. In his detailed treatment of the Nazi euthanasia program, Henry Friedlander in *The Origins of the Final Solution: From Euthanasia to Genocide* traces the origins of genocide to the T-4 program that targeted mentally retarded, physically infirm, and emotionally disturbed Germans. War permits many things. Behavior that would not have been tolerated in peacetime suddenly seems possible, defensible, and achievable. Thus, the order for the killing of these Germans was backdated to September 1, 1939, and the apparatus that developed over time included gas chambers and crematoria. The personnel who began their careers at Hadamar and other killing centers for the disabled went on to Sobibor, Treblinka, and Belzec. They soon became adept at their craft, developing into efficient killers hardened by wartime experience.

Only Jews and Roma and Sinti were killed by gassing in family groups of men, women, and children. Some 20,000 Roma and Sinti were killed in August 1944, at a time when Birkenau, the killing center at Auschwitz, which had just received 437,402 Jews from Hungary, was killing some 10,000 of them every day. Five thousand Roma and Sinti also went with Jews from the ghetto of Lodz to be gassed at Chelmno. At Treblinka, 2,000 Roma and Sinti were gassed along with some 850,000 Jews.

The written records are few. Unlike Jews, Roma and Sinti have primarily an oral rather than a written tradition, and the documentation of their fate is difficult to obtain. Thus greater still is our appreciation for this work.

The devil is in the details. Thurner works through the details—one country, one community, one victim group. She resists easy generalizations and sweeping understandings of history. Piecing together fragments from diverse sources, documents of the perpetrators, recollections of the victims, statements of bystanders, and formal records and personal memoirs, she gives us an understanding of the fate of the Gypsies in Austria before March 1938 and Gypsies within the Reich on formerly Austrian territory during the post-Anschluss period. She follows the Roma and Sinti even as they move eastward to their doom. The results are impressive. The larger picture emerges against the backdrop of solid, detailed, and historical research.

The general story is clear. It was, in the understated prose of Thurner, "not difficult to operate under old laws" for the persecution of Gypsies. Thus, the legal precedents for many Nazi actions predate Hitler's ascent to power while the impetus often came from the provinces and only then shifted to Berlin. Once the pattern of persecution began, it moved in an inconsistent and at times illogical way. The race theoreticians first had to create the foundation for the persecution of Roma and Sinti. Unlike the Jews, among whom *Mischlinge* ("half-breed") Jews were often protected, Germany's racial thinkers believed that the half-breeds were even more threatening to Germany than those Gypsies who had not intermarried. Consequently, full Gypsies were protected for a time, whereas half Gypsies were victimized much earlier. For racial thinkers, Gypsies presented yet another problem; because of their origins, they were considered Aryan, but outsiders. The word used was "asocial."

Roma and Sinti were less central to Nazi ideology than the Jews; nonetheless, the fate planned for them was quite lethal. As noted later in this book (chapter 2), one racial thinker stated that "the fact that this second most important foreign racial group does not form as strong a racial menace as the Jews is due to their small number, their mental inferiority and their asocial way of life which could not penetrate into the leading stratum of our people as the Jews did." The Germans were less fearful that the Roma and Sinti would undermine or endanger the German people as a whole the way Jewish intellectuals supposedly did. They were regarded as "more of a pest than a danger." Still, Thurner documents the German attack against the Roma and Sinti decree by decree and camp by camp, tracing the journey from persecution to "extermination through work" and gassing.

Perhaps the only element of Nazi anti-Gypsy policy that remains unclear is whether indeed there was a decision to impose a "final solution to the Gypsy problem" on the meaning that the words "final solution to the Jewish problem" would take on by the summer of 1942, namely, the systematic elimination of all Gypsies—men, women, and children—everywhere. I think that this is the major difference in the fate of the two communities. There are indications of parallels in the fate of the two communities, but Thurner does not demonstrate a consistency of policy and fanatical determination in the anti-Gypsy policy that characterized German efforts against the Jews.

Still her work is very important for understanding the nuances and details of German policy toward Roma and Sinti and their ultimate fate in the Third Reich. It is a work well worth pondering, a model of what kind of scholarship is required for us to gain a more complete picture of all that happened as the Nazis attempted to impose their new world order.

Michael Berenbaum
Survivors of the Shoah Visual History Foundation

Editor/Translator's Introduction

Some years ago, Professor Steven T. Katz suggested that I might consider translating Erika Thurner's book, *Nationalsozialismus und Zigeuner in Österreich*, into English. Dr. Thurner is an Austrian scholar who has devoted considerable energy and scholarly effort to the illumination of the plight of the Gypsies in Austria during the Nazi rule. Since her research for this book, she has become quite an advocate for the human rights of the Roma and Sinti, who continue to experience social discrimination not only in Europe but also worldwide.

The purpose of this book is both modest and ambitious. The extensive, painstaking study focuses on two central areas of Gypsy persecution in Austria—Salzburg and Lackenbach. The author illuminates the reality behind the benign-sounding designation "camp." Much of the research is archival, both from the extensive files of the Archives for the Documentation of the Austrian Resistance (DÖW) and from unpublished original documents located by the author in Gypsy camp Salzburg in August of 1981.

Until this study appeared, little was known about these two camps. In fact, until then, the existence of a Gypsy camp in Salzburg had not been discussed in the literature. And even this study, in German, is not accessible to most English-speaking scholars. In the fifteen years since the publication of the book, general public awareness of Gypsy suffering has increased both in the United States and in Austria, also spurring scholarly interest in the topic. Interest has grown especially in the United States since the establishment of the United States Holocaust Memorial Museum in Washington, D.C., which features Gypsy persecution in its exhibits and educational outreach efforts. Even though Austrian Gypsies numbered only about eleven thousand, a tiny fraction of the estimated five million worldwide, their suffering nevertheless provides us with an understanding of Nazi attitudes and policies toward this minority population.

I would like to add a word of explanation regarding the translation. All translations are to a degree interpretation. I hope that I remain true to the author's intent in my rendition. Most of the changes I made are not textual, but technical, concerning footnotes, chapter numbering, subchapters, and further divisions within chapters. Many names of organizations and administrative offices as well as titles are given. At every first mention, the German name as well as the English translation are provided. Any further mention uses only the English translation. A list of the most frequently used abbreviations is provided. First mentions of book titles, journals, and articles are immediately followed by an English translation. Additional references use only the German title.

The word "Gypsy" has been outlawed in Austria. Current Austrian usage refers to Roma and Sinti, actually specific tribes. I have placed the word Gypsy in quotation marks only at the beginning of the book so as not to distract from the text, but I remind the reader that the word's pejorative history does not allow us to use it without qualification.

We not only translated the book but also expanded and updated it. Since the original publication, new information has come to light concerning Gypsy camp Salzburg. Chapter 3 is therefore supplemented by an updated study of this camp. Throughout the book, information was corrected and brought up-to-date. We also updated the bibliography and added a number of pictures, many of which have not been previously published, to illustrate the written information.

Although much time has passed since my initial consideration of the project, I am grateful to many individuals for encouraging and supporting me throughout the various stages. Ms. Nicole Mitchell, my patient editor, who is now the director and editor-in-chief of the University of Alabama Press, expressed an early and enthusiastic interest in the project, suggesting I discuss it with Dr. Sybil Milton. I am grateful to Dr. Milton for suggesting the inclusion of photos and for providing us with an English glossary of Nazi terminology and SS ranks on which I have drawn for this edition. Dr. Milton also supplied us with a list of publications in English for the bibliography. Professor Jack Nusan Porter provided valuable criticism and generously shared his knowledge of Gypsy resources and literature with us. I would also like to thank Professor Steven T. Katz for his long-standing, enthusiastic support and ongoing encouragement to complete this project.

We are deeply grateful to Dr. Michael Berenbaum, president and chief executive officer of the Survivors of the Shoah Visual History Foundation, for providing the foreword and for placing this study in the overall context of Holocaust and Gypsy scholarship.

Completion would not have been possible without the encouragement and support of the University of Tennessee, Knoxville: the College of Arts and Sciences, the Department of Religious Studies, and especially my department head, Professor Charles H. Reynolds, whose faith in my work has given me the strength to persist. Several individuals within the department sacrificed their time and energy for this project. While I was in Israel in the summer of 1994, Mrs. Joan Riedl word-processed the entire manuscript. Joan's many queries as well as her native command of English contributed greatly to the quality of this translation; her knowledge of Austrian culture helped clarify locations and expressions (Joan's late husband, Dr. Norbert F. Riedl, was from the Burgenland). I am greatly indebted to Joan for the many hours of dedicated work on this project and for her thoroughness in double-checking my translation. In the final stages I was ably assisted by Mr. Bradford Smith, my teaching assistant during the 1995–1996 academic year, who patiently attended to the many complicated details of final editing. Mr. Barry Danilowitz, my 1996–1997 teaching assistant, cheerfully cooperated and, through his computer expertise, greatly facilitated the adjustment of thousands of details and the processing of nearly eight hundred endnotes so that we could bring this project to closure. Mrs. Debbie Myers, our departmental secretary, lent her invaluable support in many different ways. To all, many thanks for sticking with this project to its completion.

New energy at the right time is always appreciated. During the final phase, the manuscript was competently and amicably channeled to production by the University of Alabama Press's new senior editor, Curtis L. Clark. Thank you, Curtis!

Finally, I would like to express my gratitude to Dr. Erika Thurner for permitting me to translate her work and for cooperating graciously and cheerfully in the considerable revisions and queries. As Erika indicated in her own introductions, not only is the research into Gypsy persecution fraught with difficulty, but also the publication of such works takes great effort. We have experienced our share of obstacles in giving birth to the American edition as well, and I am very appreciative of the enthusiastic acceptance of the project by the editorial board of the University of Alabama Press.

Now that we have succeeded in filling the gap, it is our hope that this book will not only give readers a better understanding of the results of stereotyping that occur even today but also educate them about Gypsy persecution during the Nazi era, especially that experienced by Austrian Gypsies. The cruel sufferings and senseless deaths of this relatively small group may be multiplied by the millions for the varied victims whose lives the Nazis deemed "unworthy of living."

Dedicated to my children Richard Hugo, Christina Hanah Aviva, son-in-law David Johanan, and his sister Pamela Penina Sarah. May you never suffer persecution.

Gilya Gerda Schmidt

Author's Introduction
to the American Edition

More than a decade has passed since the German edition of *Nationalsozialismus und Zigeuner in Österreich* has been published. Not only was the research regarding this oppressed, particularly taboo Holocaust difficult, but also the publication of Nazi crimes against the Gypsies took and continues to take great effort. For years these activities by individuals and institutions have been ignored and/or boycotted by society and politics. The social marginality of the Gypsies and the lack of interest by the majority complement each other.

Even established historical scholars showed only a very limited interest in the "fate" of societal outsiders. Thus, the study of the Gypsies remained an insignificant, marginal theme, especially when scholars refrained from mythologizing and romanticization. Still today the Nazi Holocaust involving the Roma and Sinti hardly penetrates the societal consciousness in Austria.

In spite of this ignorance, research and study continued within as well as outside the university setting. In Austria, especially young scholars focused on the interwar period (1918–1938) and on the period of the Second Republic (1945–1990), as they set a regional focus.[1] The studies and papers that have appeared [since the publication of my book] brought out a number of factors and complexities; essentially they have confirmed the insights and theses of this 1982 dissertation on the Holocaust.[2] Smaller corrections regarding the Lodz transports of 1941 and the Salzburg camp resulted from [the discovery] of later sources. These additions and changes have been incorporated into this English edition.

Among the more recent publications, emphasis shall be given to the 1993 *Gedenkbuch der Sinti und Roma* (Memorial Volume for Sinti and Roma). Although this volume of sources compiled by the State

Museum in Oswiecim [Auschwitz] did not result in a new insight, it documents the names of the 20,843 persecuted [Gypsy] men, women, and children who were murdered in Auschwitz-Birkenau. Concentration camp numbers and numerical totals are thereby personalized through brief biographical data. At least this book allows the victims a place among the survivors and descendants.[3]

Jews and Gypsies were equally affected by the racial theories and measures of the Nazi rulers. The persecution of the two groups was carried out with the same radical intensity and cruelty. The Jewish genocide received top priority in planning and execution—this because of the different social status of the Jews and also their [larger] numbers. Due to their smaller numbers, the Roma and Sinti were [for the Nazis] a "secondary" problem.

The Jewish Holocaust as well as the Gypsy murders were affected by the tensions, even contradictions, between ideological and economic motives. Although the Gypsy genocide was intended from the beginning, the element of "forced labor" played an important role when places and methods of implementation had to be decided. At certain times and in certain areas (specifically concentration camps and factories), economic rationales governed decisions [concerning the direct murder of Gypsies], but even here the economic logic was early on affected by the genocidal intent ("extermination through work" in the concentration camps). In the persecution scenario against the Gypsies, the element of labor played an additional role beyond those motives already mentioned. The Roma and Sinti who had been designated as "unwilling to work" by the Nazis were not only to be punished and ridiculed through this forced labor but also destroyed. The Nazis took revenge for the Gypsies' actual or perceived freedom even before their murder. They were forced into the mold of the absolute German way of life and virtues through restriction of mobility, forced labor, slave labor, punishment, and humiliation.

Recently, in spite of limited interest by the majority culture, some action has been taken and supported by previous research results as well as those parallel to this research. In the two central areas of persecution—Lackenbach and Salzburg—memorials have been erected (1984, 1985). A small group of Roma/Sinti and non-Gypsies protested against past injustices and the concentration camp pensions denied them. Even if late, this activity resulted in reparations. In 1988, an amendment for Roma/Sinti reparations was passed.[4] Since the end of the 1980s, several Roma and Sinti organizations have been formed. Their most important success to date has been the recognition of the Roma as the sixth ethnic group in Austria, a feat that occurred in December 1993. This act means the assurance of minority protection and promotion by Austria.

Steps taken in recent years—or these late successes—could, however, not offset the developments since 1945. After the Second World War, Roma and Sinti were banned into anonymity or social marginality with predictably negative consequences. Due to the uninterrupted discrimination that continued after 1945, a majority of the Roma and Sinti suffered disadvantages in all cultural spheres of life. They were not accepted and recognized as an ethnic minority until 1993. As a marginal group they fulfilled the role of and continued to suffer as scapegoats. Until recently, this happened in the form of discrimination in everyday life.

A short time ago, the attacks against the Roma reached a new, sad level. Four young Burgenland Roma became the victims of a right-wing murder attack in the still existing Gypsy ghetto Oberwart, which is located in the southern part of the Burgenland. The cowardly bomb attack—a political attack that resulted in the greatest number of victims since 1945—has created an unexpected public forum for the topic of the Gypsies.[5] What had been impossible for scholarship and long-term educational efforts to achieve has happened in a flash assault via television and the print media that lasted for days. The focus also included a small part of the persecution history.

But will the persecution of the Roma be a topic only for a few days? The memory of our fast-paced age is short-term. There is little time for an examination of long-term misdevelopments and of our own poor attitudes. And yet, the results surrounding the bomb attack in Oberwart give us hope for the future.[6] Funeral ceremonies for the murdered men turned into a public demonstration of solidarity. Solidarity with the Roma—against their persecutors and murderers—that has never happened before!

Author's Introduction
to the First Edition

For many people, the persecution and murder of Austrian Gypsies seems to be a marginal problem, in magnitude as well as in political importance of the group. Throughout the centuries, hardly another ethnic minority has been characterized as negatively as the Gypsies. In spite of serious reservations, in this volume the a priori discriminatory term "Gypsies," which is used in a clearly pejorative manner in everyday language even in the United States, is employed. For the historian, the problem arises again and again regarding to what degree the terms from this period may be used or should be replaced by new ones, created by the victims themselves or by scholars. In our case, the alternative would be Sinti or Roma, but this creates the danger that through the use of these terms the connection to the predecessors, who were persecuted as Gypsies, will be lost. Since the sources use this term, it would be necessary to produce a translation of sorts that might be confusing.

National Socialism's Gypsy politics occupy a rather subordinate place in [Holocaust] scholarship. This is in large part due to the fact that Gypsies are often denied the opportunity to articulate their experiences and that those who deal with this problem meet with only a minimal response. But with the choice of this topic I also do not wish to go to the other extreme. Gypsies are a group who were exposed to racist persecution by the National Socialist regime, and it is precisely the example of this group that helps to illuminate the character of fascism.

Already long before National Socialism, Gypsies were given the epithet of "asocial," and Ernst Tugendhat correctly notes that this prejudice is "merely the reflex of our own asocial way of life": "We call them asocial, because they do not wish to assimilate into our society which glorifies individual achievement."[1] The unfortunate side effect of this social prejudice was the lengthy post–World War II debate over reparations for the persecuted Gypsies, and there is no doubt that the Gypsies suffered a great injustice in this juridical maze.

The theme of this study will be the reality behind the benign-sounding designation "camp." In this context, it was imperative for me to deal with the problems of the typology and terminology of these "camps." This does not mean a sterile classification and categorization. Rather, the resolution of this question [of typology and terminology] can illuminate the meaning of the camps for the victims. In this context it was especially valuable to include the eyewitness accounts of the victims, for only through these reports can we grasp the human dimension.

One could hardly imagine this kind of study without the pioneering efforts of the recently deceased Selma Steinmetz. As early as 1966 she published in German the first scholarly study of the National Socialist genocide of the Gypsies.[2] Leopold Banny, dentist in Lackenbach, provided valuable tips that allowed me to use hitherto unknown source material from the onetime headquarters building [in Lackenbach] for this study. An additional precondition [for this study] was the rich holdings of the *Dokumentationsarchiv des Österreichischen Widerstands* (DÖW) [Archives for the Documentation of the Austrian Resistance] and consultations with their scholars. It would be impossible to name all those individuals who furthered my work in many different ways, and I would herewith like to express a collective thank you.

Abbreviations

AVA   Allgemeines Verwaltungsarchiv [General Administrative Archive]

BMI   Bundesministerium des Innern [Federal Interior Ministry]

DÖW   Dokumentationsarchiv des Österreichischen Widerstandes [Archives for the Documentation of the Austrian Resistance]

IfZ   Institute für Zeitgeschichte [Historical Institute], Munich

IMG   Internationaler Militärgerichthof [International Military Court]

NSV   Nationalsozialistische Volkswohlfahrt [National Socialist Charity Organization]

RAB   Reichsautobahn [national expressway]

RM   Reichsmark

RMdI   Reichsministerium des Innern [Reich Interior Ministry]

RKPA   Reichskriminalpolizeiamt [Reich Criminal Police Office]

RSHA   Reichssicherheitshauptamt [Reich Central Office for Security]

WVHA   Wirtschaftsverwaltungshauptamt [Central Office for Economy and Administration]

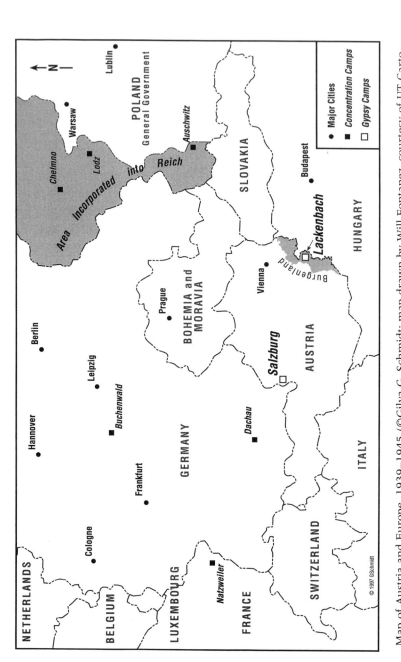

Map of Austria and Europe, 1939–1945 (©Gilya G. Schmidt; map drawn by Will Fontanez, courtesy of UT Cartographic Services Laboratory, 1997).

National Socialism
and Gypsies in Austria

1

Comments on the State
of the Literature and Sources

There was no "Gypsy" scholarship before the end of the eighteenth century. In German-speaking lands, extensive study of such topics began in the nineteenth and early twentieth centuries. Philological studies predominated. They contributed significantly to the clarification of [Gypsy] origins. In the thirties and during the Nazi period, "scientific" writings justifying racial theories predominated over anthropological studies. These kinds of [Gypsy] studies found expression in crime and race studies. They served as the handmaiden to the executive branch. So-called Gypsy specialists put themselves and their biologically and racially motivated studies in the service of the persecutors. This resulted in a whole array of fascist publications that were nearly identical in terminology and message.

Gypsy studies, Gypsy scholarship, and Gypsiology are concepts that emerged after 1945, that is to say, surfaced once again at that time. The majority of the Gypsy scholarship, which was scientifically and socially sanctioned, seamlessly appropriated and continued the Third Reich ideologies. As a result, these scholars insisted on a perpetuation of the outmoded, decidedly prejudicial, Gypsy image. Even if the Nazi period was condemned as a time of injustice, trivialization of fascist Gypsy persecution abounded. At times, this [trivialization] went so far that the work of Nazi race theorists, who had provided the theoretical basis for the persecutions, was defended. These publications attempted exclusively to prove the racial inferiority, asocial attitudes, and criminal tendencies of this outsider group. Based on evidence of criminal activity, the internment of the Gypsies was to be justified within the framework of "crime prevention."

During recent years a change in orientation has become noticeable. This reorientation has been brought about by a new approach in scholarship and a wider interest in Gypsy-specific publications. The thrust came primarily from social historians, sociologists, and social workers in the German Federal Republic, who have tried to consider the desires and ideas of the Gypsies, guided by the realization that the Gypsy has to be a voluntary partner in the study and not [only] the subject [of the study].

The situation of sources on Gypsy persecution and murder during the National Socialist period is extremely difficult. Although international pressure forced German postwar society to produce explanatory studies on the extermination of Jews and provide reparations and mechanisms for coping with the past, there was little interest in making the crimes against the Gypsies public. Rather, in order to escape reparations claims, the tendency predominated to interpret forcible actions by the National Socialists as necessary police measures.

In the war crimes trials, the topic of the Gypsies was almost entirely bracketed, at most mentioned peripherally. The trials of the doctors were the only exception. Here the Gypsies also were a more frequent subject of the proceedings because of their importance as "guinea pigs."

Surviving Gypsies themselves were hardly able to contribute to an elucidation of their fate. The reasons point to the continued discrimination against them. In addition to their limited opportunities due to illiteracy, their credibility as witnesses was doubted by government officials as well as by historians who used them as informants. This distrust, documented in the following 1977 statement by a German Gypsiologist, still overshadows the most recent past: "The inclusion of oral testimony by Gypsy witnesses into a chain of evidence is no less problematic, especially concerning events which occurred a generation ago. . . . While I do not wish to assert that eyewitness reports of persecuted Gypsies are a lie, it is a fact that, during centuries of suppression, our Gypsies recognized certain behavior patterns as conducive to survival, so that they, for instance, choose to answer what they think we want to hear."[1]

However, memoirs and recollections are of extraordinary importance, even if there is the possibility of error and subjective interpretation.[2] This is particularly true for the Nazi period, when opponents of the regime, resistance fighters, and other prisoners could not write down any notes. Thus, the eyewitness testimony of the Gypsies about their persecution can be verified on the basis of the extensive, international concentration camp literature. In this context it is, however, problematic that the accounts of the Gypsies play only a marginal role in the reports of other former concentration camp inmates.[3] Even if the total isolation of the Gypsies in the family camp Auschwitz-Birkenau occurred for spatial reasons, they were seldom integrated into the camp community in other camps. They ranked on the lowest rung of the inmate hierarchy and were even here a minority that was discriminated against. The clever strategy of the Nazis to manipulate one inmate category against another had repercussions beyond the Nazi period. Regrettably, former inmates continue to perpetuate Gypsy stereotypes and prejudices in the reports of their camp experiences.[4] And yet, these memoirs play an important role in the completion and verification [of the Gypsy accounts].

Extensive efforts to obtain access to all pertinent materials in German archives met with little success. In the State Archive in Nuremberg all documents regarding the war crimes trials were accessible; the *Institut für Zeitgeschichte* (*IfZ*) [Historical Institute] in Munich contains copies of the holdings of the *Bundesarchiv* [Federal Archive] in Koblenz. Unfortunately, however, the state of sources on the topic of Gypsy persecution during the Nazi period is extremely poor in the Federal Archives. The Federal Archive in Koblenz responded that "merely widely dispersed individual references, decrees and other texts on Gypsies can be found in some files."[5] In addition, [the Federal Archives] contain decree collection No. 15, "Crime Prevention Measures." This collection contains the only preserved RKPA [*Reichskriminalpolizeiamt* = Reich Kripo Office] decrees concerning Gypsy persecution.[6] Almost all of the ordinances against the Gypsies were of a secret nature. The majority of them "disappeared partly due to the events of the war, and partly through destruction by leading SS [*Sturmstaffel* = stormtrooper] officials based on orders of the Reich Central Office for Security (RSHA)."[7] Publications of the Internationaler Militärgerichtshof [International Military Court] (IMG) provided additional documentation. The 901 defense documents in the war crimes trials of the primary criminals were published in forty-two volumes (Nuremberg 1947–1949). Unfortunately, even this source is of little help where the fate of the Gypsies is concerned.

The attempt to obtain Reich Criminal Police Office documents via DDR [German Democratic Republic] archives also failed. The Central State Archive in Potsdam merely contained copies that were also available in other archives.

The situation regarding the files at Criminal Police headquarters in Vienna was equally discouraging. Since all matters concerning Gypsies, such as camp admissions, transfers, deportations, and similar matters, were administered centrally at the Vienna office, those files would have been of special significance. The impetus for an inquiry into the pertinent files in Austria came, in 1968, from the Dutch Institute for War Documentation. The negative result was as follows: "The files that were housed in the building of the BPD (Federal Police Headquarters) in Vienna were completely destroyed in a fire during a 1945 bombing raid."[8] In addition, we could ascertain that, in 1938, the files of the former International Criminal Police Commission were transferred from Vienna to the Reich Central Office for Security in Berlin and there probably perished "in the confusion of the war."[9] In the *Österreichische Staatsarchiv* [Austrian State Archive] *Allgemeines Verwaltungsarchiv/AVA* [General Administrative Archive], we discovered only one file regarding the establishment of the central office. The Bürckel files there (files of the Reich Commissioner for the Reunification of Austria with the German Reich) provided a few additional references.

The establishment of contact with Israeli and Polish archives as well as with former victims in those countries[10] failed repeatedly because of distance and language barriers. However, accessible Polish material on the Gypsy camp Auschwitz (*Auschwitz Anthologien, Hefte von Auschwitz* [Auschwitz Anthologies. Auschwitz Journals]) and on the Lodz ghetto was used.

Finally, it became possible after all to secure unpublished original documents and to use them for this study. Thanks to Mr. Leopold Banny, a Lackenbach dentist, who years ago wrote an article on the Gypsy camp in Lackenbach [see Bibliography, Unpublished Sources], permission could be obtained from the then owner of the former headquarters building to search the location for still extant documents. This building, lone relic of the Gypsy camp, is about to be torn down. In the postwar period it was first used as a place of business and then as a residence. During a personal visit in the summer of 1981 and after the demolition of the ceiling and of several walls, I found numerous papers from the one-time camp leadership and administration. These documents contribute significantly to our knowledge of Camp Lackenbach.[11]

Extensive preliminary work in this area has been done by Dr. Selma Steinmetz. Above all, she was able to add to the material that had been collected in the Archives for the Documentation [of the Austrian Resistance (DÖW)],[12] especially through her personal contacts with numerous Gypsy families. With her publications on the topic of Gypsy persecution, she became the pioneer in objective [Gypsy] scholarship within the realm of the German language. The trial records of camp leader Langmüller, as well as the first part of the Lackenbach camp diary, which was found in the Vienna state court in 1975, provided important sources. Personal discussions with Dr. Steinmetz and with Lackenbach residents, as well as a perusal of the Lackenbach community doctor's morgue report, provided further information. The picture was completed by detailed correspondence with Professor Johann Knobloch who in 1943 carried out linguistic studies in the Lackenbach camp and by the reports of Dr. Emil Szymanski, the lawyer who represented many Burgenland victims in matters of compensation.

The *Bundesministerium für Inneres* (BMI) [Federal Interior Ministry] also possessed important material. The files that were put at my disposal were based on the inquiries by German authorities in reparations proceedings. For a reconstruction of the conditions in two camps, Lackenbach and Salzburg, many depositions, especially testimony from prisoners and from guard personnel, were collected. These documents provided the foundation for the chapter on the Salzburg Gypsy camp; [they are] all the more important because the appropriate Salzburg authorities were not able to provide additional materials. In 1954, the BMI informed the Bavarian *Landeskriminalamt* [State Criminal Authority], "There are no documents whatsoever about the occupants of this Gypsy camp either here or at the *Bundespolizeidirektion* [Federal Police Headquarters] in Salzburg. Rather, those were at that time sent to the former *Reichszentrale zur Bekämpfung des Zigeunerunwesens* [Reich Central Office for the Containment of the Gypsy Vermin] at the *Reichskriminalamt* [Reich Criminal Authority] in Berlin."[13]

The results of attempts to obtain excerpts from state service registers, that is, police records via the *Landesgendarmeriekommando* [State Police Headquarters] in Salzburg, are hardly worth mentioning. We were able to consult some police reports,[14] witness testimony, as well as articles in the regional press as sources for the mood in the interwar period.

2

Ideological Foundations and Legal Ordinances Regarding the Persecution of Gypsies

When the Nazis came to power in 1933, the arrests of Gypsies increased rapidly, and the punishment for even minor crimes was unusually harsh. For the time being, the National Socialist regime was able to operate according to the old laws against the Gypsies. The anti-Gypsy legislation inherited by the Nazis was in part based on statutes from the fifteenth century. "The Weimar period, the first democracy on German soil, ended with this legacy, on the basis of which the Nazi authorities could operate for a long time without [instituting] new laws."[1]

The Gypsy genocide was by no means a consistent and logical plan. The race theoreticians first had to create ideological-"scientific" foundations for a Gypsy law. For this process, they could fall back on the racial materials and the records of the criminal police during the last few decades.

In times of unrest and distress, the persecution of ethnic minorities and other stigmatized groups increases in extent and intensity. "In moments of change, of social upheaval and political uncertainty, the 'Gypsy problem' gains almost immeasurably in importance."[2] In earlier centuries, this minority had been stigmatized and persecuted for one single reason or for a few reasons. Now, the fascist ideology multiplied and focused on a number of instances of hatred, of prejudice, and of the need to destroy this as well as other minority groups.

The racial theory, which reached back to already existing prejudices that had originated long before fascism, turned out to be a contributor to prejudicial false arguments.[3] The Gypsies, as incarnations of free spirits, were especially suited as objects of persecution. Desires and especially sexual fantasies were projected onto them. The despised group became the scapegoat for one's own repressed desires.[4] In addition, the Gypsies' nomadic way of life was seen as a challenge to the German sedentary way of life. As a consequence of the collective dissatisfaction with the regulated narrowness of a sedentary life, the host people reacted with irrational antipathy.[5]

The perception of the Gypsy personality as an object of law as well as of the natural sciences was a new phenomenon in National Socialism. The notion of race gradually became the center of the National Socialist dictatorship. The theory on which it was founded was based on traditional racial theories, which were diluted by resentment and feelings of hatred.

The National Socialist racial propaganda concentrated almost exclusively on negative statements about "subhumanity." "If the Hitler regime did little for the establishment of nordic racial ideals, it concentrated all its energies on the persecution and destruction of the peoples and ethnic groups whom it defamed as 'inferior.' "[6] The Gypsies provided the race ideologists with some difficulties in their efforts to incorporate them into a racial system. On the one hand they were considered "Aryan" because of their [Asian] Indian heritage, but on the other hand they were seen as "outsiders," like the Jews. However, they were counted among those outsider groups who were included under the category "life unworthy of living"[7] from the beginning. This attitude toward cultural dissidents who were to be murdered and no longer forcibly reeducated meant a decisive radicalization [of their status]. "Those groups who had been classified as less talented and predestined to servitude by the 19th-century race theoreticians, those whom the contemporaries of colonial imperialism had considered as born subjects [vs. citizens], those became for the National Socialist ideologues natural enemies, with whom the Aryans engaged in a struggle predestined by the 'law of blood,' which could end only in the annihilation of one of the opponents."[8]

The anchoring of racial thought in the legislative area ran parallel to the propaganda. "Already in 1933, a primary effort was underway towards a 'new law' that would create a completely new penal code 'in the spirit of the National Socialist *Weltanschauung*' and its 'high-minded evaluation of the ethnic community.' "[9] Everything was to be subordinated to the protection of the *völkisch* values, the safeguarding of the nationalistic way of life. Those who in any way threatened this new order (apparently or actually) had to be eliminated.[10]

In this revisionist atmosphere, concessions were made to certain stylistic flaws in the *Rechtsstaat* [constitutional state founded on the rule of law]. It was no longer the individual who was the highest good, but the securing of a nationalistic way of life.[11] The individual became a thing, an object to be put in the service of the collective.

In 1935, Gypsy persecution was theoretically ushered in with the introduction of the Nuremberg laws.[12] According to Stuckart and Globke, "As a rule only the Jews . . . and the Gypsies are of foreign blood in Europe."[13]

The differing statements by Nazi ideologues regarding the threat that Gypsies posed to the *Volks*-community by their "blood foreign to Europe" revealed the abstruseness and contradictory nature of German racial theory.[14] Here it was less a question of the scientific evaluation of the "Gypsy race" than of the task to ascribe racial inferiority to the "Gypsies." The fact that this "second most important foreign racial group" did not form as strong a racial menace as the Jews "is due . . . to their small number, their mental inferiority, and their asocial way of life, by which they could not penetrate into the leading stratum of our people as the Jews did."[15] The social position and economic situation of the Gypsies were not considered competition to German culture. "The primitive Gypsy ways will never undermine or endanger the German people as a whole the way Jewish intellectuals do."[16]

The Gypsies were considered more a pest than a danger. Any danger stemmed mainly from a mixing with "German blood."[17] Here the Nazis warned earnestly against raising half-breeds, "who pair the free spirit of the Gypsies and the lack of moral and social constraints with the higher intelligence and activity [of the Germans] and thereby become highly criminal and extremely dangerous individuals."[18] Other race scholars doubted whether the Gypsies still existed in a racial sense at all and suspected that "Gypsy" was merely a catch-all term for "all vagrant, begging, neglected, asocial and criminal elements."[19]

In the postwar era, this disagreement on the evaluation of the "Gypsy menace," whether as a racial-political or asocial problem,[20] formed the basis for a legalistic dispute. The question was whether the Gypsies were initially seen by the Nazis only as asocial beings or whether they were persecuted for racial reasons from the beginning. "It is deeply shameful that there is a hair-splitting discussion in our time on whether the Gypsies murdered by the Nazis were actually victims of the National Socialist racial madness or objects of [so-called] crime prevention measures. In this connection, the main point is not only and not primarily the fact that the asocial tendencies which the Nazis attributed to the Gypsies were based on the National Socialist racial theory, but that it is against the very concept of a *Rechtsstaat* to rob human beings of their freedom or to kill them because one expects their future behavior to be contrary to law."[21]

Within the framework of fascist minority politics, the issue was not only the "prevention of inferior primitive genes from entering into the body of the German people." We can discern a ruler-oriented intent that went beyond an ideological framework already in the Gypsy persecutions of the prewar period. The economic aspect played a decisive role in the forcible integration of single and collective objectors via the camp system.

The first step in this direction was the decree on "Crime Prevention Measures, dated December 14, 1937."[22] This decree of the *Reichsministerium des Innern (RMdI)* [Reich Interior Ministry] legitimized "preventive political arrest" as the new instrument [of the state]. The perversion of this preventive principle consisted of its application to eradicate all actual and apparent sources of danger rather than [only] all actual dangers. "Internment in a concentration camp was . . . not seen as punishment for the victim, but rather as an objective safeguarding measure, which had only a limited relationship to the individual's guilt or innocence."[23] That this arrest campaign against [so-called] asocial people also affected Gypsies can be discerned from the guidelines of April 4, 1938. According to the guidelines, this group of individuals (beggars, vagrants, Gypsies, prostitutes, and alcoholics) "was to understand that the National Socialist state does not tolerate any kind of endangering of its *Volks*-community."[24] This was the preamble to the first arrests and incarcerations of Gypsies in concentration camps. After the annexation of Austria, the criminal police also "initiated arrests there for the purpose of crime prevention"[25] based on a Reich criminal police office decree dated March 31, 1938. From this time forward criminal authorities successfully searched for "elements who were afraid to work and asocial," which was not difficult with the massive unemployment that then existed.[26]

Thus, the Gypsies were at first included in the larger circle of "asocial" persons. This classification was only a temporary solution, for it has been "proven without a doubt that already then the Gypsies were discriminated against for racial reasons, even if the scheme of extensive racial persecution had not yet been worked out in its final form."[27] So, for instance, already on October 6, 1938, the Reich criminal police office in Austria ordered the families of imprisoned Gypsies excluded from the support of the NSV [*Nationalsozialistische Volkswohlfahrt* = National Socialist Charity Organization] in the same way that families of imprisoned Jews were excluded. This is one of the numerous cases in which certain measures were instituted in the newly annexed areas to the Reich, whose implementation was delayed for tactical reasons in the *Altreich* [Germany].[28] Just how much these concentration camp internments in the prewar years were influenced by economic motives can be seen from the fact that the criminal police were actually given a specific arrest quota before a certain [arrest] campaign.[29]

The first decree directed only against the Gypsy group was the "basic decree" of December 8, 1938.[30] It demanded "the regulation of the Gypsy question according to racial characteristics." In 1936, the Eugenic and Population Biological Research Station was established under the leadership of Dr. Robert Ritter (from 1937 on, it was called Eugenic and Criminal Biological Research Station). The thorough work of this office and the concentration of Gypsy criminologists in Berlin[31] were to provide the preconditions for this regulation. In addition to police registration and rigorous restrictions of their freedom of movement, "racially pure Gypsies and half-breeds" had to submit to racial evaluation.[32] The results of the analyses were intended to serve as the basis for a future Gypsy law. By spring of 1941, Ritter's office had already arrested twenty thousand people. On the basis of this information, Ritter arrived at the conclusion that 90 percent of this "negative social select group"[33] consisted of half-breeds. "In contrast to the Jews, the Gypsy half-breeds (are) socially 'more inferior' . . . than those who are racially pure."[34] According to

Ritter's negative judgment of the Burgenland Gypsies, "the approximately 8,500 sedentary Gypsies of the Burgenland also stem from such a mixture, which resulted from a relationship of Gypsies with the lowest elements of the most diverse peoples and races of southwestern Asia and southeastern Europe. By far the greater number of these so-called Gypsies is nothing but a Gypsy-like mixture of vermin that has hardly anything in common with the real Gypsies."[35]

On the basis of an anthropological survey of more than one hundred adult Burgenland Gypsies carried out in the years 1937 and 1938, Karl Moravek concluded that "it causes great difficulties to describe these more closely according to physical characteristics and to rank them on a racial basis." His results that differed from other research stated "that almost 10 percent of the examined Gypsies show quite pronounced Nordic characteristics."[36]

"After learning of Ritter's findings, Himmler conceived of a notion for a special regulation which he was willing to push through the party against all kinds of resistance, but whose realization was thwarted by the progress of the war and which today can be reconstructed only with difficulty."[37] If one ignores the obstacle which the course of the war presented for Himmler's plans, then one may assume that he consciously declined legal support so as to forestall interference by the law and the authorities. A Gypsy law formulated in 1939 was never made public; rather, the Gypsy question was tackled by means of police enforcement. "Under the cover of the general state of emergency caused by the war, the National Socialist leadership could pursue its aims much more easily and more quickly via police measures than through laws which, no matter how strict, would have made radical measures even more difficult."[38]

After the Gypsy basic decree was passed, the arrests happened with great speed.[39] Thus, after this point, individual criminal police stations instituted "Gypsy departments."[40] In addition, the hunt for this stigmatized group continued.

The "preventive measure to fight the Gypsy plague in Burgenland" of June 5, 1939, was the first large-scale campaign that affected only Gypsies. This measure was motivated by the economic consideration to utilize the three thousand Gypsies and half-breeds who were "unwilling to work and to a special degree asocial" in camps.[41] Two thousand males over the age of 16 were to be sent to Dachau,[42] and one thousand females over the age of 15 were to be sent to Ravensbrück.[43] It is difficult to determine today whether this number was actually reached.

In the period that followed, additional steps against the Gypsies were superseded by ordinances dictated by the war.[44] For example, a Reich criminal police office decree of July 7, 1939, ordered the arrest and incarceration of all persons "not worthy of serving [in the military]" in the event of mobilization. In addition, it was decreed on August 11, 1939, that in case of war the planned police supervision would become preventive detention. "However, these decrees did not mean that all Gypsies were taken to camp immediately after the beginning of the war; only that the ropes of the ordinance net tightened."[45] Additional decrees that were based on war-related security measures followed, such as the border zone ordinance[46] and the prohibition against fortune-telling.[47] These were measures that could not have been delayed until the long-term solution to the Gypsy question was adequately prepared ideologically as well as practically. However, at the same time, other orders were given that can be seen as steps to the realization of the planned general solution. The arrest decree of October 17, 1939, is to be seen in light of such an end goal.[48] From this time on, the Gypsies were no longer allowed to leave their current place of residence. Between October 25 and 27, 1939, a large-scale arrest campaign and census were ordered. At the same time the criminal police stations were instructed to prepare collection camps for those who would be detained later.[49] This decree was the preparation for the deportation of the Gypsies from the Reich to the *Generalgouvernement* [part of Poland occupied by the Nazis, but not incorporated into the Reich].[50]

After the conquest of Poland, the plan to send all those "foreign to the [German] people" to Poland took on concrete forms. Initially, the fate of the Gypsies was also connected with the intended installation of a gigantic slave state, in which all "subhumans" from the Reich would be collected and utilized. "To the organizers of internal security, Poland seemed an excellent opportunity to cleanse the German people for once and for all."[51] Already on September 21, 1939, [Reinhard] Heydrich, on the occasion of a meeting with his chiefs and leaders of the *Einsatzgruppen* [special killing units], was able to announce that Hitler had approved the deportation to the East, which was to be carried out within a year.[52] Resettlement campaigns from Austria to Poland, based on the incarceration decree, had already occurred before the arrests began. Beginning on October 20, 1939, one thousand Jews capable of working were to be resettled twice a week to construct a shanty town in Nisko.[53] On October 16, 1939, Eichmann suggested by telegraph to [Arthur] Nebe, the chief of the security police, "The simplest method is . . . to attach to each transport a few railroad cars with Gypsies."[54] He furthermore announced that "on Friday, October 20, 1939, the first transport of Jews leaves from Vienna. Three to four wagons of Gypsies can be added to this transport."[55] This activity was then stopped after the second transport. The planned shanties also were not built; instead, all of the 1,383 deportees were simply driven away—after their money and documents were taken from them. Only twenty-two people from these transports are believed to have returned.[56] Evidence is lacking as to whether railroad cars with Gypsies were indeed attached to these transports.

Governor Frank [of the *Generalgouvernement*] is said to have objected strenuously to the threatening burden for his administrative area. At a meeting on March 4, 1940, he was able to state with relief that they had changed their minds about the great resettlement project: "They completely dropped the idea that 7-1/2 million Poles can gradually be transported to the *Generalgouvernement.* It is now merely a question of deporting 100,000 to 120,000 Poles, approximately 30,000 Gypsies, and a number of Jews to be fixed at will."[57] However, a change in plans resulted in the resettlement of merely twenty-five hundred Gypsies from the German Reich to the East in 1940.[58]

A further campaign planned for Austria—all Gypsies from the "Ostmark" were to be deported to the *Generalgouvernement*—was also not carried out. On April 15, 1940, it had been announced that "all other Gypsies from Niederdonau and Vienna were to be brought to Burgenland, so that those also could be arrested during the joint campaign."[59] Even before this could happen, these plans were again discarded. They [the Nazis] had decided to put off the final solution to the Gypsy question.[60] Given that the deportation to Poland had been seen as the best solution, and in the absence of any evidence, we can only surmise why this decision was made.[61] Besides the transportation shortage and the explanation that the exchange of Poles and Germans as well as the deportation of Jews deserved preference, "the fact may have played a role . . . that they did not yet have sufficient documentation for the racial grouping of the Gypsies."[62]

In connection with the resumption of deportations to the East in 1941, five transports were compiled.[63] These consisted of one thousand Gypsies each in Austria and Czechoslovakia. Their destination was ghetto Lodz (Litzmannstadt). Two of these transports came directly from the Lackenbach Gypsy camp.

During the period of more thorough additional preparation to solve the Gypsy problem, no larger campaigns were carried out. However, a whole string of decrees was issued. A series of decrees, from January 1942 on, successively excluded Gypsies from the army and connected organizations. After previous decrees prohibiting Gypsies from serving in the air force and in the youth corps, as of August 28, 1942, all Gypsies and "Gypsy half-breeds" were excluded from active service, as well as from the Reich workmen's service.[64] No later than spring of 1943 those dismissed were interned in concentration camps.[65] The next decree from October 1942, concerning "Gypsy chieftains," was only a farce. Himmler had not yet given up his plans to exclude the racially pure Sinti and Lalleri from the general Gypsy statutes and persecution plans.[66] His plan, to allow this privileged group "to roam in a certain area [according to Joan Riedl, he probably thought of the district of Ödenburg, now Sopron, in Hungary], to live according to their customs and traditions and to work in an occupation suitable to their tribe," reminds one of colonial reservations.[67] The preparations to realize this special plan were still in progress—the suitable group of people had yet to be determined[68]—when this decree was superseded by the next one that contained the final solution to the Gypsy question. The literature names different motivations for the exemption decree of October 13, 1942; however, there is agreement on the marginality of its importance in view of the total solution.[69]

The so-called Auschwitz decree, dated December 16, 1942, was of importance to all European countries occupied by Hitler's Germany.[70] It offered the legal foundation for the cruel act of persecution, whose goal was not only the racial segregation of the Gypsies but also their complete annihilation. In the implementation instructions of January 29, 1943, it was noted that all "Gypsy half-breeds," Roma and Gypsies from the Balkans, were to be sent to concentration camps as laborers "without consideration for the degree of mixture."[71] The destination was the Gypsy family camp in Auschwitz-Birkenau that was established especially for this purpose.[72]

From March 1943 on, more than twenty thousand Gypsies from eleven European countries streamed into this camp. A ruling that granted exemption to socially adjusted individuals, Gypsies with a permanent residence, and members of the armed forces existed only on paper.[73] "It was known that the exemption clauses were only paper decorations of these extermination decrees."[74] The racially pure, who were also exempted from the decree of October 13, 1942—like the others who were privileged—were sucked in by the campaigns if they had not taken the opportunity to go underground early on.[75] "Hundreds of soldiers, who did not even know that they were Gypsy half-breeds, were dragged away from service at the front . . . recipients of the Iron Cross . . . from one day to the next they were imprisoned behind the barbed wire of Auschwitz as asocials."[76] According to the order, this should not have happened, and in individual cases those imprisoned "by mistake" submitted petitions for release. "The criminal police strove at all cost to hide their use of measures which ran contrary to the statutes and rejected the petitions."[77]

Within the framework of this campaign, Gypsies from Austria arrived at the Auschwitz family camp. In the spring of 1943, eight transports brought 2,348 Austrian Gypsies to Auschwitz.[78] Two additional transports also contained Austrians as well as other nationalities. Thus, the total number can be estimated at twenty-six hundred.[79] In addition to the victims who at that time still lived in freedom, prisoners of the Salzburg camp as well as Lackenbach prisoners were deported to Auschwitz.[80] Smaller camps and collection points that still existed in places were dissolved.

The conditions in this totally overcrowded family camp were indescribable. By the spring of 1944, the lack of everything, especially hygienic facilities, had caused seven thousand deaths.[81] At the beginning of August 1944, the Auschwitz Gypsy camp was dissolved.[82] The 1,408 prisoners who were capable of work were sent to Buchenwald and Ravensbrück.[83] From August 2 to 3, 1944, "2,897 defenseless women, children, and men . . . were taken to the crematoria, where they were gassed."[84]

In the Auschwitz trial in 1964, an eyewitness reported on the gruesome end of this camp period: "In the Gypsy camp there was terrible excitement. Someone had called, 'The vans are coming,' and the Gypsies knew exactly what that meant, because many SS-men had lovers among the Gypsy women, and when they had been drinking they told everything quite freely. I hid in the bushes and saw how the Gypsies—men and women—were beaten. Boger was among them. I also saw how children who had hidden under cots were pulled out and taken to him. He abused them verbally—they were four, five or seven—pulling some of them up by the legs and smashing them against the wall."[85]

In the years from 1942 on, additional decrees—besides this horrible Auschwitz decree—were issued. These show, on the one hand, that the free areas for the few Gypsies who were not yet interned in camps because of such special statutes were continuously reduced; on the other hand they are evidence that the Gypsies, at least from this point in time on, were legally completely equal to the Jews. A Reich Security Office decree of March 28, 1942, regarding "labor-related legal treatment of Gypsies" extended all special statutes for Jews in the areas of labor and society also to Gypsies. In addition to other disadvantages, they were no longer entitled to wages in time of illness. They furthermore had to pay a special tax in addition to their income tax.[86]

The decision by the police to adjust punishments that were too mild through "special treatment"[87] also concerned the Jews and Gypsies, as well as the Russians and Ukrainians.[88] For the execution of their sentence, "asocial elements" were to be handed over to Himmler for "extermination through work." In addition, in October of 1942 it was agreed that in the future the courts would leave Poles, Russians, Jews, and Gypsies to the SS. This decision was made with the justification "that the justice system can contribute to the extermination of members of this group only to a small degree. . . . I believe, however, that the handing over of such people to the police can achieve much better results, because they can take measures independent of the legal penal system."[89]

The courts also had the opportunity to exterminate members of this oppressed group for insignificant crimes. This can be seen in the case of Johann Walter,[90] who, on April 3, 1944, was sentenced to death as a dangerous habitual criminal with the following justification: "The protection of the public from this hardened criminal demands his extermination"—he had stolen 300 RM and eleven chickens.[91]

The "twelfth ordinance of the Reich civil law" introduced the complete equalization of Jews and Gypsies in matters of citizenship.[92] In addition to the impossibility of becoming German citizens, they also lost the status of protected individuals. In April 1943—a time when the Gypsy transports to Auschwitz had already been under way for two months—such ordinances hardly touched upon the individuals any longer. They can at best be understood as retroactive justification.[93] A letter from Himmler to the highest Reich authorities in the spring of 1944 characterized the situation. Because of the rigorous application of the Auschwitz-decree—without considering exemptions—the number of still "free" Gypsies was so strongly reduced that the diverse prohibitions became superfluous.[94]

3

The Situation of the Gypsies in Salzburg before 1939 and Gypsy Camp Salzburg (1939–1943)

The Administrative Treatment of Gypsies in Salzburg before the Establishment of the Camp

Gypsy persecution had been a centuries-old practice before the Nazi ascent to power. Especially those measures taken in the beginning did not differ significantly from the acts of persecution already practiced. However, the attitude of the host people to the Gypsies was not always the same. The reaction to arriving Gypsy groups depended on a given socioeconomic situation. The hostility toward Gypsies who were seen as alien to the people varied according to economic, social, and political circumstances.[1] This is the reason that the Gypsies of the 1920s and 1930s were, on the one hand, seen as members of a cohesive, upper-level social group with its own laws but, on the other hand, as racially inferior criminals and asocial individuals.[2] The afterglow of the nineteenth-century operetta stereotype of the Gypsy baron meant that the Gypsy as traveling salesman, juggler, bear tamer, or fortune teller was still met with a certain degree of empathy. But the tendency to destroy the Gypsy minority as a "foreign body" within the sedentary Western culture existed at all times.

In the tense economic situation of the interwar years, the negative image of the Gypsies began to dominate. The state of consciousness for the solution of "this problem which mocks the present time"[3] was already created. If one can take the attitude of the Salzburg leaders, which is expressed in several police reports,[4] as a barometer for the mood of the population, then the demand for persecution and destruction of traveling Gypsy groups had already won the upper hand before the occupation of Austria by the Nazis.

Before 1939, there existed no permanent Gypsy camps or settlements in the province of Salzburg. At the end of 1937 it could be determined that, compared to the previous year, the Gypsy population had increased considerably. These nomadic groups were primarily Sinti from the east Austrian area.[5] In spite of this increased influx, the development was not yet seen as a Gypsy plague because the strict control of the local authorities had succeeded in driving away the Gypsies who had come. The police stations had orders to direct intruders toward the direction from which the traveling group had come or to their place of residence. For 1938 we see a somewhat altered situation. In communities along main arteries, the migration of Gypsies had increased in comparison to earlier years; in contrast, the secondary roads in the valleys showed a decrease in "Gypsy migration." In addition, one could see that after March of 1938 "motorized Gypsies from the *Altreich* rode around the Ostmark."[6]

Although it has been recorded by official sources that there were no punishable actions by Gypsies and no such connections could be made, the same report nevertheless called for a law on the basis of which owners of camp sites would have to register. The Gypsies were to be punished most severely for the slightest damage caused by their presence.[7] These measures were seen as an effective means of fighting the "Gypsy plague."

The intensification of the situation in which the individual districts no longer felt that they could handle the arriving Gypsy groups had to do with the "Tyrolean solution of the Gypsy problem." The tactics of the Tyrolean authorities undermined the return policy that had so far been practiced in the province of Salzburg. "The police stations in Tyrol apparently received the order to prevent the immigration of Gypsies under all circumstances. This, however, leads to very unpleasant occurrences here because the Gypsies who arrive can no longer be sent east."[8] The Gypsies who were sent from Tyrol to Salzburg without prior communication were mostly those who had secretly come to Tyrol from the *Altreich* and who, in addition, had no citizenship. In order to again rid themselves of these Gypsies, the Tyrol police tried to deceive the Salzburg villages. Thus, entire groups were walked to the border and then "chased" to the other side.[9] In another case, the displacement occurred by train.[10]

In a police report from Weissbach near Lofer, the following incident is documented: "Josef Schöpf, the Gypsy, told me confidentially that during the night of May 19 to 20, 1939, all 27 persons were transported by truck from Walchsee in Tyrol directly across the border to the Lindenallee [a place] outside of Lofer and unloaded there. They were accompanied by two policemen in civilian clothing. According to Gypsy Schöpf, upon unloading, the policemen told the Gypsies not to tell where they had come from and in what way they had been brought there. In order that they would keep silent on this matter, the Gypsies were given cigarettes by the policemen and a snack."[11] Since these methods, costly to the villages, were "not a satisfactory method to get rid of the Gypsy vermin,"[12] they [the villages] asked for legal measures for the purpose of radical cleansing.[13] At the beginning of 1939, using "Portschy's writings"[14] and the experience related therein as support, namely "that this race shrinks from steady and productive work, even flees from it, when not otherwise able to get out of it,"[15] a law was requested that corresponded to the arrest decree of October 1939. The response to noncompliance was to be deportation to forced labor camps, reeducation camps, and old age and nursing homes. Individuals without citizenship were to be sent to concentration camps. In addition, a radical solution was demanded through "sterilization of all Gypsies who already have a record because of theft or other crimes for self-enrichment or moral transgressions, even if convicted only once before. On the whole, sterilization (is) to be employed liberally, for this evil must be dealt with at its root."[16]

At this point in time, when the main content of police reports consisted of internment orders, it was reported from the city of Salzburg that there were more Gypsies arriving there as well as in the districts bordering on the city "because more male Gypsies work in the construction of the *Reichsautobahn* [national expressway], etc."[17]

Already in January of 1940 a decreasing tendency in Gypsy migration for 1939 could be verified. "This strong decline in Gypsy migration seems primarily connected to the existing severe measures[18] which have been passed to fight Gypsy migrations. If these measures continue to be enforced, the migration of such Gypsy hordes ought to eventually come to an end."[19] This end came about with the opening of the Salzburg Gypsy camp in 1939. Now Gypsies no longer had to be deported across the district borders, but to the internment camp established specifically for this purpose.

The Founding Phase of Gypsy Camp Salzburg[20]

So far, the existence of a Gypsy camp in Salzburg has not been discussed in the literature. According to the sources, one may conclude that, after Lackenbach, this is the second-largest Gypsy collection camp using forced labor practices. "The camp was officially called Gypsy camp Salzburg and this is how we answered the telephone."[21] Selma Steinmetz, in her monograph, mentions the Salzburg institution.[22] In addition, in the Archives for the Documentation of the Austrian Resistance, there is a file mentioning the Gypsy camp in Salzburg-Leopoldskron.[23]

From documents of the Federal Interior Ministry, the camp history can be reconstructed as follows. At the beginning of the 1950s, inquiries received by the Federal Interior Ministry regarding the existence and function of the camps in Salzburg and Lackenbach increased. The central question—here asked by the Ministry of Justice in Baden-Württemberg, the state court in Tübingen and the Bavarian state criminal authority in Munich—was, "did the Austrian Gypsy camps Salzburg and Lackenbach have concentration camp character? Are the former inmates therefore entitled to a suitable compensation, or could that possibly involve compensation fraud?"[24] In October 1956, the state court in Tübingen requested a review of the information from September 1953 on the basis of a number of testimonies "asking whether, after checking these testimonies, the view can be maintained that both camps had *not* been concentration camp-like institutions from the time of their founding. The additional question was asked whether the conditions during the period when these camps existed may have changed to such a degree that later the assumption might have been justified that they were concentration-camp-like, even if not at their inception."[25]

In carrying out the instructions of the Reich criminal police office, dated March 1, 1939, which resulted from Himmler's basic decree of December 8, 1938, the criminal police station in Salzburg created a Gypsy department. As a consequence, the collection camp for

Gypsies in Salzburg Rennbahn was established in May and June of 1939. Here there are no written documents or concrete notes on how long it existed, but it seems to have been a temporary solution.[26] From the fall of 1939 on, the Gypsy camp in Leopoldskron existed.[27] After initial interrogation, the detained families including their caravans were sent to a fenced-in area in the vicinity Moosstrasse-Kendlerstrasse-Kräutlerweg-Glan. "The Gypsy camp at Kräutlerweg was established in 1939 on orders of the Reich criminal police authority to prevent the Gypsies from traveling freely."[28]

Admissions and Number of Inmates

From 1940 on, admissions came from the entire district. For instance, the Reinhardt family with approximately twenty members was arrested on October 27, 1939,[29] in Dorfgastein and later sent to Camp Salzburg. Until that time—August 13, 1940[30]—they had to work in the quarry. In the chronicles of the police station Schwarzach it is also noted that on August 13, 1940, thirty Gypsies who had been arrested in October 1939 were sent to Salzburg.[31] The wording of the corresponding entry reads: "(By) order of[32] the Chief of the SS and Chief of the German Police [Himmler] . . . the Gypsies in the individual districts were picked up and detained for arrest on October 25, 26, and 27, 1939. On the arrest day, there were 30 Gypsies including children in Schwarzach. . . . They remained in Schwarzach almost a year. . . . By order of the criminal police, the Gypsies apprehended on October 25, 1939, were sent to Gypsy camp Salzburg."[33] Those Gypsy families who, at the time of their arrest owned a caravan, continued to live in it for the time being; later they moved into barracks that had been erected for them or that they had erected themselves, as did the others. In the summer of 1940 the camp was expanded; two large rows of barracks were erected.[34]

According to the documents of the police directorate Salzburg,[35] the camp area stretched over half a square kilometer and had to accommodate eighty to four hundred Gypsies (including children).[36] Several testimonies provide documentation for this figure. Assistant policeman Georg Widl names seventy to eighty inmates; his information covers the period January to July 1942. Adolf Laventin was in camp from December 1940 to April 1, 1943. He remembered approximately three hundred fellow inmates.[37] Karl Eberle, interned in Camp Salzburg for three and one-half years, thought that the number three hundred people was realistic and does not exclude the possibility that it might have been more.[38] A retired policeman who worked for the criminal police during the Nazi period added that "from October 1939 on, approximately 380 Gypsies were stopped in the district of Salzburg and were transported to the nearby established Gypsy camp 'Marienbad' at the beginning of 1940."[39] One can therefore assume that the usual number of inmates was three hundred to four hundred and that a smaller number—as mentioned by Georg Widl, for instance—was temporary.

In the spring of 1940, Nazi producer Leni Riefenstahl came to camp and chose Gypsies to portray smaller roles and to work as extras in a film production in the fall of 1940. Those chosen participated in the production of the movie *Tiefland* (Lowland) in Mittenwald/Tyrol. Probably thirty people, along with supervisory personnel, were involved; they were absent from camp for approximately a month.[40]

Retired police officer Pilz reported on another incident that drastically reduced the number of inmates: "One day all the Gypsy children were taken away from their families in Camp Salzburg and taken to the police prison. However, the reaction and excitement among those concerned led to the cancellation of this action."[41]

Living Conditions in the Camp and Forms of Forced Labor

In the wooden barracks every family (approximately eight to eleven people) was given a boxlike room; in it there was [only] a cot. The other family members had to sleep on the floor. "Since we had our own possessions, we did not receive blankets and other necessities from the camp."[42] Likewise, they wore civilian clothing; they had no regulation camp uniform.[43]

The sanitary facilities were approximately as needed. There were no deaths or illnesses in camp that went beyond the norm.[44] There was no sick bay, nor did a doctor come to the camp. If they were able, those who were ill had to walk on foot, under guard, to the doctor or hospital.[45] Severe cases were sent by ambulance. Pregnant women also were sent to the hospital to give birth.

In the early period, food was sent by the city inn; later there was a camp kitchen in which some Gypsy girls had to help. "Ordinarily the food consisted of a stew with fish and cabbage. For breakfast we received coffee and dry black bread, or a soup consisting of fat, flour and water for lunch, and in the evening [we received] stew. Ordinarily, there was not enough to eat."[46]

Testimony on the subject of labor allows us to conclude that there was a forced labor relationship in Gypsy camp Salzburg. The former inmates reported that all men who could work had to work outside the camp, while the women did jobs in camp and took care of the children. The men, in addition to working on river regulation, also participated in building the national expressway.[47] Several comments let us conclude that women occasionally also performed work outside the camp. Women from the Gypsy camp were seen working in the peat fields and also in the Glan river regulation.[48]

Josef Krems, whose later deportation to Auschwitz is documented in the files of the Arolsen missing persons service, first worked for several firms outside the camp. He testified that in the fall of 1940 the camp was encircled by police; the inmates were no longer allowed to go to their previous work places. "From this time on they had to march to their work places (river regulation) as a group. Besides clothing and food, they received no wages."[49] Friedrich Eberle, also in camp, confirmed the testimony of Josef Krems. "He merely added that he received no wages, but a little bit of cigarette money for the so-called forced labor."[50]

Senior criminal officer [Ludwig] Nessl noted that all Gypsies able to work were "used" as laborers by diverse companies outside the camp, especially for river regulation. Those unable to work and children supposedly were cared for by the state free of charge. In addition, those who worked are alleged to have received wages of the same amount as normal wages, which they were free to spend.[51] The fact that the men had to provide for themselves as well as for family members and children allows the fairly certain conclusion that forced labor conditions existed. In addition, one can interpret Nessl's wording, "all Gypsies able to work were used as labor," to mean there was no choice.[52]

It seems credible that the work detail would leave camp under guard. Here there are several variants regarding the strength of the detail, but these differing details might have to do with the time period and length of time that informants spent in camp. However, there also were situations in which Gypsies were allowed to leave the camp by themselves. For instance, purchases in town were made by Gypsies. They received this privilege only because in this situation escape was possible but virtually hopeless. Escapees hardly had a chance to go underground and were taken back to camp.[53]

In contrast, reports that "permits to leave camp were given out freely and generously" (L. Nessl) apparently were a distortion.[54] All former inmates and assistant policemen who gave testimony stated that leave permits were given only in exceptional situations. "Permission to leave was not given as a rule, only in a very few cases. . . . I only know of one case. Otherwise only kapos received such permits in order to go on urgent errands for the camp."[55]

Guarding and Punitive Measures

A mass of contradictions brings up the question of guarding and the connected restriction of freedom. The testimony of the inmates, but also that of the assistant police,[56] is in drastic contrast to the descriptive accounts by Ludwig Nessl. According to his version, guard duty by the state criminal police in the first years was carried out by one policeman; after a few escape attempts the guard detail was increased to four policemen. In the final years, three watch towers were established. The camp gate was open during the day.[57]

Assistant policeman Widl took the following position regarding this subject: "During my years of service (January to July 1942), the guard detail consisted of one policeman and six assistants. The guard room was at the gate and one could see from the room who came and went. At the gate, no guard was posted. . . . During my tour of duty, there was no guard tower, we also had no machine guns."[58]

Lambert Brandner, assistant policeman from August 1940 to April 1943, speaks of two watch towers, which were manned by an armed guard as well as mobile guards. In addition, the camp was encircled by a two-meter-high barbed wire.[59]

On the basis of Josef Krems's portrayal, guard duty by policemen began in the fall of 1940.[60] Former inmates A. Laventin and K. Eberle reported more significant restrictions of freedom; however, they did not make any distinction in time.[61]

It is especially difficult to come to a conclusion regarding the question of punitive measures and mistreatment. Surely a specific form of punishment contributed to keeping the camp order intact. Physical punishment may have been individual acts carried out by guards.[62] However, the bunker was a fixed instrument that was being used. The official position on this subject—represented by L. Nessl—probably did not reflect reality: "Punishment for infraction against the order was only house arrest, that is to say, a few days imprisonment in the police prison. No police mistreatment became known. Gypsies surely would have reported this, since they were not shy by any means."[63] It is probably closer to the truth that "house arrest was no punishment for an infraction against the order, but a permanent condition"—as assistant policeman A. Netbal testified.[64]

The Dissolution of Salzburg Camp

An official notice from the year 1954 tells us that at the end of 1943 or beginning of 1944 the camp was dissolved and that "no details (could) be obtained . . . about the fate of the Gypsies after the dissolution of the camp."[65] In a retired police officer's memoirs we read, "The majority of the camp inmates was deported by rail to a concentration camp. At the end of 1940 and beginning of 1941 they were escorted to the Salzburg railroad station on foot, minus their belongings which remained in the camp. At the same time a small group from "Marienbad" camp was sent to a collection camp in Laxenburg near Vienna.[66] We do not know what happened to the Gypsies sent to a concentration camp, that is to say, to Laxenburg."[67]

Both reports are incorrect about the date of dissolution. In addition, we do have information about the fate of those concerned. At the end of March and beginning of April 1943, the majority of the Salzburg inmates was deported to Auschwitz. A small group remained at most another week in Salzburg.[68] Afterward they were sent to Lackenbach.[69] We know from the already cited sources, as well as from additional Lackenbach sources, that the Reinhardt family, consisting of seven members, came to Lackenbach. Whether additional people from Salzburg arrived in Lackenbach can no longer be verified.[70] The file card collection of Camp Lackenbach is incomplete; only the first part of the camp diary still exists, and it ends on February 4, 1942.[71]

In the illegal "inmate calendar from Gypsy camp Auschwitz-Birkenau," five Gypsy transports from Austria are recorded in April 1943—one of these from Austria and Germany; which one absorbed the Salzburg inmates can no longer be determined.[72] However, written sources and oral reports confirm that a portion of the Salzburg Gypsies actually was deported to Auschwitz. Josef Krems's Auschwitz stay is documented in the files of the Red Cross missing persons service in Arolsen.[73] Karl Eberle also was deported to Auschwitz-Birkenau with his wife and children. After he spent a week in the Gypsy camp there with his family, he was sent to a work detail.[74]

After the dissolution of the Gypsy camp in April 1943, the Gypsy question was solved at least for the district of Salzburg. From that time on, Gypsies from this area who had not already been imprisoned were sent directly to Auschwitz.

AMENDED PRESENTATION OF GYPSY CAMP(S) SALZBURG: SALZBURG-MAXGLAN/ LEOPOLDSKRON OR SALZBURG-RENNBAHN

From sources that were discovered later on as well as additional interviews, it is possible today to present a somewhat different picture of the Salzburg camp(s). For this reason, we are including the author's slightly shortened chapter on "Gypsy Persecution in Salzburg" from the publication Widerstand und Verfolgung in Salzburg 1934–1945.[1] *In comparing the two studies (1983 and 1991), the arduous reconstruction of the history of the Gypsy Holocaust can be followed clearly.*

It appears that this chapter of National Socialist history was completely forgotten in the postwar period. During preparatory work for the publication *Widerstand und Verfolgung in Salzburg,* additional writings on the Gypsy camp Salzburg/Maxglan (or also Leopoldskron, Kräutlerweg, Marienbad) surfaced. Subsequently, the files of the persecutions could be amended and expanded through oral sources, such as interviews with eyewitnesses. Thus, the chapter "Gypsy Persecution in the National Socialist Show District Salzburg" took on shape and became increasingly complete. The places of action continued to remain dark. Discovering the camp location(s), at that time not "disfigured by a memorial plaque,"[2] occurred through teamwork. Together with residents of Anrain, whose memories still worked—who did not feel incapacitated by responsibility or guilt— the camp location at Schwarzgrabenweg could be identified (for those who know the location; it is between Kendlerstrasse and Moosstrasse).[3] This is private property, farmland without any structures. No material remains give any indication. The camp barracks had already been leveled before the end of the war.[4]

The topographic reconstruction of the Salzburg Rennbahn area followed a similar pattern. In 1940, the horse stalls of the Aigner racetrack had served as temporary housing for the Salzburg Gypsies. Today this location is filled with houses (Ignaz-Rieder-Kai, Johannes-Filzer-Strasse). Most of the residents have moved here from elsewhere and hardly know about the former racetrack with people crowded into horse stalls.

On the basis of the written sources that are available today, we can trace the beginnings of the Nazi Gypsy persecutions up to the establishment of Camp Salzburg-Maxglan/Leopoldskron in 1939 and 1940 clearly. There are no extant documents from 1941 on, with the exception of a document concerning the dissolution of Camp Maxglan in March 1943.[5] This chapter as well as the future fate of the inmates can only be followed through postwar sources and already existing research results.[6] For this research, the victims' reparations files belong to the most important sources—in a twofold way. They provide facts and also give an impression of the nearly unbroken tradition of enmity and prejudice toward Gypsies. The testimony of the victims was granted only "a small degree of probability." The testimony of the perpetrators and accomplices, on the other hand, weighed heavily.[7]

The Establishment of Detention Camps

A conference convened by the head of the Security Office, [Reinhard] Heydrich, on September 21, 1939, decided that all Gypsies who lived in the *Grossdeutsche Reich* [Germany and Austria] were to be resettled in the *Generalgouvernement.* This campaign was preceded by a "detention decree," dated October 17, 1939, that had been ordered by Heydrich in a secret express letter at the behest of Himmler and once more tightened the net of persecution.[8] The police stations and criminal police centers were instructed to register those Gypsies in their administrative area, and to find accommodations for them. From this time on the Gypsies were no longer allowed to leave their current place of residence. At that time, 110 Gypsies lived in the city proper; they were already being concentrated in a collection camp in Maxglan/Leopoldskron. The living conditions in this barbed-wire camp were so disastrous that they provided a danger not only for the camp inmates but for the surroundings as well. The influx of Gypsies into the city continued in spite of the detention decree. The number of camp inmates increased during the subsequent months to 160.[9]

Initially, the Gypsies could still move around relatively freely. For some it was possible to continue existing work relationships. They worked on the national expressway or for diverse construction firms. However, most did not have work opportunities and therefore also no income possibilities. They had to rely on welfare organizations. Especially villages resented this financial burden. They wanted to get rid of the Gypsies and send them to the Salzburg camp. At that time district Salzburg registered fourteen Gypsies, Hallein thirty-nine, and Pongau forty-five.

The criminal police station Salzburg tried to meet the increasing expressions of annoyance and the accumulation of complaints through rigorous handling of admissions to concentration camps. Since two-thirds of the victims were women and children, and since they often could not manage without the men as providers, the consequences of this method were minimal. So, for instance, the head of the Salzburg criminal police, SS Major Böhmer, regretted that "young men aged 15–18 or pregnant women could not be housed or did not wish to be placed."[10] In addition, arrangements were made to protect at least the city itself from Gypsies. They were only allowed to enter for a limited time with special passes. This regulation brought out the farmers. They protested against the disadvantage of the farms that bordered on the city, "which become hunting grounds for the Gypsies, while the city population is spared from this plague," and demanded equal treatment that was propagated in the ideology of the *Volksgemeinschaft*.[11]

The chain of complaints would not stop, but threatened to escalate. With the depiction of these difficulties, the criminal police sent an appeal to the Reich Central Office for Security in Berlin. In addition to the hint of "increased hatred of the population and gravest concerns regarding toleration of the extensive Gypsy plague in Salzburg for much longer," the danger of the Gypsies through fortune-telling and eventual defeatist statements was pointed out. As a way out—and for lack of other possibilities—a central forced labor camp with police guard was being debated.[12]

In early summer of 1940 the consultations regarding the expansion of the Salzburg camp began. The plan was to collect all the Gypsies from the entire district with the continued welfare support of the responsible local office. These preparations were interrupted by the notice of impending deportations of all Gypsies of the Ostmark to the East. From this time on the first transports of Gypsies to Lodz and Belzec began.

The Salzburg criminal police definitely did not want to miss the opportunity to rid the community of all Gypsies (approximately 270). They did everything to fulfill the necessary conditions—arrest of Gypsies through questionnaire and medical exam. For better and smoother management, Gypsies were to be incarcerated in a collection camp immediately (also those from the villages). SS Battalion Leader Böhmer turned to the police and the SA [Brown Shirts] and SS for guard details.

The camp in Maxglan/Leopoldskron was much too small. A suitable place was needed as a transit camp. In order not to miss this favorable opportunity, Böhmer appealed urgently to the responsible offices "since there is no chance to get permission for a late transport for the Gypsies of the district Salzburg."[13] A provisional collection camp was arranged in time in the horse stalls of the Salzburg *Trabrennbahn* (racetrack). However, shortly before the chosen date, the campaign was cancelled because of "transportation difficulties." The Gypsies were to remain until further notice, till the end of the war, in the location where they now lived.

Expansion and Tightening of Camp Conditions

When the deportations to the East were cancelled, no one stated specifically what would happen until the "final solution." In Salzburg they decided to continue the internment. Since no one knew when "the end of the war" would be, the expansion of Camp Maxglan now became necessary for the larger number of persons. The racetrack area had to be cleared at the latest by September 10, 1940.

With the installation of a strictly guarded camp with the character of a forced labor camp, the authorities connected to earlier plans. The city was to provide the additional space. In addition, for the camp expansion and support of the inmates a cost appropriation according to homeland and jurisdiction was intended; and a contribution for the guard installations was expected from the Reich criminal police office. A letter to that effect was sent to Reich criminal police chief Nebe at the beginning of September 1940. The anticipated labor from all Gypsies was expected to lower the cost of upkeep considerably; perhaps some day the camp might be self-sufficient.

Reasons against a return to earlier conditions included the danger of escape; better guarding possibilities; prestige (after all, the liberation of a group of people who had been under police surveillance for some time could harm the image of the police!); and the greater political significance of district Salzburg. They feared that in the meantime the Gypsies might have heard of plans for deportation to the East. A need for this camp was justified because of the possible escape of Gypsies from the persecution measures of the National Socialist regime. Even before an express letter of October 31, 1940, from the Reich Interior Ministry legitimized this situation, the authorities in charge—the Reich governor, the district leader, the SS and police officers, the president, the commissioner, the lord mayor of Salzburg, the director of the labor office, and the criminal police station Salzburg—had agreed "to collect the Gypsies in a concentrated manner, to put them under guard and to assign them to forced labor."[14] Administration was the responsibility of the district capital, and guarding and supervision were the responsibility of the criminal police station in Salzburg. The planned unification of the entire administration in the hands of the criminal police did not fail because of the unwillingness of the police, but because of bureaucratic obstacles.

The return transport of the Gypsy inmates from the racetrack to Maxglan was coupled with an intensification in camp regulations. Two large barracks were erected, and the campgrounds were surrounded by a two-meter-high barbed wire fence. A relatively open camp had turned into one with concentration camp–like character. From this time on the camp was strictly guarded.[15]

All capable inmates had to work hard. Wages went into the camp treasury, so that those unable to work, as well as babies, could also be cared for. In Nazi terminology, these measures were defined as "education in the idea of community." The guarded work details were used for river regulation, building the national expressway, peat cutting, and agriculture. In addition to the daily chores in camp, women, older people, and children had to do projects at home. Daily camp routine was marked by forced labor, poor nourishment, very primitive and inhumane accommodations, and the greatest possible degree of restriction of personal freedom.[16]

Internal organization showed structural elements of large concentration camps. Inmates with camp experience were released on probation and used as assistant guard personnel. The psychological pressure on these supervisors provided an important disciplinary instrument. They tried to maintain camp order on threat of readmission to the concentration camp. The rest of the inmates were threatened with diverse punitive and educational measures—not listed in detail—including the ultimate deportation to a concentration camp. Physical beatings were not specifically ordered, but used.[17]

The approximately three hundred camp inmates in Salzburg had to live under these conditions for about two and one-half years. Already after the first few months there were "positive" results. The work assignments were extremely favorable. The Gypsies received high assembly line wages and surpassed the pace of the free workers. The orders and future contracts far outweighed the expectation of the camp administration.[18]

In addition, a new source of income opened up in the fall of 1940. The Nazi producer Leni Riefenstahl had requested, or rather handpicked, Gypsies as extras and for small roles in her film *Tiefland* (Lowland) shot in Mittenwald.[19] Though it would have been impossible to refuse her because of Hitler's support of her, this intermezzo also had advantages. In the fall of 1940 and in summer of 1941, a group of Maxglan inmates (forty to sixty people, including numerous children) were sent to Krün near Mittenwald for a few weeks under the supervision of two police officers (perhaps also more). The agreed-upon "good wages" went into the camp treasury. Other rewards in the form of clothes, shoes, and pocket money also benefitted the [camp] community. For selected inmates the film production brought some diversion. Conditions were also somewhat more pleasant than in Camp Salzburg. Production demands were nevertheless enormous, especially for small children, and accommodations were horrendous.[20]

Auschwitz-Decree and Dissolution of Gypsy Camp Salzburg

More than two years before the end of the war, the "Gypsy problem" for Salzburg was completely solved. With the publication of the Auschwitz decree of December 16, 1942—Himmler's order to detain the Gypsies in Auschwitz-Birkenau and to exterminate them, just like the Jews—Salzburg was able to rid herself of her Gypsies. In instructions from January 1943, "Gypsy half-breeds, Roma and Balkan Gypsies" were moved to the center of persecution and extermination. Special regulations for "socially assimilated and pure Gypsies" were nothing more than a piece of paper, and they hardly protected victims from transportation to the Gypsy family camp in Auschwitz-Birkenau (Section B IIe). Many memoirs and documents further confirm that different selection instructions were (could be) worded very loosely. In general, local authorities saw the decree as an opportunity to cleanse a particular city (or region) completely of Gypsies. In case of doubt, victims were scrupulously assigned to deportation.[21]

At the end of March and beginning of April 1943, Camp Salzburg was completely cleared. The majority of camp inmates was transported to Auschwitz. A small group was deported to Lackenbach in Burgenland a week later. While those few who were sent to Lackenbach were able to stay there until the end of the war under conditions similar to those in Camp Salzburg, the transport to Auschwitz meant death for the majority of Gypsies. The Salzburg inmates were among 2,760 Austrian Gypsies who arrived in Auschwitz-Birkenau, Section B IIe, in spring 1943. In part, these Sinti and Roma were gassed there during the dissolution of the camp in August of 1944. The others were sent to work or to other camps as medical "guinea pigs"—if they had not died of diseases. There they died or had to participate in the death marches from the eastern camps to within the Reich during the final months of the war. More than two-thirds of the eleven thousand Austrian Sinti and Roma did not survive National Socialism.[22]

4

Discrimination and Persecution of the Burgenland Gypsies

The Social and Economic Situation of the Burgenland Gypsies in the Interwar Period

In Burgenland a completely different situation existed. At least to a degree, the Gypsy politics of Maria Theresia and her son, Joseph II, had a seminal influence on the nature of Austrian Gypsy settlements. Because of the repressive measures [used], the plan for settlement—within whose framework the Gypsies were to be given a certain degree of rights—was not suited to achieve successful integration.[1] Thus the success of the campaign was moderate. Settlement succeeded somewhat only in western Hungary, today's Burgenland. The approximately eight thousand Roma[2] who lived there before the Nazis came to power were descendants of these "forcibly settled Gypsies," that is to say, Gypsies who had already lived a sedentary, or partially sedentary life, for two hundred to three hundred years before.[3]

However, giving up the nomadic way—sedentary life in small houses—was a far cry from integration or assimilation. The economic conduct of the Gypsies was determined by the prevailing conditions in the host country. Thus, many were forced into continued mobility by the necessity to make a living. Even after giving up their nomadic way of life, they remained an outsider group, a foreign body, that was banned to the lowest rung on the social and professional ladder. There are censuses from the time of [Empress Maria] Theresia that identify more than half the Gypsies as migrant workers.[4]

During the economic crisis, which began with the collapse of the monarchy and dominated the interwar years, Austrian peasants themselves lived to a large degree at the edge of minimal existence. Gypsies, as the poorest of the poor, often were forced not only to beg but to steal. Dostal describes this "so-called parasitic or asocial behavior" of Gypsies as a defensive behavior into which they were forced in order to live at all.[5] As a result of punishment for these lifesaving crimes, Gypsies were subsequently forced into criminal behavior. This led to a deepening of the [existing] attitude that was based on prejudice and stereotypes. Hate campaigns in the local press further intensified the hostile atmosphere. At times, some reports even contained actual depictions of their situation: "The life situation of the Gypsy is really pitiful. If he works, he often receives used clothing as pay. How should he have any money? Because of his lack of education, he is always paid at a lower rate for his work. But even a Gypsy feels the terrible economic need of our time on his own body: he finds no work. Now, when many thousands of people are out of work, we are supposed to have abundant work for Gypsies?"[6]

Advocate Szymanski, who represented many Burgenland Gypsies in matters of reparations, testified as follows: "If one considers that the . . . Burgenland population of Gypsy descent was understandably particularly affected by this economic situation and therefore was often unemployed for long stretches of time, then I can say that, on the basis of my investigation into the legal files of many Burgenland Gypsy clients, the Nazi assertion is correct that these persons are to be ranked as 'criminals'—in contrast to the rest of the population. Objectively, evaluation should have shown that there was no essential difference between the two groups of persons."[7]

The miserable accommodations of the Gypsies were also a theme that was repeatedly used as an argument for the urgent solution of the Gypsy question, as well as to illustrate their asocial nature. "They [their houses] are incredibly dilapidated structures of clay and wood . . . even the word shack is actually much too nice a term to characterize these dirty holes."[8] However, after the Gypsy expulsion of April 1943, Nazi sources noted that by far not all Gypsy shacks corresponded to the above picture: "The question now arises what we are to do with Gypsy shacks that become available. Since there are many Gypsy shacks too nice to simply tear down without consideration, it is necessary to consider precisely what to do with them."[9]

Anti-Gypsy Attitudes in Burgenland before 1938

In his *Denkschrift* [polemical publication] of August 1938, Tobias Portschy, an amateur race researcher, published suggestions for a radical solution [to the Gypsy question].[10] Already before [the *Anschluss*] he had agitated as an "illegal" [National Socialist] against the Gypsies, as he explained in his publication: "As a consequence of this behavior by the illegal National Socialists, the entire Burgenland population really recognized the significance of the Gypsy question."[11]

Already very early on, the police became active "on its own initiative" in the area of Gypsy discrimination. In a May 1930 article of the *Freie Burgenländer*, we learn that "on its own initiative the police had already managed to accomplish several things, for example the registration of all Gypsies. . . . The fingerprinting of all Gypsies over 14 went hand in hand with this registration process."[12] This registration office was already established in 1928 by the federal police commissioner in Eisenstadt.[13] Thus, considerable advance work was being done in Burgenland in the 1930s for the Nazi bureaucracy. By 1938, approximately eight thousand Gypsies had been arrested.[14]

In the next edition of this publication there is mention of a Gypsy law,[15] which in essence already fulfills all of Portschy's demands, with the exception of the sterilization program. "According to available information the federal chancellor's office is working on the draft of a Gypsy law. The law which is being drafted will probably be of a primarily police nature and will therefore not suffice for the Burgenland, so that in the expansion of such a legal framework a state law will become necessary which responds to the specific Burgenland situation."[16]

The main demands in Portschy's notations are sterilization and internment in forced labor camps because the Gypsies "have been proven to be genetically inferior and are definitely a people of common criminals."[17] [Regarding] prohibition against sexual relations with non-Gypsies and equality with Jews, Portschy wrote, "Sexual relations between Gypsies and Germans as a crime against racial purity must be countered by the severest laws. Those who know the Gypsy character will have to put them on a par with the Jews in every respect."[18] He demanded the exclusion from military service and prohibition of school attendance for Gypsy children, with the rationale that compulsory school attendance leads to disaster for Gypsies. "The Gypsy is *a priori* clever and a liar, already today our legal system does not find it easy to deal with him, yet this will become downright catastrophic in a few years if compulsory education for Gypsies is continued. Then we will equip about 20,000 to 30,000 Gypsies with mental tools.[19] . . . Those who will be able to use their brains better as a result of education will become ringleaders of the entire Gypsy colony, not for a good purpose, but for evil."[20] However, passage of the corresponding legal decrees did not occur. The radical suggestions "for a solution to the 'Gypsy' question" by Portschy and others largely agreed with the persecution program of the Nazis, or, rather, they preceded and influenced it.[21]

Legal and Administrative Measures against the Burgenland Gypsies during the National Socialist Regime

After these representatives of antidemocratic and nationalist thoughts were able to realize their long-existing plans, the installation of the Nazi power apparatus in Austria and citizens' prejudices and ideas could become legal norms.

Already in March of 1938, the first persecutions began under Portschy's leadership. In addition to decrees that banned public musical performances and school attendance[22] and that took away the Gypsies' voting rights[23]—and apart from the deportations of smaller groups to concentration camps that started in that year[24]—in August 1938 an ordinance was put into effect in Burgenland on the basis of which all able-bodied Gypsies could be compelled to forced labor.[25] Thus, the possibility of forced labor existed already before the establishment of such camps. "As we were able to find out . . . recently[,] broad measures were passed to facilitate the rounding up of Gypsies and their utilization for productive work."[26] This forced labor was later intensified even further. In order to keep Gypsies from fleeing their workplace, they were to spend their free time on the weekend in the community jail.[27]

Apart from the Lodz deportations, which were the first form of final solution, one can basically state that, until the Auschwitz decree in January 1943,[28] the persecution measures were formulated in such a way that they, in addition to complete abolition of rights as well as isolation, guaranteed the Gypsies' availability as labor. From spring 1943 on, their murder was given precedence over economic considerations.

Because Portschy's ordinance to exclude Gypsy children from school attendance started a discussion of the subject and eventually predated a central decision, we will briefly address this issue. In fall 1938, at the beginning of the school year, the prohibition was made public in the official state newsletter.[29] Some school authorities paid heed to the injunction, and others sent a query to the Ministry in Vienna to help solve the conflict.[30] Because the Vienna Ministry did not receive an answer from the Reich Ministry in Berlin until June 1939, individual state school officials were instructed to make the number of school-aged Gypsy children public and to provide information on settlement patterns "to aid in a uniform decision regarding public education of Gypsy children."[31] On principle, they wanted to adhere to the school attendance regulations for Austria and provide education for Gypsy children, either through the establishment of Gypsy classes or by hiring a traveling tutor. The school directors reacted negatively and predicted the failure of such a project because "we will not be able to find a teacher who will take on this kind of service."[32]

The decree by the Reich Ministry in Berlin for Austria that was issued in June of 1939[33] did not actually see a possibility to deny Gypsy children with German citizenship an education. "Because there is not a large number of [such] Gypsy children, it will not be possible to establish special schools for them. However, based on the danger which these children constitute for their German fellow pupils morally and otherwise, they can be denied school attendance."[34] This formulation, which left plenty of room for individual initiative, quickly ended any school attendance by Gypsy children. "Consequently I instructed the principals to immediately submit individual petitions based on previous behavior of these Gypsy children, recommending admission or exclusion from school. The petitions have now been submitted; without exception they call for exclusion because of the moral endangerment of German children."[35] With the establishment of the Gypsy camp in Lackenbach—at the most a year later—these questions became moot.

Efforts in the *Altreich* also aspired to follow the path that Portschy had begun: "Exclusion already begins in the classroom; in addition to the Burgenland, West German cities also adopted this measure. There still is no separate Gypsy law."[36] They had to wait for such a decree until November 1941.[37]

5

Camp Lackenbach

Establishment of the Camp
and Basis for Internment

"On the basis of repeated demands by the general population, the Meierhof in Lackenbach was turned into a collection camp for Gypsies of the border district Oberpullendorf. The intent was to keep all Gypsies in this camp under constant surveillance and to send them from there to work places as needed."[1] With these words the establishment of the collection camp, holding camp, and forced labor camp was justified to the public. Although Nazi propaganda took public sensibilities into consideration to a certain degree, the already planned—and partly executed—incarceration[2] of this minority group was not primarily a wish of the population but a decisive step of the Nazi politics of persecution.

With the internment decree of October 1939, the leading criminal police stations were given the order to establish collection camps in which the Gypsies were to remain until their final deportation.[3] The fact seems worth mentioning that "the impetus to follow through with the urgent solution of the Gypsy question via inconsiderate detainment of the Gypsies in closed camps (came from Austria)"[4] even before there were concrete instructions regarding this matter from the Reich. In his *Denkschrift,* cited earlier, Portschy demanded the establishment of forced labor camps in addition to massive restrictions for nearly all areas of life.[5]

On November 23, 1940, a Gypsy camp was opened in Lackenbach in Burgenland. The actual opening was preceded by a special delivery letter from the Reich Interior Ministry, dated October 31, 1940, to the leading criminal police stations in Austria. They were informed that the planned relocation of six thousand Gypsies of the *Ostmark* to the *Generalgouvernement* would not take place in favor of a different solution after the war. Precisely for that reason it was necessary to establish appropriate collection camps and to introduce the men to jobs.[6] "The representatives of the autonomous administrative districts Bruck on the Leitha, Eisenstadt, Lilienfeld, Oberpullendorf, St. Pölten and Wiener Neustadt, the Lord Mayor of the city of St. Pölten, as well as the authorized administrative representative of the province of Vienna . . . today agreed to unite into a *Zweckverband* [Voluntary community-wide Association] for the purpose of establishing and maintaining a Gypsy camp in Lackenbach near Oberpullendorf. On the basis of this agreement the legal status of the Association will be governed by the following organizational statutes which are based on the legal ordinances that govern Voluntary Associations."[7]

On the basis of this agreement the planned camp was established on the premises of an inoperative Esterhazy estate—the [estate] Schaflerhof was leased for this purpose. Expenditures for the establishment and upkeep [of the camp] were to be covered by members of the Voluntary Association in proportion to the number of Gypsies who arrived from their areas. In addition, it was expected that the camp would be self-sufficient through the [outside] labor of the Gypsies as well as the camp's own agriculture. For Gypsies who were admitted to Camp Lackenbach from other areas of Austria, the appropriate representatives had to pay the established share.[8] Since the Voluntary Association was held responsible for the financing, the supervision of receipts rested with the audit department of the Oberpullendorf budget office.

All other tasks belonged to the responsibilities of criminal police headquarters in Vienna, as for instance, apprehension and admission. "Admission to the said camp occurred for purely racial reasons."[9] The incarceration was first justified on the basis of the Gypsies' asocial character, and they were stamped as asocial on the basis of their race. Many of the persecuted did not understand the restrictions to their freedom of movement, for they neither shied away from work nor were they transients. At the time of their internment they had either worked or owned property; they had no criminal record.[10] "We were taken there . . . from our decent houses and caravans to misery and to filth."[11]

Camp Administration

Supervisory Personnel

The administration of Gypsy camp Lackenbach was subject to criminal police headquarters in Vienna, Supervisory Department IIb, under the leadership of the then administrator, Reich commissioner for criminal matters, Kapphengst, and his deputies, Thiele and Zaucke.[12] The official stamp of the one-time internment camp makes clear the direct authority of the central office in Vienna: "State criminal police, criminal police headquarters Vienna, Gypsy camp Lackenbach."[13]

Criminal police personnel on active duty from Vienna also provided leadership personnel, the camp supervisor, or his deputy, in Lackenbach. The most important administrative positions were also occupied by civil servants from Vienna.[14] The camp supervisor had ultimate authority in camp and was the highest official dealing with the councilmen—representatives of the Voluntary Association—and the employers. However, in the decision-making process, his authority was marked by strong dependence on the Vienna office. Fragments of correspondence point to a lively exchange.[15] Certain incidents are also documented in the first part of the camp diary, from January 4, 1941, to February 4, 1942.[16]

Hans Kollross was the first camp supervisor in Lackenbach.[17] At the time of his appointment, he was a noncommissioned officer in the criminal police with the rank of an SS Second Lieutenant. In April 1941, when the mass admissions began, Franz Langmüller, a noncommissioned officer of the criminal police, was assigned to him as deputy. While the explosion-like increase in inmates required more personnel, the camp supervisor also needed a competent deputy in the event of his absence. Such occasions arose due to meetings in the Vienna central office or because of inspection trips to external work places.

After the death of Kollross in January 1942—he died during the typhus epidemic that ravaged the camp—Franz Langmüller took over camp command until he was transferred to the Waffen-SS [elite guard] in Poland in September 1942.[18] The time in which Langmüller acted as camp commander left the most negative memories for those concerned. His feared regime of terror netted him a trial with a resulting conviction in the postwar period.[19] The conditions at that time in Lackenbach—the devastating typhus epidemic had reached highest proportions and the building of housing was only in the beginning stages—were accepted as explanations for his tough stand and contributed to a milder sentence.

On September 1, 1942, Fritz Eckschlager, commissioner of the criminal police and SS First Lieutenant, took over supervision of the camp. Beyond the general observation that treatment improved and beatings were abolished, there was little concrete testimony about him. Professor Knobloch spoke of him as "an amiable personality"[20]; his deputy and successor, Julius Brunner, also gave a favorable deposition.[21] The beginning of Fritz Eckschlager's term of office coincided with the abolition of every form of physical disciplinary measures. It can therefore be stated that approximately two years after the establishment of Camp Lackenbach, a definite liberalization took place. Whether this development, isolated from other events, was due only to the new camp commander, or was also the result of a general easing of the reign of terror in forced labor camps, cannot be assessed due to a lack of sources.[22]

The last camp commander was Julius Brunner, a noncommissioned officer of the criminal police and SS Second Lieutenant. He held that post from September 1943 to the beginning of April 1945. Because of his appointment as deputy a year earlier, he was well acquainted with Lackenbach conditions at the time he began his office. Also, in this work, his statements, documented in the sworn testimony of 1957,[23] were consulted again and again for elucidation and confirmation of events. Why was his testimony given such weight as historical state's evidence?

Julius Brunner functioned for the longest time as camp commander—nineteen months. Altogether, he spent almost three years in Lackenbach. Because of an interim two-month period as camp administrator at the beginning of 1941, he was able to make comparisons, especially concerning housing.[24] The credibility that he was given is primarily due to the fact that surviving Lackenbach inmates praised Brunner, a positive evaluation that was confirmed by reports from other contemporaries.[25] However, one must not fail to consider that the initial situation with all of its iniquities allowed for the second phase to be perceived as orderly and bearable—the inmates had in the meantime reconciled themselves to camp life. But it would be a mockery to portray the change in the inhumane forced labor camp with its concentration camp–like features as one that made this a pleasant refuge.

Guard Personnel

Guarding of the camp was not the same during the entire period of its existence; it was subject to change. One can ascertain that it became more lenient during the course of the years. Here the following mechanism became effective. Due to improved living conditions and a more humane camp leadership, the Gypsies accepted their fate almost without resistance.[26] The camp leadership rewarded this resignation with further liberalization. However, in addition to the hopelessness of a life in freedom, the initial sanctions, which largely had broken the resistance of the inmates, must not be forgotten.[27]

An approximate picture of guard measures and personnel can be created only by stringing together the various testimonies. However, the subjective factor shall also be considered, namely, what these repressions meant to the prisoners.

In the beginning, the camp was strictly closed off and surrounded by pointed fence posts. The exterior guard consisted of a police unit that was put together by the police station Lackenbach. These were reserve policemen and former policemen. In the 1952 BMI report, one policeman on active duty was mentioned as well as approximately twenty reserve policemen.[28] Nikolaus Reinprecht, business manager, stated the following numbers in his testimony: "In the beginning three men stood guard outside the camp. . . . Only during the epidemic was there an increase of guards. . . . There were continuously four men."[29] Guarding was carried out in such a way that a group of guards patrolled the outside of the camp along the fence. There also was a camp gate.[30] "The camp was surrounded by guards. There were guards with guns. And all around a fence . . . whoever would go near the fence was shot."[31] Guard personnel as well as strangers were forbidden from entering the camp.

Camp commander Langmüller's testimony that there supposedly were no strict restrictions is definitely not true.[32] Precisely during his time, we can read in the diary that even small children who left the camp without permission were punished by having to kneel for hours.[33] Likewise, the diary entry conveys to us how difficult it was to leave the camp without being noticed: "Three Gypsies broke a hole in the wall that separated room 8 from room 7 and thus entered room 7. From there, an old door leads to room 6, whose roof is not covered. By this route they reached freedom."[34] A general opening up of the camp was achieved by Brunner only in 1944. He was able "(to convince) his superiors to reduce the police guard, so that the camp was completely unguarded on one side."[35] Johann Bocdech, director of the Stoob ceramics factory, reported that he saw no trace of guard personnel during a visit at the end of 1944.[36]

Johann Knobloch, the Austrian philologist, gave the following testimony regarding the topic of "guarding" in spring 1943: "At the camp gate there was a guard who did not check those who came and went particularly well, since they were probably familiar to him. I myself did not leave the camp for this entire period; but I believe that I did not have to show my papers when I came and went because I was accompanied. I was picked up from the train station by car. . . . There were no guard towers."[37]

For the period that was covered in the diary,[38] we learn that the guarding of the camp was very important. Not only the responsible councilmen inspected the guard unit, but also officials from Vienna came to Lackenbach for guard inspection.[39] Several times there were criticisms: "At 6 PM, a councilman visited the camp, he complained about guard personnel in the guard room, since both conversed conspicuously with the Gypsies Martha and Erna. Another inspection at 9 PM revealed additional problems. The light was still on and the Gypsies conversed with each other loudly. The guard personnel did nothing about it, and it needs to be stated generally that the guard personnel is useless."[40]

"A report was sent to the police station as well as to the KPL [*Kriminalpolizeileitstelle* = criminal police headquarters] in Vienna regarding incidents between the assistant policemen sent for guard duty and the Gypsy women."[41]

In order to stop this deplorable state in the camp, such as "disobeying orders regarding night time quiet, or smoking in the sleeping quarters"—a night watch of camp elders was instituted—"nine camp elders and orderlies take turns with half-nightly shifts. Camp elder Karl Berger is responsible for the organization."[42]

Camp Self-Administration

Similar to large concentration camps, the inner organization of Camp Lackenbach was also structured on the principle of self-administration. Responsibility for the execution of orders was delegated largely to inmates. The camp leadership primarily supervised. Although in Lackenbach the overall structuring was not as rigorous as in other camps—with a hierarchy of camp elder, block elder, room detail—camp elders or "Kapos" were responsible for the maintenance of camp order.[43] Originally, the function of camp elder was carried out by Rupert Papai and Franz Horvath. Although we learn from the diary that on January 7, 1941, both were relieved of their duties "because of repeated non-compliance with their duties," their names also appeared thereafter with this title. In a further entry, Rupert Papai and Alexander Sarközi are named on an equal level as camp Kapos.[44] In addition, on March 14, 1941, Karl Berger was mentioned as camp elder. According to the diary, he was supposed to have been deposed as camp elder on July 7, 1941, because of "suspicion of various dishonesties." "Eduard Kreitz was appointed camp elder."[45] And yet, Karl Berger's signature is on a food requisition dated August 7, 1941[46]; otherwise there are no additional details about him.

As was the case with other camps, Lackenbach may also have had several camp elders after expansion, that is to say, increase in admissions. In April 1941, nine camp elders and orderlies[47] were assigned to night watch duty. It was their duty to see that quiet prevailed during the sleeping hours.[48] In addition, camp organizers were detailed to the groups that had to work outside the Meierhof.

During the entire internment period,[49] Alexander Sarközi had the function of a camp elder. His activity during the Langmüller administration earned him the reputation of a sadist. In Langmüller's trial, he was heavily indicted by witnesses because, as Langmüller's enforcer, he frequently ordered beatings. "The execution (of the beatings) occurred through Gypsies on orders of the camp administration."[50] Already on December 14, 1940, Sarközi, son of the community clerk of Unterwart, was sent to Lackenbach from concentration camp Mauthausen "together with five other Gypsies."[51] He was then eighteen years old; his wife also was part of these first admissions in November 1940.

In camp there also was a Gypsy advocate, named Lumpo (Schneeberger). How his role and his influence affected the camp conditions can no longer be ascertained.[52]

Another witness in the Langmüller trial, Jakob Schneeberger, was Kapo of a work detail.[53] Sepp Brantner was also mentioned as Kapo. The supervision of the inmates at work was carried out via guards from the camp leadership and through Gypsies, who were designated as foremen by the camp administration.[54]

As far as internal administration was concerned, there were deviations from the large internment camps. There the office work was done by prisoners—for instance, file keeping, assignment of living quarters, drill preparations, allotment of rations, and so forth. Lackenbach, on the other hand, had office help from Vienna for this purpose. From July 7, 1941, supervisory official Josef Hajek was responsible for all record keeping; from then on he also kept the camp diary. Roman Neugebauer took care of financial matters, and Nikolaus Reinprecht came to Lackenbach to run its business operations.[55] For ration allotments, a Lackenbach woman, Elfriede Pekovits, was responsible.[56] She began her work in the camp on June 13, 1941. At the time of the epidemic, her father took over this job.[57] In September of 1941, Therese Hlavin, from the employment office in Oberpullendorf, was assigned to the camp administration as a clerk.[58]

If and how many additional Gypsies were given administrative responsibilities cannot be ascertained. The comment that more intelligent persons who were able to write were chosen as camp elders leads one to conclude that they also had to carry out some sort of written activities.[59] Prisoners were also used as at least assistants to the camp administration. We know of a "half-breed" who performed messenger services. He lived in the administration building.[60] Another "Gypsy half-breed" from Langenthal, who was not imprisoned in the camp, had to promise to carry out trips with his car for the

Gypsy camp.[61] For this purpose the vehicle had to be especially marked because at this time Gypsies were already prohibited from using motor vehicles.

Medical Care

"The Gypsies had no health insurance. When a Gypsy became ill or disabled, he had to be supported by the camp."[62] In addition to his duties as village doctor, Dr. Georg Belihart of Lackenbach provided medical care [for the camp]. Only those Gypsies who worked outside of Lackenbach were also treated by other doctors—for instance, Dr. Hans Jahn, Oberpullendorf, and Dr. Oskar Brehmer, Kobersdorf.[63] For recuperation, they were sent to the camp.[64]

At the time of the typhus epidemic in late 1941, the provisions for and care of the sick failed completely. In this period the camp was closed off and the inmates left to their fate.[65]

Although a Red Cross barrack existed only after the expansion and improvement of Camp Lackenbach, certain "equipment for the doctor" arrived in camp already in March of 1941.[66]

It also happened that, in addition to Dr. Belihart, the local midwife was called to assist with births in camp. *Medizinalrat* (Medical Counsel) Dr. Brenner, director of the State Health Authority Oberpullendorf, and Medizinalrat Dr. Zieglauer, from the Health Authority Vienna, also inspected the camp. Urgent cases were sent to the hospital in Oberpullendorf with an ambulance or with private transportation. In the camp diary, which noted hospital stays separately, usually two or three people were mentioned. At times, the number of hospitalized Gypsies rose up to ten per day. Hospital admissions could also occur directly from a workplace outside of camp.

Developmental Phase of the Camp

When the first admissions took place in November 1940, the locale that was intended for the family camp was in a hopeless state. The beginning conditions were more than primitive. Besides the concrete former estate building that was occupied by the camp leadership, there were only stables in the Hasenberg[67] area. Straw beds that were fixed there served the incarcerated Gypsies as living and sleeping quarters. Julius Brunner, the last camp commander, who already at the beginning of 1941 spent some time as a replacement in Lackenbach, gave the following report on conditions: "At that time the Gypsies were housed very primitively in former sheep pens. I considered these accommodations as below human dignity. . . . Sanitary facilities (were) completely missing at this time."[68]

The Sinti families who had come to the camp with their caravans had an advantage over the other prisoners. They could continue to live in them, and, as a result, they were in better shape.[69] During thawing conditions and in rain,[70] the families that were crowded together in the pens suffered from completely soaked sleeping facilities.

The outbreak of a typhus epidemic, caused by the miserable living conditions, at least gave the impetus for expansion and improvement of the camp. "For fear of typhus, Langmüller ordered the building of barracks. Here, too, Lackenbach resembled all other concentration camps: Barracks were built in order to guard against a typhus epidemic, not in order to ease life for the inmates."[71] In addition to the four new rows of barracks—three living barracks and one for health services—the headquarters building was also expanded. Materials for this project were obtained from the destroyed Jewish synagogue.[72] "In all kinds of weather, even small children had to carry stones from the burned-down synagogue to the camp."[73] "My little brothers and sisters had to carry the stones from the synagogue up the mountain."[74] A corresponding entry in the camp diary documents this event: "Feb. 27, 1941 . . . collecting stones at the synagogue."[75] In addition, supply transports arrived from Vienna.[76]

From the beginning of the camp it had been clear that there would have to be an expansion; blueprints were made, and building commissions surveyed the camp, but execution was constantly delayed. Priority was given to an addition to the office building and the business section, as well as to the expansion of the roads.[77]

The reconstruction of the camp headquarters building became reality in August 1941: "Today beginning of work on roof, demolition of roof on headquarters building, also demolition of electric line and rerouting to office barracks, now in progress. . . . Wooden barrack

for temporary housing of camp leadership was finished today. . . .
Move of camp leadership into temporary wooden barrack."[78]

Only after this were lodgings for the prisoners built. Professor
Knobloch remembers three rows of barracks: "In the first there
were Sinti from Steiermark, from Vienna and from Württemberg, in the second, Roma from Burgenland, and in the third, 'half-
breeds'[*Mischlinge*]."[79]

Expansion of Camp Lackenbach also included installation of sanitary facilities, which had been almost completely missing up to this
point in time. This was also a reason why during early inspection trips the Schaflerhof was repeatedly proclaimed unfit as a family camp.[80] Brunner also repeatedly complained to Vienna on that
account.[81]

When the inadequacies culminated during the epidemic, a rem-
edy had to be found. A diary entry from August 5, 1941, draws a
picture of the catastrophic water shortage: "Today there was a water
shortage in the camp, for the well was depleted; water for cooking
had to be taken from the river, since the well near the camp also
had become useless."[82] By the end of 1941 a new well was in operation. In 1942, additional exploratory drilling was carried out in order
to facilitate an end to chronic water shortage.[83] Camp lighting was
installed only in the middle of 1942[84]; before that, electric light existed only in the office barracks.

The BMI files contain a summary of conditions in Lackenbach
from 1952, which was consulted as documentation for reparations:
"The witnesses who were questioned all confirmed unanimously
that economic, sanitary and work conditions in the camp were completely normal, and that the Gypsies felt 'as if they were in "para-
dise." ' "[85]

Former prisoners, when questioned as to their impressions,[86] had
other memories: "Lackenbach was as bad as any large concentration
camp, even dirtier."[87] "Lackenbach was only better if one did not live
in camp, but was housed elsewhere as an outside worker."[88]

In conclusion, one can say that, by the end of 1942, housing and
living conditions—at least from a health point-of-view—had improved to the point that residence in the camp at least did not pose
any more immediate threat to life. After the epidemic had subsided,
the Lackenbach records office recorded only few deaths.[89]

Camp Population

Gypsy Classifications

The Lackenbach camp was established as a holding place for Gypsies of the border districts. Included were the administrative areas of the members of the Voluntary Association Bruck on Leitha, Eisenstadt, Lilienfeld, Oberpullendorf, St. Pölten, Wiener Neustadt, and the property administration of the Reich district Vienna. But already in the statutes of the Voluntary Association a clause had been included that was geared toward admissions from additional areas as well: "In the event that space in the camp would allow for the admission of foreign Gypsies [from outside the membership area], and if a district that does not belong to the Voluntary Association should ask for admission of such Gypsies, these Gypsies could be housed in the camp for the cost of room and board."[90]

Even if the point of origin of transports was not completely delimited when the camp opened, the category of prisoners was determined from the beginning. Although this minority [population], which could be found amply in the aforementioned territories, was clearly delimited, practical implementation was marked by those difficulties that "racial categorization" of Gypsies caused the Nazi theoreticians and Nazi authorities. Likewise, the concept of asocial behavior, under which all Gypsies were lumped together without differentiation, was difficult to grasp. The Gypsies were ultimately seen as asocial whether the definitive criteria of nomadism or laziness were true or not.

With the imprisonment of Gypsies in forced labor camps, several Nazi objectives were fulfilled simultaneously. Thus, for one, "those elements who would biologically damage the *Volk*" were eliminated from the German body of people, and second, inmates who were capable of working were not only obligated to maintain themselves but their nonworking fellow sufferers as well.[91] In addition, through concentration at one place, or in a few places, the possibility was created to proceed on short notice in the event of a final decision regarding the regulation of the Gypsy question.

With the assistance of scholars, categories were created that were to assure the apprehension of this group of people. For this purpose, the Reich Health Office founded the Eugenic and Population Biological Research Station. By the spring of 1941, under the direction of Dr. Robert Ritter, already twenty thousand race-biological evaluations had been undertaken in the Archives for Gypsy Genealogy, and the following categories had been established:[92]

1. Z = Gypsy/full [blooded] Gypsy, that is to say, authentic tribal Gypsy

2. ZM+ = Gypsy half-breed with primarily Gypsy blood

3. ZM = Gypsy half-breed with equal parts Gypsy and German blood

4. ZM- = Gypsy half-breed with primarily German blood

5. NZ = Non-Gypsy[93]

The little evidence that has survived does not allow a statement on how many Lackenbach inmates were evaluated race-biologically, that is to say, were examined according to the above categories. More concrete information can be obtained only on the basis of the knowledge of Gypsy tribes who lived in Austria at that time and their regional distribution.

According to a 1933 police census, 7,153 Roma lived in Burgenland. In 1938, their number was estimated at eight thousand.[94] At that time, Burgenland was already partitioned into Niederdonau [Lower Danube] and the administrative district Oberwart, which belonged to district Steiermark. In addition, there were approximately three thousand Sinti. These nomadic Gypsies could be found at the outskirts of larger cities, especially in Vienna, Neustadt, Linz, Villach, and Salzburg. In addition, there were splinter groups of Lovara and Serbian Gypsies.[95]

Because the majority of the imprisoned Gypsies came from Burgenland (at that time administrative districts of Niederdonau and Steiermark), the Roma constituted the majority of Lackenbach prisoners. In addition, many Sinti arrived from other districts. In April 1943, south-German Sinti arrived with a transport from the Salzburg camp.

Nothing can be said about the numerical relationship between

Roma and Sinti in Lackenbach. While in some cases the rediscovered file card files were helpful in analyzing problems, only a small portion of the files contains a notation about "race."[96] Of twenty-four people whose tribal affiliation was noted specifically, nineteen were considered Roma, three Sinti, one a "half-breed," and one a non-Gypsy.[97] Of the three Sinti mentioned, two were members of the south-German Reinhardt family; a musician, also Sinto, came from Lower Austria.[98]

Some of the imprisoned were released on the basis of a racial evaluation. These people were either non-Gypsies or "half-breeds" with primarily German blood. From a report by a representative for the Gypsy Question in the Race Political Office of the district office Niederdonau, located later on, we learn that there were very few "half-breed families" who were not arrested and interned because they were "socially almost completely assimilated." According to a report, some non-Gypsies who were erroneously admitted as Gypsies were sent to a "camp for asocial Germans."[99]

Admissions Committee

In order to provide personal data for the Eugenic and Population Biological Research Station, the installation of an extensive bureaucratic apparatus became necessary. In accordance with the Incarceration Act of October 17, 1939, full-scale arrests in Austria began. In the period between October 25 and 27, 1939, all "Gypsies, Gypsy half-breeds, and vagrants of the Gypsy-type" were to undergo checks. The first step was carried out by local police authorities and state police units. These were instructed to file a formal report (RKP No. 172)[100] with the appropriate criminal police station after completion of the identity and nationality checks. After review and possible additions through specially trained experts, the data and fingerprints were sent to criminal police headquarters in Vienna for central evaluation. The Office for Gypsy Affairs at criminal police headquarters in Vienna—the highest authority for Austria—had to add to its own archives from the information received and pass on form RKP 172 to the RKPA. In the final instance, the result of every personal identity check was in the hands of the Reich Central Authority for the Abolition of the Gypsy Vermin at the RKPA, who eventually decided upon and initiated race biological investigations.

For the group in question, these proceedings temporarily ended with the result that all of their papers were taken away from them and they were instead given a uniform ID card that they had to carry at all times for identification purposes.[101]

Criminal police headquarters in Vienna were responsible for admissions to Camp Lackenbach. Referrals from other police stations and state police occurred in consultation with headquarters in Vienna, which made the final decision in all important Lackenbach matters: "The camp command and the admission of Gypsies was subject exclusively to the criminal police headquarters in Vienna."[102]

Admissions and Camp Population

From the opening of the camp on November 23, 1940, to the end of the year, the number of the imprisoned rose to 180. Whether these first admissions happened as a result of larger transports or by individual admissions cannot be evaluated because of lack of sources; [the same is true] in the case of approximately one hundred Gypsies from Langental, who belonged to the initial population as of December 1940.[103] On December 14, 1940, a transport of six people came from concentration camp Mauthausen, among them the later camp elder Alexander Sarközi.[104] On the basis of preserved file cards with low camp numbers for this early phase, one can state that among the first Lackenbach inmates there already were women[105] and children of every age.[106]

In 1941, a year of massive admissions, April 6 marked the beginning with the most admissions. Three hundred and ninety-eight Gypsies from Mattersburg and environs were brought to the internment camp. Until the middle of November 1941, the strong flow continued. Another five admissions—among them also a larger transport from Mauthausen[107]—reached nearly the size of the first large transport. The majority of groups who arrived in camp consisted of between ten and one hundred persons. In addition, there were also continually admissions of single individuals and families.[108]

Only a few documents exist with limited value as evidence concerning admissions during the following years.[109] With the help of a few incidental facts the attempt can be made to analyze this problem. One point of departure is the knowledge of the continuous numbering of inmates. The last entry in the diary on February 1, 1942, was 2928 (camp birth Josef Karoly).[110] The highest possible number, 3210, again a birth (Katharina Schneeberger), was assigned on February 1, 1945.[111] From February 1942 to February 1945, only 282 new admissions could be confirmed, that is to say, approximately eight per month. If one considers that approximately fifty numbers in this period were assigned to births, 232 prisoners who came to the camp as new admissions remain.

At the beginning of 1942, complete isolation occurred because of a typhus epidemic.[112] In that year there were no admissions before the beginning of spring, when the danger of infection had passed.

Investigations into the establishment of another Gypsy camp in Salzburg netted facts about a Lackenbach admission in 1943. If this Salzburg institution was meant to be a temporary solution, like that in Lackenbach, the original intent was [also] followed in Lackenbach in the sense that this place remained merely a way station for those who were imprisoned there. The majority of those imprisoned in the Salzburg camp were deported to Auschwitz at the end of March and beginning of April. A small group of Salzburg prisoners came to Lackenbach. It can be said with certainty that at least seven members of the south-German Sinti family Reinhardt were registered in Lackenbach on April 6, 1943.[113]

These Lackenbach admissions on April 6, 1943, and the last assigned number 3074 (for the youngest family member, 1939) allow an additional reconstruction. A further document that reports new arrivals refers to March 31, 1944. Franziska Reinhart, referred to Lackenbach on this day together with her brother and son by criminal police headquarters, received camp number 3151.[114] Thus, for the period April 1943 to March 1944, seventy-seven admissions could be determined. Starting with this number 3151 from March 31, 1944, the difference to the last assignable number 3210 of February 1, 1945 (birth of Katharina Schneeberger), could be determined. Within these ten months, there was therefore again an increase of sixty people. A more precise count can be obtained for the months of April and May 1944. Between March 31 and May 30, 1944, seven additional numbers were assigned,[115] that is to say, in the remaining eight months, fifty-three new prisoners were added.

The number of admissions from this date until the dissolution of the camp—the end of March and beginning of April 1945—is not known. Three new admissions from the abandoned concentration camp Auschwitz can be named on the basis of a document from February 23, 1945.[116] Thus, the highest assigned number must have been above the one known (3210). It cannot be discounted that there may have been additional new admissions. The assumption that in Lackenbach there also were duplicate and multiple assignments of the same numbers—as in other camps—can be discounted. After the announcement of the Auschwitz decree, almost all Gypsies still living in freedom were deported to the family camp there. Therefore, after April 1943, Gypsies were sent to Lackenbach only occasionally.

Often, the concurrent arrest and admission of whole families or tribes occurred. However, this method was not compulsory, for when the admissions began, numerous families had already been torn apart by the arrests that had been made.[117] So it could happen that children whose parents had earlier been taken to a concentration camp were sent to Lackenbach alone.[118] Babies and small children who had been left behind had to be provided for free of charge by the criminal police headquarters in Vienna.[119] On the basis of altered regulations, these children were later taken from these homes and sent to Lackenbach. For instance, in August 1944, two children, Ludwig Mate, born March 5, 1938, and Peter Horvath, born August 14, 1939, had to relocate from a city-run orphanage to a place in Camp Lackenbach.[120]

Often the destruction of entire Gypsy camps that had existed at the edge of numerous villages was undertaken. Simultaneously with Gypsy incarceration, their habitations were erased: "The Gypsy habitations are to be removed in such a way that no traces are left, therefore, above all, foundations are to be completely removed."[121] The completion of such operations was entered into the camp diary with the stereotypical commentary: "At 6 AM, 14 Gypsies were brought from the police station St. Martin, and the camp there was emptied. They were given camp Nos. 705–718. . . . Today the Gypsy habitation in Weppersdorf was destroyed and the people admitted to this camp (15 people). They were given camp Nos. 684–698."[122]

Former Lackenbach inmates remembered their forced admission: "We were approximately 10 families in Mörbisch, we were maybe

100 people here on the lake. On a Sunday in August, 1941, we were picked up, I'll never forget the day; to leave home at 5 [in the morning] . . . criminal police and SS men came from Mörbisch, with guns."[123]

"One night the SS came to town. Trucks drove up and whole families were loaded at random. When this happened, almost all Gypsies hastily left the village. I moved to Gisshübel near Vienna and lived there in a sublet. . . . In 1941, I was arrested in Gisshübel, along with my wife. We were taken to the collection camp Lackenbach in Burgenland."[124]

Eugen Hodoschi, a seaman with the navy in Norway, was to be taken to Buchenwald after his discharge in the fall of 1942. His plea to be at least sent to his family in Lackenbach was honored due to his merits as a German soldier.[125]

One aspect that, in the postwar period, supplied arguments against the actual Lackenbach conditions were some voluntary requests for admission. If one, however, considers the motives of these "voluntary prisoners," their decision can be understood, especially in consideration of their expected incarceration in a forced labor camp under conditions unfit for human beings. Thus, single individuals or parts of families asked for admission because their family was already imprisoned there. These people preferred to share the difficult lot in camp with their families instead of facing their own questionable future alone.[126] This decision, therefore, must not be interpreted to mean: "Lackenbach could not have been so bad, otherwise people would not have requested voluntary admission at their own initiative."[127] In addition, the possibility to enter the camp voluntarily—at their own expense—existed for those who were released from imprisonment.[128] The assumption that these people were not offered an alternative surely must be considered.

On the basis of attempts to estimate admissions to the Gypsy camp, some statements about the number of inmates in the different periods can be made. Until April 1941, the number of inmates varied only slightly. In the three months—January, February, and March—the number grew only from 180 to 198. April 6, 1941, marked the beginning of large waves of admissions. As a result of the 398 people who came with this transport, the camp population rose to 591; continual additions followed. On November 1, 1941—

before the first 1,000 prisoners were sent to Lodz—the camp population reached its maximum with 2,335 people. After the second transport of November 7, 1941, the number again averaged approximately six hundred people.[129]

Due to a typhus epidemic, the beginning of 1942 brought a reduction to a low occupancy of less than 550 inmates. "From September 1942 until the camp's dissolution, the camp population varied between 600 and 900 individuals, of which 200 to 300 were children."[130] A review based on admissions in the last three years confirms this statement.

In establishing the camp, it was the goal of the Voluntary Association to house the Gypsies from their own administrative areas there. Accordingly, the largest groups came from places in Burgenland and Lower Austria (Lower Danube), as well as from Oberwart, which, during the Nazi period, belonged administratively to the district of Steiermark. In view of the expected expansion, they were also prepared to expect admissions from other areas. Soon numerous Viennese Gypsies arrived in Lackenbach; others came from Steiermark and Kärnten; occasionally there also were Gypsies from Upper Austria and Salzburg.[131] A small group was composed of other nationalities. Thus twenty Italian Gypsies were documented,[132] and several were from Hungary.[133] German Gypsies also were represented in Lackenbach[134]—especially from Württemberg.[135] Most of the German Sinti had already moved away from the *Altreich* before the beginning of the war. Some of them had already endured a lengthy incarceration in Salzburg before their arrival in Lackenbach. The list of Lackenbach inmates published in the appendix and compiled on the basis of discovered file cards gives a detailed listing of the birth places. These, in many cases, were identical with their places of residence.[136]

Several statements can be made about the age structure of Lackenbach inmates. The majority of file cards could be used as basis for calculations because 268 of the file cards contained sufficient information regarding age. In addition, seventy-five more names and birth dates became available as a result of relevant diary entries. Because the camp population fluctuated between six hundred and nine hundred persons,[137] the resultant age profile based on 343 statistics

Table 1. Camp Population by Age Group

Age Group	Number	Percentage
0–10 years	104	30.3
11–15 years	43	12.5
16–20 years	55	16.0
21–30 years	60	17.5
31–40 years	39	11.4
41–50 years	22	6.4
51–60 years	10	2.9
61 years and over	10	2.9

can be considered a relatively large sample. This does not include the period of the sizeable mass movements, especially from August to the beginning of November 1941. Based on the year 1943 (as an average statistic), the camp population [can be] broken down into specific age groups (table 1).[138]

Despite the high death rate among children in the first year,[139] children under age ten made up almost one-third of the camp population; when one combines children under age fifteen in one group, they comprised 42.8 percent of the population. Children and youths up to twenty years of age made up 57.8 percent of the camp population. The age profile shows a clear imbalance in favor of the younger generation. Eighty-eight percent of the inmates were not older than age forty.

The majority of those imprisoned in the Gypsy camp worked as day laborers before their incarceration, especially in construction and in agriculture. Women worked as domestics and in agriculture and the laundry. Others earned their living as craftsmen with permits for their own businesses, for example, as brick makers, plumbers, and smiths. "Until his forced relocation, Michael Horvath and his large family from Unterwart were in the brick-making business."[140]

In addition, there also were traditional [Gypsy] occupations, such as basket weaver, umbrella maker, and pots and pans repairman; for women the occupations were traveling salesperson and fortune-teller, which were still sometimes practiced in transit. Others had earned a living as drivers at fairs and as musicians.[141] Before the Nazi

time there were Gypsy bands in many Burgenland villages. In his
study, Joseph Bertha reported about an incident with the Gypsy
brass band in Unterwart that, until 1938, had played for all public
events: "It can be seen as an irony of fate that, in 1938, the brass
band accompanied the Unterwart citizens to a Nazi mass rally and
then had to resign there."[142]

Thus, already in the interwar years, many of the Gypsies had
turned away from their traditional occupations that no longer en-
sured a living. Like the other dependent, destitute population
classes, they entered into servitude. Their socioeconomic situation
resembled that of an army reserve unit. When there was a shortage
of workers, there was work for the Gypsies.

At the beginning of the twentieth century, numerous Gypsies
from Sulzriegel were given a chance to work as miners. Karl Berger[143] was able to show an affidavit that confirmed that he "had
worked in the Schlaining antimony mine for 17 years, from 1912 to
1929, and eventually was laid off because the company closed down.
. . . A second [Gypsy] was in the mine for 12 years, a third for 8
years." After the mine was closed down, numerous men were employed as servants of the spa administration in nearby Bad Tatz-
mannsdorf and women [were employed] in the laundry.[144] As a matter of course, this minority was the first to feel market fluctuations.
Therefore, the majority of the Gypsies never made it beyond the level
of itinerant laborers. Some sought a way out of their hopeless situation through begging and theft.

There are plenty of sources that mention Gypsies as diligent and
also, contrary to many witnesses, as tenacious workers. Several were
able to produce proof of a permanent job when they were admitted
that they then continued to keep after their incarceration.[145] Already
before the opening of the camp, numerous Gypsies were employed
at the Meierhof [estate] or worked as seasonal workers on other estates.[146] Quite a few had served in the German army before their
internment.[147]

[Camp] Departures

Not all Gypsies who had been sent to Camp Lackenbach were still
imprisoned there during the camp's dissolution at the end of March

1945. Already at the beginning of November 1941, big changes in the prison population occurred as a result of two large transports of one thousand people each that had been compiled directly in Camp Lackenbach [and sent] to Lodz. Later there were only smaller transports or individual transfers to concentration camps. An exact numerical count is not possible.

Great losses were caused by death. According to the available documents—camp diary, death records, registrations with the Lackenbach records office—there were 237 losses through death. However, testimony and memoirs of former inmates allow us to deduce that the detention caused more deaths. The sources for recording camp births and deaths of newborn children are especially incomplete.[148]

Numerous escape attempts led to a reduction in the number of inmates. For the period covered by the diary—January 4, 1941, to February 2, 1942—64 of 170 escape attempts succeeded. If we assume that the escape rate remained equally high over the next few years, we can assume that approximately two hundred persons left the camp by escaping.

In individual cases there also were discharges. On the basis of the incomplete records, we can neither mention numbers nor give approximate estimates. In the beginning phase, several Gypsies were released upon a review of their "racial category." In later years, release became possible when a different nationality could be proven.

In addition, a change in camp population resulted from outside labor details. This absence from the camp was in most cases only temporary. Thus, departures of larger numbers of inmates and thereby reductions in camp population occurred when whole construction details were engaged for different segments of the national expressway (September 5, 1941: 193 people, September 21, 1941: 140 people.) However, after a certain time, these, or at least some of them, returned to camp.[149] In some cases, the workers stayed at their outside workplaces and lodgings for the entire war period (for example, Stoob ceramics, brick works Walbersdorf).

In addition, specifically limited absences from camp could also occur through prison terms at other facilities. Court verdicts were rendered on crimes that had been committed by individuals before their incarceration in Lackenbach. After serving their term in the penitentiary, they had to continue their indefinite imprisonment in Lackenbach.[150]

Deportations

As already mentioned, the two largest deportations that were carried out during the existence of Camp Lackenbach were those two transports with one thousand people each at the beginning of November 1941 to ghetto Lodz (Litzmannstadt).[151] During this period in Austria, altogether five Gypsy transports with a total of 5,007 people were compiled with the destination of Lodz. The two Lackenbach transports mentioned were marked "station of origin Mattersburg." Two additional deportation trains were readied in the Burgenland villages of Oberwart and Rotenturm; the fifth train came from Fürstenfeld (Steiermark). These two evacuations were carried out within the framework of a large-scale campaign to cleanse the eastern districts. In addition to twenty thousand Jews, these comprised five thousand Gypsies.[152] For this purpose, the Gypsies were taken to Mattersburg on trucks, loaded onto railroad cars, and taken to Lodz via Vienna.[153]

The orders were given in higher places, but, according to what criteria were these people selected for relocation, and to what degree did the Lackenbach officials or prisoner overseers influence the compilation of the transport lists? It cannot be doubted that just as admissions occurred via the criminal police headquarters in Vienna, so also in this matter directives came from Vienna. In his testimony, Josef Hajek, administrative official, made the following statement on the matter: "The Gypsy holding camp Lackenbach also was a so-called transit camp for Gypsies, who were sent to us on the orders of Vienna, and, on additional specific instructions from Vienna, some of them were again organized into transports."[154]

According to an entry of November 4, 1941, in the camp diary, this method of handling the matter is at least partially confirmed. On this day, and on orders of the criminal police in Linz,[155] 301 Gypsies arrived in Lackenbach for continued transport to Lodz. According to witness testimony, especially the camp elder, Alexander Sarközi, was incriminated in having influenced the transport organization. Considering that an ordinance existed to deport all who

Table 2. Names in Transport from Linz

Camp No.	Name	Birth Date
2780	Trollmann, Johanna	12/25/28
2781	Trollmann, Franz	2/26/30
2782	Trollmann, Amalia	1/7/35
2783	Trollmann, Alfred	4/4/40
2784	Link, Franz	2/13/1894
2785	Link, Mathilde	2/24/09
2786	Link, Ida	3/14/27
2787	Link, Hildegard	4/20/34
2788	Link, Franz	3/7/29
2789	Link, Hilde	5/25/32
2790	Link, Andreas	5/10/1892
2791	Link, Maria	7/2/01
2792	Link, Eduard	4/21/22
2793	Link, Rudolf	10/26/18
2592	Kerndlbacher, Sonja	10/8/27
2584	Link, Maria	12/16/39
2583	Link, Ursula	10/27/21
2811	Seeger, Gottfried	6/5/30
2753	Demestra, Eduard	9/1/41

could not work to the East—that is to say, children, old people, and those of other age groups who could not work—there must have been a sort of selection process for those already imprisoned in camp. Franz Karall, who also accused Sarközi of putting together those transports on his own initiative, remembered the following method: "All excess camp inmates and those not able to work were regularly gathered together in the Meierhof and sent to death camps in Poland."[156]

Since the camp numbers of the 301 people from Linz who were admitted on November 4, 1941 (2541–2848) were known, 19 names of this transport could be established on the basis of file cards and other documents (table 2). (According to the diary entry of November 4, 1941, this transport from Linz was destined for Lodz [Litzmannstadt].) There is also a page of a November 4, 1941, evacuation list with an additional seventeen names.[157]

Calculating the ages of the deported with the help of these thirty-six names (and birth dates) leads to the picture in table 3. There is

Table 3. Ages of Deported and Percentages

Age Group	Number of Persons	Totals
0–10 years	15	
11–15 years	7	22 = 61.1%
16–20 years	2	
21–30 years	4	
31–40 years	2	
41–50 years	4	
51 years and over	2	14 = 38.9%

no reason to doubt the statement that the highest percentage was children, even if these figures cannot be considered representative based on the minute number available.[158] In this case, 61 percent of the children affected were under the age of fifteen. In two-thirds of the cases, these deported children were younger than ten years of age.

In the proceedings against Langmüller and Sarközi (as codefendants), the latter was found innocent in this matter. For one, his own parents were also deported to Lodz. In addition, the fact that orders and instructions had come from the criminal police headquarters in Vienna also helped his case, although another former camp inmate—who testified in favor of Sarközi—indirectly incriminated him in this matter: "I would like it to be known that I owe my life solely to the accused, for he continually saved me from [inclusion in] a transport to Lodz (Litzmannstadt)."[159]

In any case, it is certain that a selection was undertaken according to the previously mentioned criteria and that none of those relocated survived ghetto Lodz. A portion died immediately after arrival. By January 1942, the rest were murdered in Chelmno—that is how long the Gypsy camp in ghetto Lodz existed.[160] After these mass transports, only smaller groups or individuals were sent from Lackenbach to other concentration camps. In some cases, the threat of detention in a concentration camp was applied as a deterrent. After repeated, unsuccessful escape attempts, this threat sometimes became reality.[161] Likewise, refusal to work also could have as a consequence detention in a concentration camp.

The camp file card system also shed light on the fact that in the spring of 1943—that is, after the Auschwitz decree—relocations to Auschwitz took place, probably on the basis of age and ability to

Table 4. Relocations to Auschwitz

Camp No.	Name	Year of Birth	Date of Admission	Departure
?	Brand, Karl	1939	11/19/41	3/30/43
224	Horwath, Marie	1899	6/4/41	3/30/43
2147	Horvath, Emilie	1929	10/26/41	4/29/43[162]

Table 5. Additional Relocations to Auschwitz

Camp No.	Name	Year of Birth	Date of Admission	Departure
1976	Hodos, Anna	1934	9/21/41	3/30/43
119	Horvath, Helene	1919	12/15/40	3/30/43
?	Sarközy, Josef	1933	—	3/30/43[163]
1631	Sarközi, Anna	1903	—	3/30/43
3046	Stojka, Katherina	1927	—	3/30/43
28	Papay, Raimund	1922	—	4/29/43[164]

work. On three file cards, the relocation is clearly marked with a final date stamp and the destination "Auschwitz" (table 4). On the basis of that same departure date stamp, six additional cases allow the assumption that these people also were sent to Auschwitz (table 5). There are no other details that would have justified their release/departure at this point in time.

No concrete facts are known about the size of these transports. We only know that among the deportations heading for Auschwitz that were organized by the criminal police headquarters in Vienna on March 31, 1943, there were prisoners from Lackenbach. Because the camp population did not experience any dramatic changes from 1942 on, these probably were small transports.[165]

Deaths

The end of the year 1941 was marked by the outbreak of typhus in Camp Lackenbach, to which approximately 250 camp inmates succumbed. The epidemic was recognized only relatively late.[166] In the different reports the death figures vary. While the Lackenbach registry recorded only 180 deaths caused by typhus, former inmates reported about 300 victims of the epidemic.[167]

Table 6. Deaths Recorded by Month, 1941

Month	Deaths	Month	Deaths
March	1	August	2
April	2	September	6
May	1	October	18
June	1	November	54
July	6	December	60

The Lackenbach camp diary, which can be consulted as a document for the period January 1941 to February 1942, also contains different numbers. "The diary shows inaccuracies regarding births and deaths, especially of children."[168]

The death figures in the death register of the Lackenbach village doctor, which also shows entries about deaths in the Gypsy camp, allow recalculations about course of illness, beginning of epidemic, medical care, and intensity of effort to combat the disease.[169]

The outbreak of an epidemic was officially noted in the camp diary at the time when the first supervisor, Kollross, was sent to a Vienna hospital and was diagnosed as having typhus. "Tuesday, January 6, 1942: According to a telephone message from Vienna on January 5, 1942, camp supervisor Kollross was admitted to the Triest hospital and (was) diagnosed as having typhus. . . . Dr. Brenner, in consultation with Dr. Belihart, district doctor[,] . . . visited some critically ill persons and also saw the dead. One critically ill patient displayed symptoms which seemed to justify the suspicion of typhus."[170] From that day on, deputy camp supervisors and officials of the camp administration were quarantined for ten days.

The rapid increase of deaths in the last months of 1941 and the causes of death in the death records allow the conclusion that the epidemic began earlier (table 6).[171] In the column "basic ailment and immediate cause of death," the most frequent causes of death were: diarrhea/undernourishment, weak physical condition, whooping cough, pneumonia, and tuberculosis. Children's diseases, such as measles or smallpox, together with undernourishment, ended in death. Older people died of old age, blood clots, paralysis of the heart, stroke, and so on. From July 1941 on, "diarrhea" is the dominating entry, superseded in December 1941 by "influenza." Dr. Belihart had received instructions from the authorities to list "influ-

Table 7. Deaths from Epidemic by Age Group

Time Period: 3/12/41 to 12/1/41+

Age Group	Numbers	Percentage		Total	
0–1 year	21	23.1			
1–3 years	41	45.1	68.2%		
4–10 years	14	15.4		83.6%	
11–15 years	3	3.3			
16–20 years	0	—			
21–30 years	2	2.2			
31–40 years	2	2.2			
41–50 years	1	1.1			
51–60 years	1	1.1			
61 years and over	6	6.6	7.7%		

+ The explanation for the chosen time periods follows in the text.

Time Period: 3/12/41 to 1/12/42

Age Group	Numbers	Percentage		Total	
0–1 year	28	15.9			
1–3 years	47	26.7	42.6%		
4–10 years	15	8.6		51.2%	
11–15 years	8	4.6			
16–20 years	4	2.3			
21–30 years	5	2.9			
31–40 years	10	5.8			
41–50 years	15	8.6			
51–60 years	16	9.2			
61 years and over	27	15.4	24.6%		

enza" as cause of death.[172] This circumstance allows the conclusion that they understood clearly, at least from the beginning of December, that "acute diarrhea" was an infectious disease to which not only babies and small children who were barely capable of survival succumbed.[173] Especially old people whose bodies were already weakened by inadequate nourishment in camp could no longer fight off illness.

There were, however, deaths from the epidemic in all age groups. A tabulation of the deaths, determined on the basis of information in the death records, documents the age proportions (table 7). Until the beginning of December the deaths occurred mostly among children—the percentage of babies zero to three years of age was 68 percent and that of the four-to ten-year-olds was 15 percent—but later there was a shift. The number of older people rose disproportionately (it tripled for people over age fifty-one). The least number of deaths occurred in the age group twenty-one to thirty. With ninety deaths (51 percent), the mortality rate of children was still disproportionately high.

When asked about the situation during the epidemic, Dr. Belihart testified: "I immediately notified the health authorities and refrained from working in the camp for the period of the typhus epidemic. Later, after approximately three quarters of a year, I again resumed my duties as doctor in the camp."[174] The period of his absence from the camp was not mentioned. A careful study of death records allows one to draw the corresponding conclusions.

When the death entries began to increase in October and November 1941, the entry notebook was left behind in the camp.[175] Entries in the [following] categories were made in the camp—"police station number, day of viewing, name of deceased/description of place of residence, occupation and position, religion, marital status, day and year of birth, place of birth, political district/province, place of registration, date of death (or stillbirth), day of funeral." Before that time, everything fell under the jurisdiction of the doctor; until then the death entries were handled exclusively by Dr. Belihart. Thereafter, it was presumably the task of the administrative officials or also of the Kapos; the book shows three different handwritings for the succeeding period.[176] The two remaining columns—"cause of death and attending physician"—were filled in by Dr. Belihart only later. From January 4 to 13, 1942, the notations were handled exclusively by the camp secretary. Thereafter, Dr. Belihart again took possession of the book; those who died in the Gypsy camp were no longer entered. The doctor came only once more—on January 6, 1942, previously cited—for an inspection and official confirmation of the diagnosis in the camp, not for the treatment of the deathly ill.

Thus, the inmates were imprisoned and left to themselves. "For an indefinite time, until the identification and [subsequent] disappearance of the symptoms, the Gypsy camp was completely isolated."[177] Healthy Gypsies who worked outside also were called back from their place of work, detained in the camp, and also exposed to the danger of infection.

The measures that were taken document that they were implemented on the basis of safety considerations for camp leadership and administration and the population at large but that the lot of the inmates was not considered. The mass deaths in the quarantined area were of interest only insofar as they posed a threat to non-Gypsies. Any kind of medical treatment and care was stopped[178]; instead the guard was tightened: "Police lieutenant Körbl from station Lackenbach was ordered by the commission to instruct the guard unit that, in the event of escape attempts by inmates, they should shoot to kill."[179] In addition, the guard detail was increased. Reports by victims shall serve to give a picture of the slow death in camp: "In the first years we were plagued by lice, they were also carriers of typhus. When one was ill, he stayed on his cot, to live or to die. They wrote on the barracks: Attention, danger of typhus!"[180]

"There was typhus in our camp. In the morning when I woke up, I looked at my neighbor. I said to him: Get up. He was dead."[181]

"Without medicine and without doctor. . . . And every night, each night, 5, 6, 7, 8, 9, 10 people . . . died. And we wheeled them out to the Jewish cemetery."[182]

Often, the corpses were collected for days in an old Gypsy cart before they were thrown into mass graves and covered over in the Jewish cemetery.[183] But already before the isolation and the total cessation of any medical care, 60 percent died without a doctor's care. Of the 175 Gypsy deaths in the death register, 106 died "without an attending physician."[184]

The numbers of those who died in the last quarter of 1941 approximately agree in both the camp diary and the death register. January 1942 was the last month in which the diary was fully kept. This period shows forty-four dead and seventy-four ill. For January 1942, the Lackenbach register recorded forty-five deaths.[185] On the basis of this source, the further course of the epidemic, that is to say, the period of its decline, can be reconstructed. In February 1942, there were only nine deaths; in March there were five. Between one and three deaths per month were recorded for the remainder of the year 1942. Thus it can be ascertained that the epidemic receded before the onset of spring.

Table 8. Age Distribution, 1942 Deaths

Age	Number	Age	Number
0–1 year	4	21–30 years	6
1–3 years	1	31–40 years	11
4–10 years	8	41–50 years	5
11–15 years	5	51–60 years	6
16–20 years	4	61 years and over	13[189]

Another figure demonstrates the decline of camp inmates at the end of 1941 and beginning of 1942. After the deportation to Lodz at the beginning of November 1941, the camp population leveled off at five hundred to six hundred people. In these months about 10 percent of the camp population died.[186] From February 1942, the already mentioned death list of the Lackenbach registrar[187] provided the only documentation on the deaths that subsequently occurred in Gypsy camp Lackenbach. The writings found in the headquarters building also contained fragments of a death list. Because it consisted of only two pages—there are deaths listed on January 17, January 18, and March 5, 1942—it is of no value as evidence. It can, however, be concluded that internal notes were made by Kapos or camp elders.[188] Due to the still numerous deaths in January 1942, the death rate for the total time period of 1942 is still high; with a total of only six births, the excess is on the side of deaths (table 8). For this year, the death rate is somewhat higher among children and older people than among those of other age groups.

From 1943 on, there is again an excess of births. In this year, there are eighteen births versus six deaths. In 1944, there were twenty-four newborns and only seven deaths; for the beginning months,[190] three newborns and one death were noted.[191]

The clear break that can be ascertained for all areas of camp life—change in camp leadership, improvement of total life circumstances—can also be noticed in an examination of child deaths in the camp. In the beginning phase, the chance for a newborn to stay alive was extremely small. Either babies already carried the typhoid fever germ within them at birth or they were so weakened as a result of insufficient nutrition and insufficient hygiene that they succumbed to the illness. As already noted, the percentage of deceased babies (zero to three years of age) in the overall death rate was especially high (time period: March 12, 1941, to January 13, 1942—43 percent). In 1941, twenty-nine births were registered in camp. According to the death records, twenty-three babies (zero to one year) and forty-four small children (one to three years) died in the time period March 12, 1941, to December 31, 1941.[192] In 1942, only six children were born—surely as a consequence of the devastating typhus epidemic. Four children died before completion of their first year (age group zero to three years: five deaths).

After the epidemic subsided, there was a decline in child mortality. At least babies had more of a chance for survival in the improved circumstances—if they were not already destined to be sent to a death camp. In 1943, eighteen children were born, and only one baby died. In 1944, there was again a small increase in child mortality: out of twenty-four births, five babies died even before completion of the second month. In addition, in this year two two-year-olds died.[193] In 1945: [there were] three births and one death—a child of less than two months died in February 1945.[194]

The birth rate for the entire internment period results in negative numbers: seventy births versus 250 to 300 deaths. For the period March 12, 1941, to January 12, 1942, alone, seventy-five children below the age of three died; twenty-eight of them had not yet completed the first year.

Escapes

The most frequent reaction to the inhuman conditions in Camp Lackenbach was escape. As the SS people in concentration camps were ordered to prevent even thoughts of escape from arising through deterrent punitive measures, so the Lackenbach commander also was instructed to prevent attempts of escape at all cost. Therefore, this crime was punished with the toughest camp measures. According to orders from the central office in Vienna, those recaptured were to receive a certain number of lashes.[195] The camp diary, which noted repeated escapes and recaptures, also noted other punitive measures. In addition to the "beatings on higher authority," which were described as "grasping with tweezers," an unsuccessful escape attempt ended in solitary confinement, denial of food and/or additional heavy labor.

There were, however, also successful escapes. Some prisoners were able to hide until the end of the war; others escaped further persecutions through flight to Hungary. Julius Hodosi, who succeeded in hiding for some time, describes the actual escape: "I worked in road construction. We ate breakfast next to a forest. Once there was an opportunity, and I fled into the forest. After approximately three minutes, my absence was noticed. I was chased, but I was able to throw them off. During my escape I also came to Hungary. Near Ödenburg, I again entered Austrian territory and managed to get to Mattersburg, from where I went to Vienna by train, illegally of course."[196]

The most important precondition for a successful escape was assistance upon reaching freedom. There were some locals who attempted "to protect and to hide their Gypsies."[197] The majority of the population, however, was much too intimidated by the threatened reprisals. The expected consequences frightened them away from supportive actions,[198] which for some escapees would have been lifesaving. For instance, Johann Horvath, who fled on December 17, 1941, died of exposure in the hospital in Oberpullendorf.[199] Others were not capable of escaping detection by the alerted police indefinitely without the help of strangers and returned to camp voluntarily.[200]

For some, escape attempts had unpleasant consequences. After their capture by criminal police or state police, they were deported to large camps such as Ravensbrück or Auschwitz.[201] After his escape from Lackenbach, Alois Fröhlich from Vienna and his first wife and two children were sent to the concentration camp Auschwitz-Birkenau. He escaped death in the gas chamber because of his job as a founder in the Dora factory.[202]

But all measures were not enough of a deterrent, nevertheless, to chance an attempt at escape, and many an inmate who was subject to the prescribed punishments after his recapture tried it again or even several times. Numerous files document these incidents; the stamp "escaped" is noted on many files more than once.[203]

The percentage of escapes cannot be determined. Escape attempts are noted for 18 of 275 people on the available file cards. However, after checking these documents, one suspects that the files were not kept with the same thoroughness all the time. Therefore, escapes were not entered continually. Numbers are available only for the period of the diary. In the thirteen months in which the diary was kept, 170 reported escapes were entered. Sixty-seven fled directly from camp, and 103 used the more favorable situation at work or on the way there. In 104 cases, the end point of such endeavors was Camp Lackenbach. Either escapees were caught by patrols or they surrendered voluntarily. Sometimes fellow prisoners turned in escapees, thereby ending the escape attempt prematurely, that is to say, thwarting it from the beginning. "Yesterday camp inmates No. . . . escaped. However, they were detected by two Gypsies who happened to come from work at St. Martin and returned to camp by nine PM."[204] Presumably it was the expected sanctions that led to such uncomradely behavior, for, if inmates were suspected of complicity by the camp management, they were punished by the withholding of food.[205]

On the basis of available sources, it is also not possible to determine whether there was an increase or decrease of escape attempts over the years. On this subject, camp leader Brunner said, "Escape possibilities were always given in camp. The Gypsies fled individually as well as in groups."[206]

Some documents allow the reconstruction of measures undertaken when an escape occurred. First, the camp management sent an arrest request to the criminal police headquarters in Vienna.[207] Vienna published the names of the escapees in the search bulletin. If the escapee was still listed in the search bulletin due to an earlier proceeding, a new entry was not made. "However, on the basis of that search, a search request was initiated in the search system of the criminal police headquarters."[208] If there were hints of a possible escape destination—for instance, the home community[209]—the corresponding police stations were notified. If the escapees were caught and returned to camp, the criminal police was notified by a form letter.[210]

In searches, individual criminal police stations worked hand in hand. District borders also did not pose a problem in returning escapees to the place from which they had fled.[211]

Discharges

For the release of inmates, only two reasons were accepted. Inmates had the chance to regain their freedom if they could prove their "Aryan descent," that is to say, their "primarily German blood" (ZM-),[212] or if they were considered "foreign Gypsies."[213]

In Camp Lackenbach, a number of Hungarian Gypsies were imprisoned. They could obtain a discharge only if they succeeded in regaining their Hungarian citizenship. "I helped a number of camp inmates to complete the formalities to regain their Hungarian citizenship, a precondition for release later on."[214] These surely were only individual cases; on the existing 275 file cards,[215] five such discharges are noted (table 9). The two first mentioned—Maria and Veronika Sarközy—were in camp for one and three-quarter years, the others even two and one-quarter years, before it was determined that they had been robbed of their freedom "without just cause." After one and one-half years of imprisonment, Eleonore Pfaffl, Camp No. 364, born on February 20, 1898, in Eisenstadt, was released in December 1942. It was possible to determine that she was not a Gypsy.[217] The boy, Erich Papai (Camp No. 1602), together with his mother and three sisters, was allowed to leave Lackenbach after barely a month. They were able to prove their "Aryan ancestry."[218]

Some entries in the camp diary noted that several reviews and race-biological evaluations were undertaken. For instance: "Tues-

Table 9. Discharges—Hungarians

Camp No.	Name	Birth date/place	Date of Admission	Date of Discharge
1804	Sarközy, Maria	11/10/34 Pressburg	9/21/41	6/4/43
1799	Sarközy, Veronika	6/19/1891 Kisleg	9/21/41	6/4/43
2112	Weingartner, Ella	2/22/32 Langental	10/26/41	2/23/44
2111	Weingartner, Ladislaus	2/24/27 Langental	10/26/41	2/23/44
?	Hodoschi, Theresia	3/20/06 Kaisersdorf	10/26/41	2/23/44[216]

day, May 6, 1941: Requested Camp Nos. 532-535 for race-biological evaluations"; or "Friday, May 16, 1941: today, at the request of the Eisenstadt commissioner, the following Gypsy half-breeds were released."[219]

In addition, some discharges were initiated by the criminal police headquarters in Vienna. However, they were not explained in detail in the respective diary entries.[220]

Whether a discharge always occurred with the intervention from outside, or whether it was possible for inmates to effect an investigation of their case on their own initiative, cannot be ascertained.

Internal and External Forced Labor

The founding statutes of the Voluntary Association called for the camp to be self-sufficient through the work of the Gypsies. Therefore [the camp administration] endeavored to find work for all inmates.[221] Those men who were fit to work were to be employed in suitable jobs primarily outside the camp, while women and minors were employed in jobs they could carry out at home and by helping in the camp.[222]

At the beginning, jobs consisted primarily of the kind of work necessary to maintain the camp and to maintain themselves. In addition to the usual maintenance of the home (the cooks also were inmates),[223] the fields that belonged to the camp had to be tended, the saw mill had to be operated, and wood had to be collected.

They also immediately began to improve the access roads to camp. However, this work was carried out not only by men but also by women and children. For example, the road from Lackenbach to Unterfrauenhaid was a frequent building project of Gypsy women.[224] That such work was considered heavy labor, even by the camp administration, can be seen from a diary entry that notes that work on the access road is punishment: "Since, during the morning hours, several orders given by the camp leader were not carried out . . . in the afternoon [the inmates] worked on the access road as a punishment."[225] In addition, a number of inmates were assigned to the initial camp renovations.

Because of the continuation of the war, the acute shortage of workers triggered a request for imprisoned Gypsies. Although the intent to place Gypsies with suitable outside companies had existed from the camp's inception, there soon were farmers and manufacturers who came to the camp to hire labor. Thus, the Lackenbach Gypsies were employed in the most important branches of industry. The existence of some firms, that is to say, the full realization of their potential, depended on the labor of Gypsies. For example, the Lautner brick works in Lutzmannsburg would have had to cease production without Gypsies: "The district leader of district Oberpullendorf objected to the recall of Gypsies from the Lautner brick works in Lackenbach, since production of the company would have to cease."[226] The development was such that, at least at times, more and more inmates were employed outside the camp. Only a small group of people necessary for the maintenance of the camp were left in camp.

Types of Work

Criminal police headquarters in Vienna had the privilege of deciding labor assignments. There it was determined which projects were to be given priority.[227]

Most important were the building of the national expressway, road construction, and other public building projects; river regulation; and dam construction in Kobersdorf, Oberpullendorf, Trausdorf, and Klostermarienburg. These projects were carried out under the supervision of the firm of Kuschel and Haagen, Vienna.

As already mentioned, brick works needed Gypsies as workers: Julius Lautner, Lutzmannsburg; Josef Heinz, Oberpullendorf; and the Walbersdorf brick works Matisz in Mattersburg; also, the basalt works in Oberpullendorf and the ceramics factory in Stoob [used Gypsy labor].

Young people and children were sent to work on estates and in forestry. They went, for instance, to the estate of Baron Rohonczy in Oberpullendorf, to the Haidhof in Parndorf, to Ernst Kautz in Unterpullendorf, and to the estates in Kobersdorf, Strebersdorf, Ritzing, and Nebersdorf.

The mill works of Alfred Schmidt, Drassmarkt, and the Thies mill in Neutal also depended on the labor of Gypsies. Smaller private firms, innkeepers, and agricultural enterprises were also allotted Gypsy prisoners.[228] By the end of 1941, 370 people were employed for the construction of different segments of the national express-way.[229]

Up to this time, approximately 160 Gypsies were employed on estates and in forestry, and approximately 40 Gypsies worked in quarries and brick works.[230] One must take into consideration that those workers were also counted who had left their place of work through escape. Also, inmates often were withdrawn from one employer and given to another. Some files show as many as five different places of work. A majority of the inmates worked in more than one place of employment during their period of incarceration.[231]

Length of Work Days and Working Conditions

The work day lasted between eight and eleven hours. On a list from the construction firm Kuschel and Haagen, the daily work hours of twenty Gypsies who were employed in the construction of the dam at Oberpullendorf were noted in detail. From this list, one can see that they worked nine and one-half hours from Monday through Friday and five and one-half hours on Saturday.[232] Johann Bocdech, business manager of the Stoob ceramics factory, gave the following information about regulation of working hours there. "Work started at seven in the morning and ended approximately at 5:30 PM; in October/November, when the days got shorter, work ended already from around 4 PM. The lunch break was daily from 12 to 1."[233] Whether and how long they worked on Saturdays cannot be ascertained from his and others' testimony.

The most frequent time frames were from 7 AM to 5 PM, with half an hour or one hour for lunch. However, it could happen that Gypsies who were sent to nearby workplaces as day laborers had to work an eleven-hour day.[234] The documents indicate that the length of the work day did not change over the years and that the lengthening of the war did not lead to an increase [in work hours].[235]

In camp, forced labor conditions existed. All inmates capable of working had to do heavy work: "I . . . had to do heaviest work in a clay pit."[236] Or, "And I had to work very hard, in the forest and in road construction. In addition, I sometimes had to transport corpses: I had to take between 15 and 20 corpses to the Jewish cemetery, and in the evening I had to play music for the camp administrators."[237] Especially women and minors were physically abused when assigned to work in quarries, road construction, and similar work. In spite of this, work outside the camp was preferred to that within. "Those who were lucky enough to work outside the camp had more freedom than we in the camp."[238] The conclusion that those who worked and lived outside the camp had a better life is part of most memoirs. And yet, these "privileged individuals" also had to remember constantly that their life was forcibly regulated and that they themselves could not make any independent decisions. The desire to give up a disagreeable workplace was thwarted by the threat that the individual would be sent to a concentration camp.[239]

Little is known about the treatment of inmate workers by employers or foremen. A diary entry for the early period gives the impression of strict discipline. Thus, a Gypsy woman was punished because she transgressed against the injunction of silence during work.[240] Those working in road construction also were prohibited from speaking with passersby; they had to turn away when local residents or former acquaintances passed by.[241] "Supervision . . . during the work period was carried out by guards of the camp administration and by Gypsies who were designated as foremen by the camp administration."[242] In the beginning, there was no work detail that left camp without a guard. If there was not sufficient guard personnel, they would rather forego the work: "Work on the Meierhof was terminated today, since the work has to be carried out outside of town and there is no guard personnel available."[243]

At an outside workplace, guarding had to be secured as well. This was the responsibility of the employer.[244] For the transport of a larger group of workers to more distant workplaces, the camp supervision needed to supply guards. The number of guards for such enterprises varied. For example, when, on September 5, 1941, 193 Gypsies were sent to the RAB [national expressway] in Baden, a guard supervisor and ten camp orderlies were ordered as escorts.[245] A group of eighty Gypsies who went to the forests to collect wood was also supervised by a guard supervisor and a certain number of orderlies.[246] Other details that worked on nearby estates and in forest administration were usually accompanied by camp orderlies.[247]

When Julius Brunner took over the camp administration, guarding was also relaxed outside the camp, and the majority of Gypsies performing forced labor was thereafter also unguarded at the workplace. From then on they no longer were subject to their supervisors and employers without recourse. "I strictly forbade camp elders and foremen to mistreat their fellow inmates. I protected Gypsies who were employed outside the camp against abuses by their employers and removed them from their job, if necessary."[248]

If there was no supervision by police toward the end of the war, there was spot-checking by the camp commander.[249] However, such controls at workplaces outside the camp had already taken place under the first camp commander, Kollross.[250]

It is due to the unevenness of guard details and the forcible relaxation of the same in the last years that testimony on this issue shows discrepancies. While some reported that there was no supervision at the workplace, others felt that they were constantly watched by the mere presence of the foremen.[251] J. Bocdech reported that the mobility of Gypsy workers in the Stoob ceramics factory was barely restricted,[252] while inmate Raimund Frost remembered "that in the last years the fence to the factory premises in Stoob was reinforced."[253]

If workers were absent from their jobs for a longer time because of illness—if they needed to be hospitalized or returned to camp to convalesce—the employers could request replacement workers.[254] According to a diary entry of July 6, 1941, an exchange of workers was sometimes also approved on the grounds of unsuitability or danger of escape: "The lessor of estate Kobersdorf exchanged Elisabeth Horvath, camp No. 299, because of illness, instead camp No. 294 was sent"; October 11, 1941: "From RAB Alland were returned: 11 women because of uselessness (No. . . .) and three women because of danger of escape."[255] What sanctions waited for these inmates cannot be ascertained from the documents, but the thought comes to mind that they did not earn a better workplace by being returned to camp.

If all of those capable of working were employed for any and all jobs, the conditions were not the same for all. On the one hand, the extent of the expected performance varied from company to company; on the other, there were differences due to the different types of work, combined with individual tolerance.

For those inmates who were not housed in the immediate vicinity of the firm, travel back and forth was an added hardship. For instance, Gypsies who were employed in the Stoob ceramics factory had to walk five to six kilometers to the clay pit every day (sometimes they were allowed to take the early train, according to J. Bocdech's testimony), and after nine and one-half hours work they again had to walk the same long way to Lackenbach.[256]

Employers were not empowered to grant vacation or other benefits. In some special cases they could approach the camp commander with specific suggestions, and he would make a decision in the case.[257]

Compensation

"For their work the Gypsies received no pay, except for a small allowance of 4 to 6 RM [Reichsmark] per month. If desired, I am willing to attest to the above fact to any authority."[258] Foremen and camp elders received somewhat more, between 10 and 14 RM.[259] However, the employers were obligated to pay the full local wages for the work of the Lackenbach Gypsies.[260]

The Voluntary Association laid down the following guidelines for the accounting procedure: 10 percent of the wages earned were to be given to the worker for pocket money; the rest was to be sent to the camp cashier. This accounting procedure can also be found in a diary entry of March 23, 1941: "The accounts are settled weekly, the people receive ten percent of their earnings from their employer weekly."[261] On this subject, former inmates said: "For the hard labor we got nothing except 3 to 8 Marks monthly which served to buy the three cigarettes per day which the camp allowed."[262]

Some of the blue file cards, whose reverse side shows the notation "pocket money," also show amounts of 2, 3, or 8 RM. In connection with this information, one also regrets the incompleteness of the record keeping. The entries all date from 1941; later there were no more entries in this column.

The discovery of wage stubs, work contracts, and account statements allows some conclusions to be drawn regarding hourly wages. The construction firm of Kuschel and Haagen paid an hourly wage of 0.48 RM to women, slightly below the rate for men at 0.56 RM. If one figures the monthly allowance from that, then women received 10 RM and men 12. Agricultural concerns paid up to 0.50 RM per hour. For inmates who worked in inns or in private homes, the camp received 3.50 RM per day; here the daily work hours were not always given.[263]

According to the diary, quarry workers—men as well as women—received an allowance of 5 RM: "June 11, 1941. Payment of pocket money to the quarry workers, 42 people at 5 RM = 210 RM."[264]

Farmers had to pay between 10 and 20 RM monthly to the camp treasurer for those inmates who lived completely on their property[265]; for children this amount dropped to 5 RM per month. In some cases it was sufficient that children, hired for guarding cattle, received room and board.

The highest hourly wage is recorded on an employment confirmation for Johann Galatsai, who was employed by the Walbersdorf brick works.[266] He earned between 0.60 and 0.66 RM. His fate, which is illuminated by two confirmations from the firm, can be seen as an example of the arbitrary nature with which admissions to the Lackenbach forced labor camp occurred. Johann Galatsai, born in 1888, had, since 1904, worked satisfactorily [for the Walbersdorf brick works], with [only] minor interruptions. Despite this, he was sent to the camp on April 6, 1941.[267] On May 26, 1941, the leader of the labor office in Oberpullendorf came and asked for ten men for the brick works Matisz (Walbersdorf), "among them also Johann Galatsai-Horvath."[268] J. Galatsai then worked again as a stoker in the brick works from June 1941 to March 1945. The difference was that now his pay went to the camp treasury: "Wages were paid every two weeks as follows: In a 14-day pay period, Galatsai earned—110 hours at 0.60–0.66 RM; from that Galatsai received 10 percent pocket money—6.60 RM—and food from the prisoner of war kitchen of the Matisz brick works in Walbersdorf. The difference had to be sent to the administration of Camp Lackenbach."[269]

We learn from the diary that in the beginning months it occasionally happened that workers who did very heavy work and who were especially diligent were given special rations. There were free cigarettes or sometimes, for those doing extra heavy labor, additional rations of bread: "Friday, January 24, 1941: 1) 15 Gypsies, who do extra heavy labor in the saw mill and on Meierhof, today received 10 cigarettes gratis from the camp commander as recognition for good work. 2) From today on, the Gypsies who work on the Meier-hof (six men) as well as those who work in the saw mill, receive one loaf of bread as an additional ration."[270]

Child Labor

Precondition for Camp Lackenbach was that the inmates were able to work. Therefore, the transports that went from Lackenbach to the East carried primarily older people and small children.[271]

Those file cards that also give information on forced labor obligations state an age below forty for almost all those employed. In a few cases, forty-five is the maximum.[272] The material at our disposal has too many gaps to allow a generally valid statement. However, memoirs and writings give an impression of the child labor practiced there.

Ten-to thirteen-year-old children, boys as well as girls, were sent as workers to agricultural enterprises, to river regulation, and to the silk worm industry.[273] In some cases the businesses did not have to pay any salary at all to the camp treasury. It was sufficient when the children earned their keep with their labor.[274] Often they were not spared from heavy, physical work. Rosalia Karoly remembers her sad childhood in Lackenbach: "I was then 12-1/2 years old . . . we were sent to Lackenbach. Already the next day we were sent to work, I received a locksmith uniform and wooden shoes which were much too big; we had to work on river regulation, also the children. I was given a cramp-iron that was bigger than I was. Already on the first day I came back with a bloody face, so I was beaten. I always had to work with the adults, but my food rations were for a baby."[275]

Children who stayed in camp had to help with housework. Others were sent to the surrounding forests to collect wood. The inhumane conditions under which this work was carried out show the extent of the brutality—"In winter it was the order of the day that barefoot children had to fetch bundles of wood for heating."[276]

The preserved contracts, which were drawn up between the camp administration and employers regarding children who were to enter into a working relationship, give the impression of a slave trade.[277] If one considers that those working outside the camp had a freer life, children who were employed by farmers also had a better chance for survival. This is especially true for the last years. Camp commander

Brunner endeavored to increase the number of Gypsies who worked in companies and for farmers so that they would not starve in camp.

Nothing definite can be said regarding either a minimum age or the existence of regulations. The available documents allow us to conclude that children under age ten were not contracted out.[278]

Camp Living Conditions

The previous topics already gave detailed descriptions of the Lackenbach situation. On that basis we know that the first months after the camp's establishment were especially hard for the inmates because of inadequate housing. If a sizable number tried to get away from camp life by escaping, some others saw the only way out in suicide.[279]

With the arrival of ever greater masses of people, the living conditions deteriorated increasingly; the outbreak of the typhus epidemic then led to an escalation [of the deterioration]. At the end of 1941, several deaths and funerals took place daily.

Subsequently, the camp administration tried with reduced manpower to build a functional camp life by creating appropriate housing. Unfortunately, we know from reports about punitive measures in the Langmüller period that the reestablishment as well as the maintenance of order was to happen forcibly—by physical punishment instead of by the removal of bad conditions. Everyday life in camp was marked by hard work, inadequate nourishment, and reduction of personal freedom to a minimum.

With the onset of camp commander Eckschlager's administration in September 1942, every form of corporal discipline ceased. "I can confirm that the Gypsies were always treated properly and humanely by criminal police commissioner Fritz Eckschlager, and that he always tried to improve their situation as circumstances allowed. . . . I myself always treated the Gypsies humanely and with consideration and never mistreated them."[280]

Daily Routine

An exact timetable of the daily camp routine has not survived. Since work started at 7 AM, we know for sure that the day in Lackenbach began early. Those inmates who worked in the Lackenbach clay pit had to first walk the five to six kilometers there.

Lunch in camp was eaten only by those who worked in the immediate camp area or on Meierhof. Lunch was taken to the inmate details who worked in the surroundings, on the access road, or in the forest.[281] Details who worked in more distant workplaces did not return until evening. For the majority of camp inmates the day ended at 5 PM, and from 8 PM on nighttime quiet prevailed. Only those men who "did heavy labor outside the camp were given permission to stay up until 8:45 PM."[282] This ordinance applies to the first months of 1941. Nothing can be said about its maintenance and strict adherence in later years. However, an event from spring 1943, reported by a visitor, shows that the inmates took more liberties: "They had a celebration. It was evening and the Gypsies gathered in the barracks farthest from the administration building. They played the violin and young girls danced to the music. In order not to be disturbed by camp guards, the Gypsies posted guards themselves; however, they did not have to report intrusions."[283]

Weekends, which began on Saturday afternoon, were different. But even on these days, certain work needed to be done. Women had to do laundry during their spare time; men collected firewood in the forest.[284]

Sometimes inspection tours provided some variety in the monotonous daily camp routine. Visits by representatives and mayors of the immediate environment were frequent. If there were inspections by [a delegation from] criminal police headquarters in Vienna or even by high officials from the *Altreich*, the camp orchestra might have to play.[285]

Life in Lackenbach was different only for small children. Since mothers often were assigned to work details, the children were taken care of by a matron. Two of them we know from the diary: Helene Steiner and Maria Weinrich.[286] Professor Knobloch remembered that there was a camp teacher in his time. "She complained that there were not enough visuals. She would have liked to have pictures and blackboards for her work."[287]

If one takes the existing figures into consideration—most of the time there were between two hundred and three hundred children in camp—the impression grows that [the figures] must relate only to the smallest [children], that is to say, only a fraction of those present, who were watched by one matron or teacher and thereby were somewhat sheltered from the reality of camp life. The life of the older children, at least those from ten years of age on, was similar to that of the adults. They had to carry out the work assigned to them.

A short-term change occurred in the spring of 1943. Suddenly there was an interest in the language and the folklore of the inmates. For this occasion, a linguist came to camp for ten days. The preamble to this period began with an order by Heinrich Himmler in September 1942. Himmler never quite wanted to subordinate his own thoughts and plans regarding the future of the Gypsies to those of the general party line. His "genealogical research" was to establish a positive connection to the Gypsies in Germany.[288]

Within this project, the Vienna orientalist, Professor Christian, was given the task to research the various Gypsy dialects. He delegated this task to his assistant, Johann Knobloch, and obtained permission for him to carry out these investigations in Camp Lackenbach.[289]

Professor Knobloch himself reported on his presence in Lackenbach:

> My stay in Lackenbach lasted only 10 days. In this time period, I lived in camp. . . . Permission for my work in the camp had been obtained for me by the director of the Institute for Oriental Studies where I worked as a war replacement for the assistant who was on active duty. At first, the camp directorate thought that each individual informant should be sent to an office where I could work. I noticed immediately that this atmosphere was not conducive to my undertaking. Thus, I expressed the wish to the commander, who had an agreeable personality, to visit the Gypsies in their barracks as their guest. This established an atmosphere of trust. . . . I took turns working with all inmates, but concentrated my efforts on those who were good story tellers. . . . I spoke with many camp inmates freely; unfortunately not all were suited for the linguistic studies. Of course, with suitable individuals I worked for hours. Since I have not published all materials by far, I can only say that I have information from at least a dozen informants.[290]

Housing

We already reported on the primitive and poor housing in the early [camp] stages. Even though we have no concrete information about the dimensions—except that the camp was soon over-crowded—we know from diverse sources that there were at least twelve dividers in the sheep pens and that room two became the kitchen.[291] The cramped conditions of the living quarters during the mass admissions become clear when one learns that approximately two hundred individuals were squeezed into one room.[292]

After the establishment and enlargement of the camp, the Gyp-sies were housed in newly erected barracks that also were heated sufficiently in the winter months.[293] We have a detailed report by Professor Knobloch on the interior of this barracks-like facility: "A hallway in the center, to the right and left the rooms. . . . As far as I can remember, every family was assigned a room. The families were together. There were no further divisions within the rooms, but one could divide them with curtains. In the rooms, I could work at the table which also was the dining table for those who permanently worked inside the camp. . . . They slept in beds."[294] The compilation of room lists was part of prisoner registration. It guaranteed super-vision without problems.

Nutrition

With their admission to camp, all of the Gypsies' food ration cards were taken from them as well as those for clothing, which were handed over "to the Lackenbach municipal authority for further dis-posal."[295] At registration for communal meals, the cancellation of their food ration cards was confirmed.[296]

The poor quality and insufficiency of the camp food is not only documented by testimony from former inmates, but entries in the camp diary also hint at the precarious shortage of food in various ways: "Wednesday, May 28, 1941: Today we could only cook a clear broth for lunch, since there were no more groceries. For the eve-ning meal, we had to get flour from the mill. . . . Saturday, August 9, 1941: Today the question of groceries became extremely urgent and could only be solved temporarily through extensive efforts. A car from Vienna arrived with rice and cabbage."[297]

Ration cards that were found in the administration building from 1941, 1942, and 1945 allow us insight into camp nutrition, which is characterized in official reports as "mediocre because of the war,

Table 10. Nutrition at Camp Lackenbach

Date	Breakfast	Lunch	Dinner
8/7/41	Coffee	rice soup	soup made with flour, fat and water
8/8/41	Coffee	meat soup with noodles	coffee
8/30/41	Coffee	sour turnips with potatoes	soup with flour, fat and water+
8/31/41	Coffee	fried potatoes and meat	coffee+
1/4/42	Coffee	turnips, potatoes, meat	beef soup with sap sago
3/21/45	Coffee	potato soup	soup
?/45	Coffee	potato soup	noodle soup

+ On these two days, the two- to three-year-olds received rice cereal and milk for supper; children from four to seven were given "milk with *Schoeberl* [a doughy addition]."[299]

but sufficient, since the camp inmates supposedly received the same food rations as the rest of the population" (table 10).[298]

A closer examination of the inmate population and the use of foodstuffs allows a clearer picture of the insufficient nutrition.[300] From lunch on August 31, 1941, we can determine that with a population of approximately one thousand inmates and meat consumption of 145 kg [approximately 319 pounds], portions were less than 150 grams [5 ounces]. Babies are also included because no separate meals were listed for them. On January 4, 1942, portions were at least 200 grams per person.[301] Meat dishes, except for "meat soups," probably were restricted to Sundays; both days for which meat dishes were listed were Sundays. If one compares this to the standardized concentration camp norms—where the weekly standard for meat from August 1, 1940, to May 14, 1942, consisted of 400 grams [13 ounces][302]—one can determine that the nutrition situation in Gypsy camp Lackenbach was not better than in other concentration camps, especially not at this time.[303]

As in other camps, the most frequent meals were different kinds of soups. "These soups were tasteless and watery; nutritional value and tastiness of soups decreased even further when they had to be eaten cold. This happened very often, for instance, when the inmates only returned to the camp in the evening or at night."[304]

Knowing about the poor quality of this food, one can understand that the inmates rejected the prepared food and requested other food—especially in the early months when they did not yet accept everything without objection: "Monday, March 3, 1941: In the evening, the Gypsies who worked outside the camp began to rebel against the food and wanted to be given bacon. They repeatedly refused the food."[305]

The deficiencies in the care, also caused by the unexpectedly high admissions from other administrative areas and the undernourishment that resulted from it, were decisively coresponsible for the outbreak of the typhus epidemic. Improvement occurred only when, after the epidemic subsided, inmates were increasingly sent to outside firms and agricultural concerns to work and were in part fed and housed by the employer. Inmates who were housed with firms outside the camp were again excluded from the communal meals and given ration cards.

Due to the expansion of their business and lack of other workers, the Stoob ceramics factory also hired Gypsies from August 1, 1942, on. In the beginning, when they still returned to camp every evening, they brought their rations from camp. Then, from the middle of November 1942 on, a building that belonged to the factory was used as housing. There they had their own kitchen and cooks. Johann Bocdech testified that the approximately thirty employees (in the beginning there were seven to eight Gypsies) had ration cards for heaviest labor, that is to say, received food according to those standards.[306] Anton Schneeberger, who worked in the ceramics factory, remembered only poor food, but not ration cards for heaviest labor.[307]

"(Camp leader Brunner) allowed the people to leave the camp to work for farmers. He said they weren't here to starve. Brunner treated the Gypsies well."[308] Brunner tried to make life more bearable for the inmates through supplements from the camp's own gardens. "The food supply of the Gypsies was guided by the prescribed standards, but I attempted to upgrade it with produce from a greenhouse that was associated with the camp."[309] The two ration cards from 1945, which were signed by Brunner, show four heavy laborers listed separately. In the diary, we also find the notation that those performing heavy labor sometimes received a loaf of bread as a special ration. Former inmates predominantly remembered bad food: unpeeled potatoes, Swedish turnips, spoiled cabbage, inedible cheese, wormy legumes, and, above all, tiny amounts.[310]

Clothing

In Lackenbach, there was no uniform clothing for the inmates as in most internment camps. The Gypsies were allowed to wear their regular clothing, and the camp leadership encouraged the inmates to bring their own clothes. Some inmates used their vacation to get clothing and linens from their former homes.[311]

Taking away clothing ration cards was part and parcel of the admissions process. Accordingly, future provisions, especially work clothes, had to be supplied by the camp. For one, shipments of old clothes and sheets from the National Socialist Charity Organization in Vienna arrived in Lackenbach; in addition, the commissioner in Oberpullendorf assigned ration cards for work clothes and shoes.[312] When questioned on this theme, Professor Knobloch testified that there was no specific work clothing; "rather everyone could wear what they wanted. I remember, however, that once an older girl was scolded because she appeared in a pants suit. After that she wore a dress. Cleanliness of clothing was especially important."[313] Thus, women who had put in a fifty-hour work week had to use their free Saturday afternoon to wash clothes: "The inmates who worked out-side had the afternoon off. The women used the afternoon to do laundry."[314]

In addition to the fact that families stayed together, the wearing of civilian clothes was a decisive mark of distinction in the discussion whether Lackenbach was like a concentration camp. But in Gypsy camp B IIe in concentration camp Auschwitz-Birkenau, where families also stayed together, inmates wore their own clothes as well.[315]

Contacts with the Outside World

"Gypsies were allowed to leave the camp only with a transit pass issued by the camp administration. . . . I often made use of the right to grant leave, and in special cases vacation, so that occasionally each of the camp inmates received leave for personal reasons."[316] This credible information[317] is at our disposal for the last one and one-half years of the camp's existence. Entries in the camp diary, as well as the discovery of some transit permits in the former Gypsy camp,[318] allow the conclusion that short vacations were granted infrequently throughout the entire time of the camp's existence—mostly to regulate family affairs.

Study of the diary leads to the conviction that more leave was granted during the first few months: "Karl Berger, Robert Horvath, and Johann Kosak came back from vacation"; "Nine people were sent on vacation"; "Easter vacationers returned."[319] The permits were partly justified by special diligence.[320] However, individual notes show that these permits were exceptions. "Andreas Hodosi, camp list 21, and Josef Hodosi, camp No. 30, were given leave from March 8, 1941, to March 10, 1941, 6 AM, to go to Rattersdorf-Liebing to handle urgent family affairs."[321] This was an exception.

After May 1941, we hardly find vacations in the diary, as there are no documents about preferential treatment until October 1942. Transit passes recovered for the end of 1942 confirm short leaves from the camp to regulate family affairs (table 11). Passes were also given to those inmates who left camp for shopping or other errands: "Gypsy Ludwig Horvath, born September 5, 1906, was given a pass valid until February 19, 1941, for the purpose of picking up shoe makers' tools in Deutschkreutz."[323]

Inmates were allowed to receive visitors only under guard in a forecourt of the camp. Individuals from outside camp were not allowed inside.[324] Only those inmates who lived with their outside employers could visit their family and friends in camp on weekends. Disregarding the visiting prohibition could have unpleasant consequences for those from outside. For instance, on September 7, 1941, three people from Vienna were "admitted to the camp temporarily[325] . . . because of disregard of the visiting prohibition." For one of them the "temporary admission" became a permanent one.[326]

If visitors wanted to alleviate the permanent hunger of their relatives temporarily by bringing food, it could happen that the bene-

Table 11. Transit Passes

Camp No.	Name	Length	Signature
465	Jantschitz, Franz	10/11–10/12/42	Eckschlager
249	Horwath, Elisabeth	10/11–10/13/42	Eckschlager
100	Horvath, Marie	12/23–12/27/42	Brunner[322]

factors themselves were interned in camp. Such an incident occurred on March 23, 1941, when the quantity of food stuffs smug-
gled in raised the suspicion of the camp administration "that the two
visitors do not make their living honestly." That was reason enough
to also incarcerate them.[327]

Additional incidents can also be seen as confirmation of the already cited visiting prohibition, that is to say, restricted visiting
privilege. Thus, even families or friends from the immediate surroundings sent money and packages to camp by mail.[328] However,
the majority of the shipments came from Vienna; several packages
were sent from distant Burgenland villages; and two came from the
Altreich (Dortmund and Ravensburg). Some inmates received packages from the "Protectorate" [Böhmen and Mähren].

One can therefore recapitulate that receipt of packages as well as
receipt of money was allowed, but no information is available about
any restrictions, such as frequency, size of packages, restriction to a
certain kind, amount of money,[329] and so on.

Package stubs available as documentation allow the assumption
that the number of packages was not limited. In one case, the same
recipient (Anton Rosenfeld, camp No. 931) received within a short
time three packages, of which two arrived in camp within one
week.[330] Whether the inmate actually received the full contents—
the packages had previously been opened[331]—and whether he could
do with them as he pleased is unknown.[332] At least there is confirmation in the form of a signed package stub by the addressee.
Often this procedure was also witnessed by the signature of a camp
elder (for instance, Sepp Brandner[333] or Alexander Sarközi) or even
the camp leader.[334]

While the receipt of money shipments had to be acknowledged by
the recipient, it is not to be assumed that prisoners were allowed to
keep large sums. Several circumstances speak for a central administration of prisoner money. In camp, nothing but cigarettes could be
bought. If large amounts of money had been available, the danger of
disregard for certain injunctions by those who worked outside the
camp would have occurred—such as bartering with civilian workers and going to restaurants and movies, for example. Diary entries
report that large sums of money that were found when camp inmates were searched[335] were taken from them. Brunner's descrip-

tions of the camp dissolution also point to the existence of inmate accounts: "When the Russian troops arrived . . . I distributed . . . the deposited sums of money and documents."[336]

Financial support by relatives met with approval in all camps. For instance, in Buchenwald, before the beginning of the war, they built up a flourishing snack business from which especially Kapos and specially designated block buyers derived benefits. With the outbreak of the war, there was hardly anything to buy—except tobacco goods.[337]

Stories and notices about Camp Lackenbach allow the suspicion that the cigarette business was profitable for the administration and was allowed for this reason. For instance, when asked about their earnings, former Lackenbach inmates reported that they only received 3 to 8 Marks per month, "which served to buy the daily ration of three cigarettes in camp."[338] A sufficiently clear diary entry reads: "Sold 500 cigarettes to camp inmates, and deposited the amount of 15 RM for them in the camp register, and on March 30 entered [transaction] in accounts receivable ledger."[339]

The inmates also were allowed to write and receive letters, but all were subject to censorship. The permitted extent of actual correspondence is unclear. From the fact that the sender of money and packages knew the camp number of the inmate addressee one can derive that there must have been contact in the form of letters. If these details were missing, [the shipments] might possibly have been returned [to the sender].[340] Although correspondence between inmates and immediate relatives was allowed in all camps, it was restricted to twice a month.[341]

Even if there was no fixed limit for Camp Lackenbach, another problem kept Gypsies from using this privilege liberally. A majority of the incarcerated adults was illiterate[342] or at least so untrained in writing that a signature alone caused them great difficulties.[343] Yet, due to a hasty prohibition, even those age groups who were of school age before the camp's establishment and who in some cases had already started school remained without education. Already in September 1938, a "prohibition for Gypsy children to attend school" was announced in Burgenland, although such an ordinance did not yet exist from the Reich.[344] Other factors that prevented frequent letter writing also need to be pointed out—not enough leisure time, disinterest because of censorship, and cost of mailing.

Acts of support that were not tolerated included attempts by relatives to slip something occasionally to the inmates during their outside work. "At approximately 3:30 PM . . . two Gypsies . . . were found . . . in mildly inebriated condition. Both had been cutting reeds for brooms and, according to the testimony of both, Guntram Horvath received a 'surprise' visit from his daughter in the forest, who brought them 1 liter [1 quart] of wine."[345] As punishment and to sober them up, both culprits remained in isolation for one and one-half days, and they received no food except breakfast.

Punitive Measures

Although the diary gives only an inaccurate picture of the horrors that occurred in Camp Lackenbach, a single entry points to the degree of physical punishment. We learn, for instance, that on April 19, 1941, the culprit of a harmless transgression such as "unauthorized smoking in the sleeping quarters"[346] was beaten for 15 minutes. If one wants to get a grasp on the fate of the victims, reports of punitive measures such as these and similar ones contain enormous value as testimony. They allow one to recognize the harshness of the disciplinary measures without much imagination.

Even though there were orders from the central office in Vienna to be especially harsh in escape attempts—which was the most serious sort of offense—and to also make use of beatings,[347] instructions were so general—as they were in the large camps[348]—that inmates were to a great extent at the mercy of and subject to the terrorism of the camp leader (and his assistants).

The harsh forms of punishment, especially physical force, reached their greatest extent under the camp leadership of Langmüller and at the same time also their end. Some of the victims had a chance to speak out during the trial that resulted from his indictment in the postwar period. Witness testimony and the resultant verdict provided detailed accounts on the subject of mistreatment in Lackenbach.[349] After initial denials, the accused had to admit that he had himself given beatings repeatedly, which the court considered proof "that the accused not only ordered the beatings of Gypsies that were prescribed by the central office in Vienna and which the Gypsies received because they fled from camp, but that he himself in addition gave beatings for various reasons with a stick or with a dog whip."[350] Witness Margarethe Papai, in camp since 1940, reported on mistreatments that she herself had to suffer: "He (Langmüller) beat me to such an extent that my hand was in a sling for three months."[351] Martin Horwath remembered that Langmüller always carried a dog whip, but he also mentioned that camp elders carried out the beatings on orders of the camp commander.[352]

Two Viennese administration officials, Nikolaus Reinprecht and Josef Hajek, confirmed that there were beatings under Langmüller's command. "Mistreatment of Gypsies happened when Gypsies in camp became guilty of non-disciplined behavior or attempted to escape. . . . (They were) sentenced to beatings, which then were given on a wooden block[353] by other Gypsies."[354] "Later, however, this punishment was abolished."[355] Because Langmüller often delegated the enforcement to camp elders—and here especially to Alexander Sarközi[356]—reports predominated that could not substantiate Langmüller's participation: "The accused himself did not administer beatings, he only gave the orders."[357]

Even the then mayor of Lackenbach, Mathias Hlavin, knew that Gypsies "got beatings when they did something wrong." He himself was only in camp once or twice during the entire period but knew about it from other people.[358]

The police commander, Ingenieur Karpischek, did not accept the mistreatments in the Gypsy camp without protest: "I could not watch these things. . . . That also was one of the reasons why I was suspended from service and sent to Poland as punishment."[359]

Franz Langmüller was found guilty of "putting people, that is to say, Gypsies, in painful situations, mistreating them considerably, and offending their human dignity and insulting them during the Nazi terror period, all under the cloak of official authority."[360] He was sentenced to a year of extra security imprisonment, intensified through a hard board as bed every three months.

Even though the court was from the beginning distrustful of Gypsy testimony and often required confirmation from non-Gypsies,[361] there were accounts of incidents that were so serious that everyone felt that the Gypsies' human dignity had been violated. The court's argument stated, "Even though the Gypsies in general are considered unclean, in the opinion of the court these incidents offend against our conception of human dignity."[362] Prisoners had to empty out the toilets with their bare hands because they had no tools to remove the excrement. Others' faces were pushed into the excrement of children who had, of necessity, done their business in the camp alley.[363]

Besides beatings, which were given primarily for escape attempts,[364] the punishment most often used was solitary confinement, often in combination with deprivation of food. The inmate who was separated from the others could, in addition, be sentenced to heavy labor in camp.[365] In a diary entry of January 23, 1941, we read, "As punishment the three (escapees) were shut off in a room, and they were not given food for a few days." January 24, 1941: "Stefan Horvath, [born] September 2, 1911, who should be seen as the instigator, (continues to be) separated from the other Gypsies. . . . During the day, Stefan Horvath had to perform heavy labor in the camp."[366] These measures were also used to punish such crimes as theft from comrades[367] or complicity to escape.[368] Transgressions during working hours, for example, disregard of the speaking prohibition, leaving the work room unauthorized, or smoking when prohibited,[369] had the same consequences. A rarer method of discipline was the cutting off of hair.[370] Besides these punishments that were carried out in camp, for some transgressions deportation to a concentration camp followed. This threat—especially realized for repeated escape attempts—was meant to contribute to a reduction in the escape rate.

Only a change of course under the two subsequent camp commanders, Eckschlager and Brunner, allowed for a partial fading of the cruelties in the memory of former inmates—they were anxious to improve the situation of the Gypsies in accordance with the circumstances.[371]

Over the course of the years, the Gypsies had gotten used to camp life. It had become their home. Especially the very young ones had spent the majority of their childhood in camp. A Viennese Sinto, who had been deported to Lackenbach as a ten-year old, described his impressions when freed. When told that he was free to go, he could not comprehend what that meant: "You can go through the gate up front. It was for me as if the world was collapsing. That was impossible for me. This was my home."[372]

The camp was disbanded when the Soviet army approached. "I (distributed) all groceries and clothing in camp to the camp inmates, also arranged that they were given deposited monies and documents and initiated their freedom."[373] The Lackenbach inmates were released directly from camp and were thus spared death marches during the last months of the war. Gypsies who had survived other concentration camps or the experiments done on them had to participate in the death marches.[374] "The camp administration, consisting of three individuals, left on Thursday, March 29, 1945, via horse and carriage for Vienna."[375]

An Attempt at a Typology

If, at the beginning of the war, there still were clear characteristics of differentiation between the individual camp types, these distinctions blurred more and more as the function of the camps changed. The continuation of the war required the establishment of new priorities.[376]

Concentration camps, as chief instruments for the realization of the National Socialist terror were, until 1938, primarily places for separation and forced education of so-called enemies of the [Nazi] state and the [German] people. Already in the beginning phase they had characteristics that formed the conditions of imprisonment for their entire period of existence. Certain principles in inmate treatment, combined with a finely worked-out system of inmate hierarchy, created an atmosphere of terror. The wearing of prison garb, slave labor, and mistreatment demoralized and weakened the inmates. If, at the beginning, there were orders to do heavy, senseless work, eventually the exploitation of labor took precedence, together with the physical extermination.

Even those measures that began at the beginning of 1938 under the collective concept of "crime prevention," and which affected Gypsies as well, had economic motives. Concentration camps had functioned as detention places for [so-called] biological and political enemies of the people, while at the same time using their labor. In addition to the elimination of individuals who were a burden to the community, here laborers were forcibly recruited for certain projects.

The introductory explanation of the appropriate statute reads, "The strict execution of the four-year-plan requires the employment of all people capable of working and does not allow that asocial people withhold themselves from work and thereby sabotage the four-year-plan."[377] The economic interests of the SS were added to the political-police motive of combating the enemy. In the winter of 1941–1942, the work detail aspect became the dominating factor that determined the further development of concentration camps. "Concentration camps did not stop being places of political persecution, but, to a much larger extent, they became an especially discriminating and draconian form of forced labor."[378] In addition to these economic tasks, the concentration camps served as shielded places for criminal acts, for mass shootings, and for medical experiments.

The establishment of Camp Lackenbach served as a preparatory step for the not yet completed solution of the Gypsy question. The complete expulsion of Gypsies from society (in which the majority had not been integrated in the first place) occurred through their isolation in a camp especially for them.

The primary characteristic in Lackenbach was forced labor. Because of the intended self-sufficiency of camp life, the inmates did not in any way become a burden to the general public. They had to fend for themselves as well as take care of those family members and inmates who could not work. The use of Lackenbach inmates differed at least from the time when the economic interests of the SS dominated there. If, in other concentration camps, work was connected with total exploitation and physical extermination,[379] in most cases outside work in Lackenbach brought an improvement of living conditions for those concerned.

In this connection one can also point to a differing development for admissions. If, in other camps, the increase of admissions in later years was also caused by a lack of labor, the numerical development in Lackenbach shows a different picture. Mass admissions to the Gypsy camp occurred only in the year after the establishment in 1941. Thereafter, there were only relatively insignificant changes in the camp population. Also, with regard to death statistics, there are no parallels to the concentration camps. After the end of the epidemic in the spring of 1942, the number of deaths in Lackenbach decreased considerably.

In the concentration camps, deaths increased to such an extent that repeated circulars of the SS-WVHA [*Wirtschaftsverwaltungshauptamt* = Central Office for Economy and Administration] in 1942–1943 requested camp commanders to stop this development, that is to say, to counteract it in the interest of labor. From August 1943 on, a slight decline was to be noted.[380] In addition, the dominance of the economic factor effected a lessening of the reign of terror.[381] An additional favorable effect on living conditions in the concentration camps was provided by the course of the war. "With the continuously deteriorating situation at the fronts, which continuously accelerated the demand for soldiers . . . the composition of the guard details . . . changed. . . . The most brutal SS men have left . . . a very unusual atmosphere for concentration camp conditions developed."[382]

If several criteria that are typical signposts of concentration camps were not applicable to Lackenbach, the camp suggests an inclusion among forced labor camps on the basis of well-known facts, such as structure and organization. In part, the inner development nevertheless showed similarities [to concentration camps], so that in certain phases there were only small differences in degree.

Thus, at the time of the camp establishment, inadequate conditions regarding housing and especially sanitary facilities existed in Lackenbach. The transformation of the place into an internment camp was possible only through simultaneous expansion by the inmates. The adaptation of the buildings for camp command and administration was given priority, as was the case elsewhere.[383]

Already at the camp's opening, seasoned inmates were brought from other camps and given assignments.[384] These Nazi tactics were based on the experience that, from the beginning, terror and defamation created the "desired" atmosphere through a finely tuned system of the inmate hierarchy.

Possibilities for comparison also exist for the epidemic. If the onset was provoked by planned undernourishment and lack of sanitary facilities, there was practically no care and treatment of the sick. There were, for instance, also concentration camps in which a small number of inmates died from direct personal abuse, through shootings or mistreatments. In concentration camp Bergen-Belsen, for instance, the main causes of mass death were hunger and premeditated epidemics.[385]

In the discussion on ranking, that is to say, differentiation of Lackenbach from concentration camps, two arguments of differentiation were employed. In addition to the question of competence and guarding, wearing civilian clothes and keeping whole families together were factors. In the chapter on clothing, it was already documented that this special regulation brought no advantages for the inmates and that these exceptions also existed for other inmate categories in camps for different reasons.[386] Although in Lackenbach complete families were admitted and housed together, in many cases individual family members were deported to other camps. Other families had been torn apart because of the Lodz deportations.

The strongest argument against ranking Lackenbach as a concentration camp was the fact that the Gypsy camp was under the jurisdiction of the criminal police. Camp commanders were criminal police, and guard personnel consisted of police and reserve policemen, and they did not belong to the jurisdiction of the SS. "Combat of the Gypsy vermin" during the Nazi period fell under the jurisdiction of the criminal police—as all measures in the area of "crime prevention." However, in this connection the organization of the SS and the police during this period must be taken into consideration. On the occasion of his appointment, Himmler had announced the fusion of the SS and the police as a specific goal.[387] In a lecture in November 1941, he termed the general SS, the combat SS, and the police as "the three pillars of the SS."[388]

In Lackenbach the first two stages of Gypsy persecution were carried out—imprisonment and forced labor. Further steps of persecution, such as sterilization, use of experimental tools, and extermination, were to be carried out in other places. Lackenbach had become a transit camp to the large concentration and death camps. Threat of deportation to a concentration camp, as well as repeated deportations, governed the atmosphere and living conditions in camp.

Dancing girl: Hungarian Romni (courtesy of DÖW, Vienna).

Young woman with child in work reeducation camp Weyer on Inn, 1941 (courtesy of Andreas Maislinger, Innsbruck).

Sinti soldiers from Oberösterreich (Upper Austria) in World War I (courtesy of
Rosa Martl, Linz, and community of Hochburg-Ach).

Sinti musicians at Salzburg Inn, 1938 (courtesy of Josef Reinhardt, Offenburg
[deceased]).

Arrest and deportation, Vienna-Simmering, 1938 (courtesy of DÖW, Vienna).

Portrait photo in work reeducation camp Weyer on Inn, 1941 (courtesy of Andreas Maislinger, Innsbruck).

Portrait photo in work reeducation camp Weyer on Inn, 1941 (courtesy of Andreas Maislinger, Innsbruck).

Portrait photo in work reeducation camp Weyer on Inn, 1941 (courtesy of Andreas Maislinger, Innsbruck).

Portrait photo in work reeducation camp Weyer on Inn, 1941 (courtesy of Andreas Maislinger, Innsbruck).

Portrait photo in work reeducation camp Weyer on Inn, 1941 (courtesy of Andreas Maislinger, Innsbruck).

Children in Camp Salzburg-Maxglan (courtesy of Martin Haslauer/Erika Thurner, Salzburg).

Camp Salzburg-Maxglan/Leopoldskron (courtesy of Josef Reinhardt, Offenburg [deceased]).

Salzburg Gypsies as Riefenstahl *Tiefland* film extras
(courtesy of Josef Reinhardt, Offenburg [deceased]).

Nomadic gypsies—before 1938 (courtesy of DÖW, Vienna).

"Portschy *Denkschrift*" [1938 polemical publication on
Gypsy danger to German racial purity by Dr. Portschy]
(courtesy of DÖW, Vienna).

Gypsy caravans in Camp Lackenbach (courtesy of
DÖW, Vienna).

Female inmates at Gypsy camp Lackenbach leave for work (courtesy of DÖW, Vienna).

Burgenland Roma band, Unterwart, 1937 (courtesy of Claudia Mayerhofer, *Dorfzigeuner,* Vienna, 1987, 158).

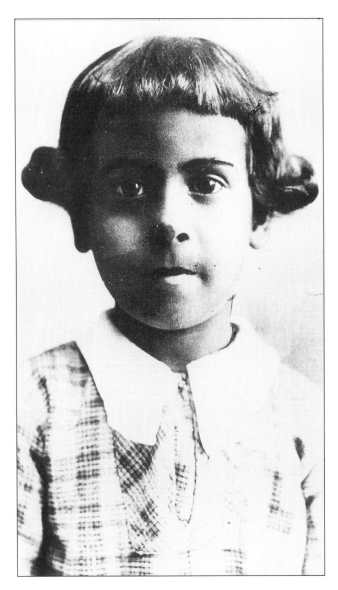

Sidonie Adlersburg, who died in Auschwitz concentration camp (courtesy of DÖW, Vienna).

Roma survivor with concentration camp number tattoo (courtesy of DÖW, Vienna).

Prisoners in work reeducation camp/Gypsy collection camp Weyer on Inn, 1941 (courtesy of Andreas Maislinger, Innsbruck).

Prisoners in work reeducation camp/Gypsy collection camp Weyer on Inn, 1941 (courtesy of Andreas Maislinger, Innsbruck).

Gypsy woman in concentration camp Auschwitz-Birkenau (courtesy of DÖW, Vienna).

Arrival of Gypsy transport in Auschwitz (courtesy of DÖW, Vienna).

Remains of headquarters building at
Lackenbach camp after the war (courtesy of
DÖW, Vienna).

Gypsy memorial in Lackenbach, erected in 1984 (courtesy of Leopold Banny,
Lackenbach).

6

Gypsy Transports from Austria to Lodz and Chelmno

When, in November 1941, the deportations east were resumed, Austrian Gypsies were also included in the transports to Lodz (Litzmannstadt).[1] From interviews that Dr. Steinmetz conducted with Viennese and Burgenland Gypsies in 1965, it can be seen that many had lost their relatives in Lodz.[2]

The reconstruction of events in the Gypsy camp of ghetto Lodz is not exactly simple. Although some documents on the events survived and were used by the Polish historian Jerzy Ficowski for his two publications,[3] they have been missing since Ficowski gave them to the Main Commission on Research into the Hitler Crimes in Poland in 1950. Martin Pollak, who in the years 1975 and 1976 tried to pursue the whereabouts of these documents for the *Dokumentationsarchiv* [DÖW] in Vienna, wrote resignedly: "Each search here (resembles) an incredible adventure, which only too often ends in nothing."[4]

The Gypsy camp, "the small ghetto in the large Lodz ghetto," existed only from November 1941 to the beginning of 1942. There Gypsy extermination in Poland began, carried out under camp conditions. The first large campaign in the fall of 1941, which included twenty thousand Jews and five thousand Gypsies, was based on the decision of the January 1940 Conference Regarding the Clearing of the Eastern Districts.[5] Eichmann's department N-B-4 in RSHA (emigration, cleansing) was put in charge of deportation of Jews, together with Gypsies from the Reich area.

Altogether, 5,007 Gypsies were deported in five transports of 1,000 persons each.[6] All five transports were compiled in Austria— two in Camp Lackenbach on November 4 and November 7, 1941.[7] For two of these transports, which began at the railroad station in Mattersburg, we can find entries in the camp diary as well as in the police records.[8] These entries apparently refer to the first and fourth transports. A list of the escort detail from a Lackenbach transport still exists. Twenty-one persons, officers and guard supervisors, had to guard the train.[9] Three additional deportation trains that arrived between November 5 and 9, 1941, in Lodz left from the following points of embarkation: Rotenturm and Oberwart (Burgenland) as well as Fürstenfeld (Steiermark). The admissions to Lodz are recorded according to sex. The last transport included 1,007 individuals, hence a total figure of 5,007 people resulted.[10]

The leader of the ghetto administration, Hans Bielow, responded with annoyance "when some Nazi authority had come up with the idea to squeeze an additional 5,007 Gypsies into his ghetto."[11] This announcement was succeeded by his complaint to the president of Lodz, Dr. Übelhör: "I was firmly convinced . . . that I would be able to turn to the monumental economic tasks of the ghetto, and I am already now confronted with the apparent *fait accompli* of having to accommodate not only 20,000 more Jews, but also 5,000 additional Gypsies in camp very shortly. If the planned deportation took effect, I would consider it my duty to point out that the ghetto administration . . . declines responsibility for the maintenance of order and security . . . especially since it sees a great danger in the accommodation of the Gypsies."[12]

For the execution of the plan, 300 square meters were separated from the rest of the area by double barbed wire. This area had to accommodate five thousand people.[13] As a consequence, within barely two months, 613 Gypsies had died or been murdered. This hermetical sealing of the camp section raised numerous suspicions, and even the *Judenrat* [Jewish Council] in Lodz was not sure whether these inmates really were Gypsies. In reports in the daily bulletin, mention of Gypsies is always in quotation marks. But there are today sufficient documents that erase all doubts.[14]

After the outbreak of the typhus epidemic, the only ones who had access and also insight into the events were Jewish doctors and burial personnel. The recorded testimony of the few survivors unfortunately is among the lost Polish documents. In addition, there is also other information that confirms the existence of such a Gypsy camp in Lodz. On the one hand, there is a November 15, 1941, request by the "labor office in Lodz (Litzmannstadt)" to mobilize 120 Gypsies "as quickly as possible"[15] for the German weapons and munitions factory in Poznan (Posen); the commissioner of Oberwart gave directions to all mayors concerning inquiries about those who had been transferred to ghetto Lodz. In this communication, dated March 19, 1942, we read that "permission to visit is not possible" and that [message came] at a time when none of the relocated Gypsies were alive anymore.[16]

In addition, a variety of documents that were found in the Lackenbach headquarters building give witness to the deportations to ghetto Lodz. Thus, one page of the main list of the transport, dated November 4, 1941, and containing seventeen names of victims, was found.[17] There is also a letter by criminal police headquarters in Vienna, dated August 18, 1944, in which information is requested on Hubert Daniel, a Gypsy. The answer of the camp directorate, dated August 28, 1944, stated that the individual was sent to Lodz (Litzmannstadt) already in 1941.[18] In addition, a diary entry, dated April 11, 1941, tells us that those 301 Gypsies who, on that day, arrived in Lackenbach from the criminal police in Linz "were destined for transfer to Lodz (Litzmannstadt)."[19]

At the beginning of January 1942, the Gypsies were sent to the extermination camp Chelmno (Kulmhof) by truck, and the "ghetto within the ghetto" disappeared. "The victims transported from ghetto Lodz to Chelmno included . . . a larger transport of Gypsies and typhus cases."[20] The transport to Chelmno happened in groups and probably lasted until January 12, 1942. Only very few succeeded in surviving this horrible death camp by escaping. Witnesses were not able to give details on length of internment and gassing of Gypsies, but it is pretty certain that no one survived. Altogether there were only four survivors in Chelmno.[21] We can in any case tell from the statistics on the Chelmno victims that the Gypsies of the evacuation transports to Lodz were murdered in Chelmno: "To this total number we can add approximately 5,000 Gypsies who were evacuated from the Lodz ghetto and killed in Chelmno"—this according to the credible testimony of witnesses G. (at that time deputy to the elder of the Jewish inmates in the Lodz ghetto) and Fuchs (at that time criminal police commissioner of the state police command Lodz.)[22] The Israeli researcher Miriam Norvich confirms almost all of these facts. In addition to the Polish sources, she was also able to use those at Yad Vashem in Jerusalem.[23]

Somewhat strange are the circumstances that influenced the decision of the relocation place. "Eichmann, who never made his own decision, who was always concerned to be 'covered' by orders, now took 'for the first time and for the last time' an initiative which contradicted his orders; instead of sending these people to Riga or Minsk . . . he directed the transport to the Lodz ghetto."[24] During the trial in Jerusalem, Eichmann could not really remember the specific circumstances, but he testified to have had choices in this matter between Lodz and the Russian territories.[25] The complaint of Dr. Übelhör, the ghetto commander, to Himmler seems more macabre: "Eichmann deceived him and his people with 'cheap tricks which he learned from the Gypsies.' "[26]

7

Gypsies as Subjects
of Medical Experiments

Motivation of the Doctors Who Participated
in the Experiments and the Interests
of the Pharmaceutical Industry

Medical experiments on human beings were justified on the basis that this way achieved faster progress and possibilities for solutions of acute problems. That these so-called scientific enterprises were connected with sadistic tendencies can be seen in the torture, maiming, and deaths that resulted. The Nazi doctors considered themselves engineers in the technological process of industrialized destruction. Any possible scruples were removed by the National Socialist ideology, which designated those individuals who were used in experiments as inferior and "unworthy of living." They restricted themselves to "the elimination of those who deviated from the norm—that which was different became deviant, inferior."[1]

The Nuremberg military tribunal judged these human experiments as "crimes against humanity." These activities "which were inhumane reality under the cover of *eugenics* or other medical research"[2] included murder, brutalities, and horrors by 350 doctors who were considered "medical criminals." "For these human experiments, the existing testimony of victims and caregivers for inmates is the almost inevitable subjective corrective to the objective medical reports and cover-up explanations of doctors who participated."[3] When one reads the defense speeches and concluding remarks of the accused doctors in the files of the proceedings, one can only concur with the above statement. Here they tortured, mistreated, and killed "only in order to save the victims from execution."[4] In "working with human material," doctors were never led by feelings other than "medical-human."[5]

Already in 1938 one could read in the *Wiener Klinische Wochenschrift* about the attitude that prevailed among doctors. For some doctors, the restriction and extermination of life seems to have become the new ideal of a community-supportive form of medicine: "We doctors now have to weed out this vermin and destroy it, in so far as that is within our jurisdiction."[6] And, "If we now have to demand sterilization in all cases that we perceive as a threat to the purity of our people, this in no way contradicts the medical spirit. . . . As fanatical followers we have to excise from our people all that is sick, impure, and destructive."[7]

From the Nuremberg trials the quote was transmitted that "narrow scientific medicine . . . was being tried, that is, 'the spirit which sees the human being only as an object.' "[8] This statement characterizes the attitude of the majority of Nazi doctors who willingly participated in human experiments, even themselves developing initiatives for the execution of experiments. Helpless victims were traded as raw material. Characteristic for this attitude that reduced the "guinea pigs" to the value of goods was the sale of 150 female concentration camp inmates to the Bayer company for medical experiments. "After the price per inmate had been set at 170 marks (the camp originally demanded 200 marks per female inmate), the deal was closed."[9] Already then it was understood that these projects violated medical ethics. In connection with the third convention of military doctors in May 1943, Professor Rose noted that "human experiments are in many cases not justified, since the results are not better than those with animals."[10] However, this conclusion did not keep him from continuing his experiments. The experimental projects increased in importance, while the treatment of those who were ill did not. The pain and unbearable suffering of the "guinea pigs" was not considered.

If one tries to understand the willingness of doctors to participate in Nazi crimes, the explanation can be found on various planes.[11] On the one hand, it was the attitude of doctors, who degraded the patients to objects and who, in their research madness, only saw the "available human material" or totally disassociated the victims from any human category. For instance, Dr. Gräfe had stated that "experiments would not be conducted on inmates, but only on Poles, and that Poles are not human beings."[12] Another aspect that enables such behavior might be the uniqueness of medical activity. Thus, medical crimes seem to defy definition "for it has still not been determined when medical activity turns into a medical crime."[13]

"A rarely mentioned and rather subconscious condition for medical crimes seems to be the emotional distance of doctors from sick people, an 'objectivity' which at that time did not keep them from maiming and killing them [the sick people] for experimental reasons."[14] This basic attitude had a decisive effect on the National Socialist restructuring of society, on the revaluation of all values. Medicine became science with a political purpose. The human experiments were legitimized sociopolitically, economically, and scientifically. Many doctors proved their capability "to replace the last traces of medical thinking with the extermination criteria of a race-hygienic and political nature."[15]

But there was no homogeneity in the attitude of doctors who served in the inmate areas and experimentation stations vis-à-vis National Socialism; likewise ambition and productivity of individual doctors were also motivated differently. There were doctors who performed their duties within the limits of the orders; others, for whom these duties became an insufferable torture, tried to get away from the concentration camp—"these vacuums without any culture" (Mitscherlich). Others, who were convinced of the strategic aims of National Socialism, for that reason participated in projects important to the war. "But there were many doctors who went way beyond that and participated actively in the destruction of entire inmate groups such as Jews, Gypsies, Poles."[16]

Thus, experiments were undertaken that, under normal conditions, are carried out only on animals. Here doctors themselves requested permission to experiment in certain camps. For instance, Dr. Josef Mengele requested a transfer to Auschwitz, with the explanation that "there he expected to find sufficient human material for his race-biological experiments."[17]

Clauberg was the most prominent doctor who was not a member of the SS and who had applied to carry out experiments in Auschwitz. His interests were in a cheap, nonsurgical method of sterilization. From preserved correspondence we know that he asked Himmler himself to be allowed to experiment on women interned in Auschwitz. For this he received permission.[18]

Since the concentration camp system was based on the exploitation of the labor of the inmates, the efficient use of scientists was a logical consequence. Hence, inmate doctors were sent primarily to sick bays and experimental stations of the concentration camps. These inmate doctors had to do all the work, while the SS doctors often limited their activities to visitations; because of their prisoner status they also could not refuse to carry out experiments that equalled torture and endangered the life of the "guinea pig." Constantly in contact with seriously ill people, they were always exposed to infection, and for many becoming fatally ill was inevitable.

In addition, many an SS doctor profited from the scientific capabilities of inmate doctors. So, for instance, the inmate doctor Professor Epstein—former professor for children's diseases at the University of Prague—and his assistant, Dr. Weisskopf, were the actual authors of the work on Noma and twin research done by Mengele.[19] For the different experimental projects, the best available experts from each camp were used. Dr. Ding-Schuler asked the SS-WVHA Auschwitz for the Lemberg specialist, Dr. Ludwig Fleck.[20] For these doctors the selection meant an improvement of their own situation—they were protected from immediate campaigns and death transports and enjoyed a better existence materially. In addition, most of them tried to help fellow inmates through their position. However, their possibilities were very limited. In general, doctors and nurses experienced the same treatment as every other work detail. There were some incidents in which the outside world was told that these inmate doctors were to blame for the deaths of patients. Such a fate befell the health building personnel of the Gypsy camp Birkenau after its dissolution on August 1, 1944: "At first we could not fathom the reason for this unexpected repressive measure. However, after some time, we found out that we were sent to the penal details because of Mengele's accusation that we killed Gypsies through purposely poor work in the hospital. We know, however, that Mengele wanted to get rid of us by assigning us to this exhaustive work."[21]

In all experiments, the connections to the pharmaceutical industry were very close. Through an immediate application to humans, the firms saved lengthy experimental series with animals. "The role of IG Farben in developing and preparing chemical warfare was so deep and far-ranging, that it saved the German army the establishment of its own chemical service which was a given for all allied armies."[22]

In order to avoid lengthy pharmaceutical experiments, experimental medicine was being tried on inmates. For this purpose, the "guinea pigs" were injected with bacteria. They were injected and fed with these preparations without exact knowledge of their effects.[23] "For instance, these experiments were carried out by Captain Dr. Vetter, who himself was an employee of IG Farben (Bayer). . . . From 1941–1945, Vetter traveled with death in his medicine bag between all the concentration camps, he showed up in Sachsenhausen, Dachau, Auschwitz and Mauthausen."[24] IG Farben tried to cover up the crimes while the experiments were under way. A conversation in the middle of 1943 between an IG Farben man, Dr. Julius Weber, and Dr. Ding-Schuler gave the impression of practical deception tactics: "IG Farben officially does not want to know about the experiments on people or artificial infection of people."[25]

The Situation of the "Guinea Pig"

Gypsies were most consistently excluded from the human sphere by all non-Nazis. That is why the doctors first thought of Gypsies when they wanted to continue animal experiments on humans under the cover of scientific inquiry and medical experiments for war purposes. The Nuremberg doctors' trial proved and confirmed a number of camp reports that Gypsies had to stand for all possible kinds of cruelty. Dr. Conti's[26] reason for the selection of "guinea pigs" was that "in war time, when millions of the best people and the completely innocent have to sacrifice their lives, the community enemy also has to make his contribution towards the common good."[27]

That Gypsies were most decidedly deprived of their humanity is proven by cases in which experimenting was allowed only under the condition that the "guinea pigs" belonged to this outsider group.[28] If their racial "otherness/inferiority" was the trigger for their incarceration, this "otherness" saved them from many an inhuman project. For this reason they probably were spared the barbaric and perverse low-pressure and refrigeration experiments of the cancer specialist, Dr. Rascher, in Dachau. Reich doctor Grawitz, in a letter to his superior, Himmler, also expressed his fears regarding the use of Gypsies for experiments "to convert salt water into drinking water (which could) possibly bring experimental results that cannot simply be applied to our men."[29] The preceding suggestion, to use "asocial Gypsy half breeds" for these experiments, was made by SS Major General Nebe.[30]

From the documents it cannot be determined or estimated how many Austrian Gypsies participated in the human experiments. Here the trail did not have to be blurred because transports that were designated for experiments were not even entered into the inmate camp journal; in the death records only the number of deceased experimental persons was recorded, not their names.[31] However, memoirs allow one to conclude that Austrian Gypsies were included in all those projects in which Gypsies were used as research objects.

Experimenters often declared in their defense statements that the experimental persons were volunteers. However, we can state fundamentally that the "guinea pigs" were not fully, if at all, enlightened regarding the extent and consequences of the experiments on their physiological and psychological being. Within the framework of the individual experiments there are sufficient examples that expose this "voluntary" character, or rather examples that manifest clear force.

If it really was the personal decision of inmates to participate in human experiments, then it occurred under concentration camp conditions, that is, either they did not dare to refuse in view of the alternatives (gas chamber or immediate shooting), or the acceptance was in the hope of promised advantages (better food, better work details, conditions that meant survival). If participation was obtained on the basis of these false pretenses, the willingness of the inmates during the experiments proved to be insufficient.[32] Thus, a survivor reported that he requested to be exempt from the "salt water experiments" because he already had had stomach surgery. His request was ignored.[33] A "guinea pig" who wanted to refuse the salt water experiments was fed salt water via the gastric tube. "Another guinea pig was tied to a bed with a bandage over his/her mouth, because he/she had obtained some drinking water and bread."[34] These examples demonstrate how doctors treated their victims, "whom they thought to be volunteers."

Additional arguments against voluntary consent are provided by the different sterilization attempts, such as the method of x-ray castration that was constructed in such a way that the procedure could be done unknowingly. In these cases all permission became superfluous. All those who were spared internment in a concentration camp were also forced into sterilization. Already interned persons were blackmailed into statements of voluntary participation by the unkept promise of [subsequent] freedom.

Medical Experiments

A portion of the research projects was connected with the population development intended by the National Socialists. Here two aims were pursued. On the one hand, they endeavored to develop efficient methods that were supposed to make it possible to limit so-called inferior races and nations in their reproduction. This planned elimination was in line with the programmatic intent of the NSDAP [*Nationalsozialistische Deutsche Arbeiterpartei* = Nazi Party] since its accession to power. The experimental preliminary work on mass sterilization paralleled the direct annihilation in the concentration camps. Within the framework of population-biological research, the second aim was to speed up the increase in their own so-called pure nordic race.[35]

In addition, there were experiments of importance to the war effort whose necessity could be justified on technical grounds (typhoid experiments, experiments to convert salt water into drinking water). Professor Ivy of Chicago—expert witness for the prosecution—testified at the Nuremberg trials "that 'war-related necessity' provides a basis for experiments, but does not allow a violation of rights."[36]

Typhoid Experiments

During the Nazi period, these experiments on humans were carried out in two camps: concentration camps Buchenwald and Natzweiler. Both projects included Gypsies.

From January 1942 on, diverse series of experiments in Buchenwald were led by SS Major Dr. Ding-Schuler. Eugen Kogon who, as a Buchenwald prisoner, was Ding-Schuler's camp secretary, transmits to us a diary entry on the establishment of this research department: "Since the animal experiments do not allow for sufficient conclusions, the experiments have to be carried out on humans."[37] In total, approximately one thousand people in Buchenwald were drafted for this project; as a result [of them] about one-seventh of them died. "The scientific value of these experiments was either zero or very low."[38] Documents confirm that at least thirty Gypsies suffered this fate. From correspondence between SS offices in February 1944 we can ascertain that for the testing of a Danish vaccine "in the near future 30 suitable Gypsies (will be) sent to the Institute for Typhoid Fever Research in Buchenwald."[39] Authorization for these experiments was tied to the stipulation that "the experiments had to be confined to Gypsies."[40] In Dr. Ding-Schuler's camp diary, six deaths are recorded in connection with this experiment.[41] In testing other vaccines by the firms Behring/Marburg and Höchst/Frankfurt, apparently numerous Gypsies from Burgenland died.[42]

In concentration camp Natzweiler it was not a question of testing existing vaccines; here Dr. Haagen carried out tolerance experiments with new serums. However, he did not use those patients of the camp who were ill with the disease—in Natzweiler the epidemic lasted until summer 1944. ("According to his own testimony, Professor Haagen did 'not have time' for preventive vaccination against this epidemic."[43]) Rather, transports with "suitable guinea pigs" from other camps arrived. In the documents, three such "shipments" are recorded. The first, in November 1943, composed of more than one hundred inmates, did not at all correspond to Haagen's impressions of "suitable guinea pigs," who were to be "healthy, normally nourished and in good general physical condition,"[44] for eighteen had already died during the transport. "Only 12 inmates (of 100) are in a condition which makes them suitable for the experiments."[45]

These deported persons probably were from the Auschwitz Gypsy transport, which a former inmate remembered as follows:

Three cars full of inmates in striped clothing, Gypsies. Some lay or sat on the floor hollow-cheeked, feverish and incapable of rising for weakness; the others were so weak from hunger that they could barely crawl. Between them there lay some dead bodies, who had died on the ride from the railroad station to camp. The picture in the second car was the same. The third car was half-filled with dead bodies, who were stacked on top of each other. This proved that they were already dead when loaded into the car at the railroad station. The other half of the car was filled with the remainder of the ill and weak Gypsies. I was surprised at the consideration shown them by taking them to the infirmary, but already on the next day there was an explanation. These Gypsies came from the ill-reputed Auschwitz camp, so that they could perform bacteriological experiments on them here. They were infected with the typhoid bacteria. But not all of them; a part had already died of starvation during the night. In spite of the wintry weather, the unfortunate ones had been housed for the long trip from Auschwitz to Natzweiler in an unheated freight car and were given only four days' provision, although they were en route for 14 days.[46]

In view of the fact that Haagen could not make use of these emaciated human beings [*Muselmänner*], another ninety people "who had been released from the army and the SS only shortly before"[47] were transferred shortly thereafter.

In May and June, 1944, Haagen requested an additional two hundred inmates. Whether this transport took place cannot be determined, nor which inmate category was concerned, for in these cases no entries in the inmate camp diary were made. They were immediately separated, and in the death records as well, the deceased were recorded without names. At the Nuremberg doctors' trial, the Dutch witness Nales reported twenty-nine deaths from Haagen's experimental series in the winter of 1943–1944. "In support of his testimony, he had brought along a copy of the original death records which he and others had made in camp."[48] The Salzburg resident Karl Eberle was also deported as a "guinea pig" from Auschwitz to Natzweiler: immediately after their [the inmates'] arrival in camp they were housed in a locked room in the experimental area. Shortly thereafter, the experiments began. He cannot remember details or the length of the experiments, only the hallucinations from which he suffered.[49]

Desalination Experiments

The prehistory of these experiments on Gypsies [is as follows]: from 1941 on, cases of distress at sea increased due to the aerial war in the Mediterranean and Atlantic; the biggest problem for those affected was thirst. In 1942, the Technical Office of the Air Force charged the Research Institute of Aviation Medicine with finding a scientific solution. Already in 1943, Dr. Schäfer was able to present his positive results. He had developed a method by which salt water could actually be desalinated. Still in December 1943, I. G. Farben was given the order to produce the "Schäfer solution."

At the same time, Ingenieur Berka (Air Force, Vienna) found a way to improve salt water without desalination. "While the Schäfer method entailed direct desalination of salt water, the Berka procedure would merely improve the taste of salt water, and its vitamin C content supposedly increased the capacity of the kidneys to eliminate cooking salt."[50]

Even if one could hold the war situation responsible for the necessity of the experiments, it was already known at the point when the decision was made to use primarily Gypsies as "guinea pigs" that persistent application would lead to permanent health damage or even death. In May 1944, the chief of the health inspection office, Professor Schröder, was convinced that "the Berka method would result in health damage that would lead to permanent damage at the latest within six days after ingestion of the *Berkatit* and . . . (that this experiment) ends in death at the latest after twelve days."[51]

The first experiments, carried out on soldiers,[52] brought good results for the Schäfer solution, while the *Berkatit* proved to be useless.[53] Yet, in May 1944, the Technical Office decided nevertheless to use *Berkatit*. The reason: the manufacture of the Schäfer product would have required the raw ingredient silver nitrate. This was rejected for reasons of cost.[54] The decision in favor of *Berkatit*, however, triggered controversies, and during discussions in May 1944, the decision was made to undertake additional inmate experiments. Dr. Becker-Freyseng, who voted against *Berkatit*, suggested the use of concentration camp inmates and Dachau as the place for the experiments.[55] The decision to experiment on inmates was based on the experience that at that point in time it would no longer have been possible to obtain the forty necessary "guinea pigs" from military installations.[56]

Professor Eppinger from Vienna was responsible for the experiments; they were to be carried out by Professor Beiglböck. Beiglböck fundamentally objected to working in a concentration camp, but he did not mind the use of Gypsies "since they are asocial."[57]

Reich SS doctor Grawitz gave the basic consent to use concentration camp inmates. His fears that the use of "Gypsy guinea pigs" and their "partly different racial makeup" might result in falsified experimental results were countered by Himmler with the following instructions: "Gypsies, and to double-check, three others."[58]

The letter of the health inspector to Himmler, requesting forty "guinea pigs" who had to be completely available for four weeks, expressed concern about these experiments: "From a medical point of view, and according to our current knowledge, this procedure must be seen as questionable, since the ingestion of concentrated saline solutions can engender severe toxic symptoms."[59]

Based on the statement of the accused at the Nuremberg doctors' trial, there were enough "voluntary" inmates. Those involved supposedly decided themselves to participate in the experiments. Of the one thousand Buchenwald Gypsies who "volunteered" under these conditions, forty-four were chosen and sent to Dachau. There they heard for the first time that they were to participate in the experiment. However, this consent under concentration camp conditions could be achieved merely by pretense. Onetime recruitment occurred indirectly. Gypsy inmates were to report for a better work detail[60]; another time they were offered better food before and after the experiments as a direct incentive for participation.[61]

Josef Tschofenig, head of the x-ray station in Dachau from summer 1942 on, checked the Gypsy transport in summer 1944 before beginning the experiments and excluded a number as unsuitable.[62] "There were two (2) or three (3) Poles, five (5) or six (6) Hungarians, ten (10) Austrians . . . but I know that one was a German, a semi-Gypsy. . . . Of the Austrians, five (5) or six (6) were from Burgenland."[63] The "guinea pigs" were split into four groups, and they received different quantities of solid and liquid nourishment. The nourishment was, however, in most cases limited, so that all were very weakened physically. One group had to go hungry for almost all of the twelve days.[64]

In the investigative protocols of the state police, Vienna, Beiglböck admitted that "individual guinea pigs suffered from cramps and attacks of despair"[65] but [said] that there were no deaths and [that] the "guinea pigs" were released in better condition than on their arrival. "Deaths and physical damages did not occur."[66]

The witness Josef Tschofenig gave different information. He testified that it was the norm in Beiglböck's experimental area, as in others, to pass off those inmates who were emaciated as a result of the experiments to the general area in order to blur the death figures of the experimental station.[67] "From my own experience I know of a death among the 3 (three) who came to the 'Internal' [area]. . . . I still remember him especially, because he was brought to my X-ray station on a stretcher, since he was so weak that he could no longer walk."[68]

In the doctors' trial there were two witnesses who testified for Wilhelm Beiglböck. However, a Viennese student who was a nurse on the station questioned the voluntary nature of the "guinea pigs."[69] A French medical student, also a nurse, testified that "no one died during the experiments . . . and that all were well when they left the station."[70]

There are no additional confirmations as to whether inmates died from the consequences of these experiments or, rather, to what degree the salt water experiments caused physical damage. In any case, one can see from the files that the danger that lay in the prescribed length of the experiments was known and that one also had to consider the possibility of deaths. The notes from the experiments, however, must have given a negative picture because Dr. Beiglböck found it expedient to make erasures and changes before the trial. If the changes were to provide a better picture of the patients' condition, the erasures of names prevented calling survivors as witnesses. Steinbauer[71] and Beiglböck admitted only after persistent lying that they had made these changes. They especially tried again and again to stamp Gypsy testimony as unreliable in order to be able to present their own testimony as authentic and to trivialize the experiments for lack of other proof.[72] However, this attitude was no exception, but can be seen as an example of the prevailing ignorance toward victims and the renewed discrimination[73] against victims, who ought to have received justice and whose suffering ought to have been exposed.[74]

Eugenic Experiments

The race and eugenic experiments of Dr. Josef Mengele affected especially the Gypsies. The work that Mengele carried out in the hospital of the Gypsy camp in Auschwitz from 1943 to 1945 can be summarized under the category of totally perverted medical experiments.[75]

His main interest was in twins, dwarfs, unusual eye coloration, other birth anomalies, and *Noma* research.[76] We have a reconstruction of Mengele's medical activities in the Gypsy hospital primarily thanks to secretary Tadeusz Joachimowski. He was employed as the main record keeper from the time of the foundation of the camp until its dissolution and was able to hide a part of the documents and to take them to Warsaw.[77] "Dr. Mengele had a special interest in Gypsy children. In the Gypsy camp there were over 60 pairs of such twins aged 2 to 14. In the course of the . . . experiments, almost all twins were systematically killed by injections, so that on August 1, 1944, only seven pairs of twins were left."[78]

"As far as the fate (of these) twins is concerned, it has to be made clear that, on the day of the final liquidation of the Gypsies, Mengele took 'his Gypsies' to the main camp and when they could not be accommodated there, returned with them to the Gypsy camp. There he personally shot his 'darlings' in the hallway of the crematorium and ordered an autopsy of the murdered twins for 'scientific' purposes."[79]

Elisabeth Guttenberger, herself an inmate in the Gypsy camp, remembered the fate of her relatives: "My cousins, who were twins, also served as 'guinea pigs.' After he had undertaken different kinds of measurements and given them injections, they were gassed when the last Gypsies were sent to the gas chambers. On the order of Mengele, the corpses of the twins were dissected before they were cremated."[80]

Mengele had unlimited research possibilities; he was the only twin researcher who was able to dissect his "guinea pigs" on the same day in order to compare the inner organs. He was one of those camp doctors who, beyond what was ordered, maimed and killed inmates under the cover of science.

Hermann Langbein reported about the lot of those Gypsies who had an unusual eye coloration [iris coloring]: "In a *post facto* conversation with me, his teacher, Freiherr von Verschür, admitted that Mengele had sent incredibly interesting specimens of eye pairs—pairs with different coloration—to this institute.[81] These were the eyes of Gypsies whom Mengele ordered killed because of this abnormality. When I told this to the professor, he seemed surprised and shocked. Did he never think about the source for his student's specimens?"[82]

Many children in camp who suffered from *Noma* had the possibility of living for some time, for Mengele considered this illness worthy of study. In the infirmary of the Gypsy camp, a *Noma* department was established to which forty-five Gypsy children were admitted.[83] After having undergone different therapies, the symptoms of these suffering children were documented in photographs. "Mengele took the charts of these guinea pigs with him. These patients never returned. What happened to them could not be exactly determined."[84] We may assume that for these patients, too, the crematorium was the gruesome final stop.

The serological experiments, also carried out on Gypsies, were part of the racial research and were to show the difference from "Aryan blood." In Sachsenhausen, Dr. Fischer, who had gained his experience in this matter through experiments on captured blacks, was given this task. In 1942, Fischer began to experiment with forty Gypsies; then the examination of Jewish blood was to follow.

Himmler's interest in these investigations was tremendous. On July 20, 1942, Grawitz informed Himmler that Fischer would begin with experiments on forty Gypsies. An enclosure in the form of a reprint informed Himmler of Fischer's previous race-serological experimental results with blacks and stated that "numerous additional and control experiments are still necessary before statements can be made on a practical application of the method."[85] But no results were published. Dr. Horneck, who had carried out similar experiments previously, had been ordered to the Eastern front prematurely.[86] Fischer's experiments also quietly stopped. The premature end of ambitious series of experiments was typical in Nazi behavior, thus preventing scientific anthropology. "Projects which . . . did not achieve the expected results were terminated prematurely."[87]

Sterilizations

From the legal measures to "prevent genetically defective progeny," the path led to the massive extermination of so-called life unworthy of living and finally to plans as well as to preliminary work in the sterilization of entire peoples, the realization of which was prevented only through the collapse of the Third Reich.[88] The search for a cheap, quick sterilization method for those peoples who were destined by the Fascist extermination politics to be extinguished biologically represented a pre-stage toward a final solution. In this research project, which was given priority within the realm of the other experiments, sadistic experiments with the gravest consequences were undertaken.

Rudolf Brandt, Himmler's personal expert, testified at the Nuremberg doctors' trial: "Himmler was highly interested in the development of a cheap and quick method of sterilization, which could be used against the enemies of the German Reich, such as Russians, Poles, and Jews."[89] In the pursuit of these criminal aims that served negative population politics, three experimental series existed. The plan to achieve sterilization through medication was triggered by a scientific publication about an animal experiment. The company of Madaus and Company, Dresden-Radebeul, had been successful in sterilizing animals with the extract from the South American *Schweigrohr* [tropical plant]. The thought to test this product immediately on humans was suggested to Himmler from two sides.

In August 1941, the deputy district leader of Niederdonau wrote to Himmler that the leader of the district office for racial politics there, Dr. Fehringer, intended to carry out human experiments in cooperation with the Pharmacological Institute of the Vienna Faculty of Medicine on the basis of Madaus's animal experiments. Fehringer considered the inmates of Gypsy camp Lackenbach for the experiments. Dr. Pokorny, a Munich specialist, also expressed interest in these experiments. In October 1941, he wrote a letter to Himmler in which he expressed his ideas. He thought that "the three million Bolsheviks in German detention could be sterilized."[90] From here, arrangements were made with the Madaus works via Oswald

Pohl, leader of the Main Office of the SS Economic Administration, and Reich physician Dr. Grawitz. The failure of fundamental necessities, namely the cultivation of this plant [*Schweigrohr*] in hot houses, did not allow a realization of this plan. An experimental series with mice and rats continued until 1944 and was ended without results.[91] But even in the case where these experiments would have been carried out on humans, the Gypsies in Lackenbach would have been spared participation in this project. As can be seen from a letter of October 14, 1942 (Gerland, deputy district leader of ND [*Niederdonau*], to Rudolf Brandt), Pohl considered Fehringer's suggestion to use the inmates of Gypsy camp Lackenbach for sterilization experiments as outdated.[92] Himmler had decided in favor of the suggestion "to use criminal persons who should be sterilized *a priori*."[93]

The second series of sterilization experiments was based on the principle that sterilization or castration could be achieved through the application of x-rays. Apparently from 1943 on, the execution of this method was entrusted to Dr. Schumann, using "suitable material in concentration camp Auschwitz." In the years 1939 and 1940 he had collected the appropriate experience as leader of a euthanasia clinic and expert in the euthanasia program. Preliminary work for this method of sterilization was done by the office of the Reich leader Bouhler (Hitler's private office). Already in 1941 his administrative chief, Viktor Brack, had made the suggestion to sterilize Jews with x-rays, and details regarding the experiment were brought to Himmler's attention already in March 1941: "If anyone is to be sterilized permanently, this can only be achieved by the use of such high X-ray dosages that castration with all its consequences will result. Lesser dosages would only prevent the ability to procreate for a short time."[94]

The decisive factor for the doctors was that this method was quick and could be carried out unnoticed, thereby hopefully achieving the realization of planned mass sterilization. The resultant damage and predictable side effects—damage to the rest of the body tissue and burn wounds from the strong dosages—were simply ignored. Victims were to step in front of a counter and fill out forms or answer questions while the official operated the appropriate machinery. The possibility of hiding this procedure long-term did not exist, but this fact did not cause any special discomfort. In June 1942, Brack wrote to Himmler: "I believe that it has already become unimportant whether the victims realize from the effects after a few weeks or months that they have been castrated."[95] However, experiments that were carried out under Dr. Schumann in Auschwitz resulted in the realization that castration of the male was pretty impossible in this way. In order to achieve results, "guinea pigs" had their testicles removed four weeks after treatment. Dr. Robert Levy, inmate doctor in Auschwitz from 1943 on, suspected that "the testicles were removed in order to undertake microscopic experiments to ascertain the results of the X-ray treatment."[96]

From the sworn testimony of a Polish woman, Gustawa Winkowska, we know that x-ray sterilization was also carried out on Gypsy children in Ravensbrück: "A doctor came from Auschwitz for a few days, possibly for a week, and while he was in camp, he occupied himself the entire day with the X-ray sterilization of Gypsy children, without using anesthesia."[97]

A third method of sterilization, through intrauterine inflammation, was tried by Professor Clauberg. "The method I concocted to achieve sterilization of the female organism without an operation is practically finished. It is achieved through a single injection from the entry of the uterus, and can be carried out during the regular gynecological examination with which every doctor is familiar."[98] Here, too, the "guinea pigs" were not to know about the procedure. Himmler had considered concentration camp Ravensbrück for Clauberg's work. But at his [Clauberg's] request, the experimental station was then established in the main camp at Auschwitz. The selected women were deported from Ravensbrück to Auschwitz. In the chronological table from Auschwitz on July 7, 1942, we find the following entry: "Himmler promises Professor Clauberg to provide women in Camp Auschwitz for his sterilization experiments. Methods are to be found to sterilize many people as quickly as possible in order to exterminate so-called 'inferior races,' whose labor they still want to utilize."[99] And in the chronological table from Ravensbrück for the summer of 1943 we read: "Professor Clauberg requests three hundred inmates from Ravensbrück for deportation to Auschwitz for the purpose of experimental sterilization."[100]

A collaborator of Clauberg's was Dr. Gebel, chief chemist of the Schering works. He concocted the contrast liquid that was subsequently injected into the sterilized individuals to check for results. The experiments were extremely painful and endangered the health of the "guinea pigs" extremely. "In numerous cases there were inflammations which often forced the women to lie in bed for weeks and months and in several cases caused their death."[101] "Statistics . . . as well as testimony from former inmates indicate that a portion of the guinea pigs died or were killed, with their corpses autopsied."[102]

After the liberation of Auschwitz by the Red Army, sterilized women were transferred to Ravensbrück. "They got a few hundred Gypsy women and promised them freedom if they would agree to sterilization. . . . 140 female Gypsies fell victim to this inhuman treatment, among them even little eight-year-old girls!"[103]

Most of the sterilizations in concentration camps occurred under conditions of blackmail, [that is,] under deceptive conditions. The inmates were promised freedom if they submitted to the sterilization experiments. "At the end of this year, further transports were assembled. They were divided into those who were suitable for the military and those young women and men who agreed to participate in sterilization experiments in the hope of freedom. They were promised that they would be released from camp. But the truth was quite different. Eight days after such an operation, undertaken without anesthesia, they again had to work. This killed many of them."[104]

One inmate, Gerber, formerly a nurse in concentration camp Ravensbrück, testified similarly in the Auschwitz trial: "I know that the camp physician, Dr. Trommer, insisted on it. The Gypsies were all ordered to appear before the commander, Suhren. They were told that they could get out of the camp and become soldiers, if they would agree to sterilization. But afterwards they were not released from camp."[105]

In the doctors' trial, Suhren reported that he actually received release documents for sterilized Gypsies from the Reich criminal police.[106] However, releases occurred only in the rarest cases; this is documented by numerous eyewitness accounts. In the case of the Birkenau Gypsy camp, there is a list that confirms eleven such releases: "If we also add eleven women who were released from camp after their sterilization, we arrive at the figure of 2,394 Gypsies who were still alive on the day of liquidation, or 10.4 percent of all of the Gypsies who had been in the camp."[107]

Hermann Langbein also knew of only one case in which the sterilized person was released. This was a Gypsy woman with a sick baby, who accused Mengele: "Doctor, my husband wears the same uniform as you do, and our child has to die here miserably." Mengele checked out her information. After sterilization, she and her child were released.[108]

With forced sterilization of Gypsies and other victims of National Socialism, the perpetrators went beyond existing laws. Where forced sterilization was undertaken within the framework of medical experiments, in fact without the victims' knowledge of the procedure, a definite breach of law had occurred.

According to §225 of the German penal code, premeditated deprivation of procreativity fell under the category of grievous bodily harm with a prison sentence of two to ten years. The ordinances were even stricter under Austrian law. Here the penalty of five to ten years was even higher than in Germany. Under Austrian law, procedures that affected the sexual reproductive system of a human being were unlawful even if the person in question had requested them. "According to paragraph 44 of the Austrian penal code, 'a crime was committed even against those people who themselves requested the damaging procedure.' On this legal basis, even those sterilizations that were carried out with voluntary or forced permission, are punishable. The legal breach becomes even clearer with those eugenic experiments that were being undertaken without the knowledge of the victims—as with hidden X-ray machines—or on children."[109]

When prisoners are promised freedom on condition of an operation, or when freedom is tied to such a condition, this is also forced sterilization. At the time of the first mass deportations to concentration camps, the situation for Gypsies was similar. Many were faced with the alternative of sterilization for continued temporary freedom.

The sterilizations that were undertaken on the basis of the laws passed by the Nazis also contradicted civil law. "This is also not changed by the fact that the Reich civil law denied and negated the rights of Jews and Gypsies as population minorities."[110] Already in 1934, more than 60,000 sterilizations were undertaken in Germany; by 1945 between 200,000 and 350,000 persons had become victims of this torture.

For Austria there are no figures. Here, already in the interwar years the demand to sterilize Gypsies was a central topic. After "annexation" [1938], these demands took on concrete form. In Dr. Portschy's *Denkschrift* of fall 1938, previously cited, which he also sent to the Reich Interior Ministry, sterilization of Gypsies belonged to the base pillars of the National Socialist solution to the Gypsy problem. In addition to the school ban for Gypsy children, correspondence between ministries and school authorities from 1938–1939 on also demanded their sterilization, whereby the "law to prevent genetically inferior progeny" was to be invoked. But they also understood that realization might encounter legal obstacles. "The sterilization of Gypsies desired by many cannot be carried out due to lack of legal support, since not as many Gypsies are genetically inferior as a few spot checks show."[111] However, the close association of state and party health directives facilitated that the step from "an injunction against marriage and mixing" to forced sterilization was a small one in spite of lacking legal support.[112]

Damaging Consequences of the Medical Experiments Performed on Gypsies

Sterilization was thus one of the first measures to "fight the Gypsy vermin" already in the prewar years. The victims were given the choice of sterilization or internment in camps. "After they had arrested us, we began to realize . . . now the individual families will be sterilized. I had to sign [a paper stating] that I would not be sent to camp if I would submit to the experimentation purposes of the Nazis."[113]

From April 1943 on, no unsterilized Gypsies were allowed to live outside of camp. The few who were spared the concentration camp on the basis of certain criteria, such as military dependents, Gypsy wives of German men, or representatives of certain professions, had to agree to forced sterilization.[114] In such cases, the authorities verified this information with considerable bureaucratic fanfare.[115] "All of my in-laws had already been sent to Auschwitz concentration camp, although these people had always been employed. But we only found this out months later and in a round-about way. Only one of my husband's brothers, who had been sterilized and who was a mechanic, had been spared. He was needed at the airport in Schneidemühl, and he could not be spared."[116]

Even though about half of the Austrian Gypsies survived the Holocaust, a majority of these survivors were marked by human experiments. "In 1944, the beginning of National Socialist dissolution, the entire sterilization program of the SS ended in documents about hidden failures and yet still hoped-for possibilities [of success]. The practical result: many hundreds of dead [people], many hundreds of maimed [people]."[117]

Many only gradually understood the depth of the procedures they had undergone. They were still children at the time of the sterilization, and their parents also did not enlighten them.[118] Others became victims of the hidden x-ray castration procedure. They had not only lost their reproductive capacity through this procedure. In order to achieve results, many "guinea pigs" had their testicles removed; in others, the burns had destroyed the body tissue. "During my visits to Gypsy families, I saw men and women who had been 'treated' by Nazi doctors in this manner, sterilized women and men who seemed weak. It is important for Gypsies to procreate. A childless person is useless for them."[119] Especially for the strongly family-oriented Gypsies, fertility has a special biological, personal, and social value. The inner confrontation with the loss of this essential opportunity for self-realization is especially difficult for Gypsies. The status of a family in the Gypsy community was determined by the number of children. Children were even more important for the man than for the woman. A man without a family could not be maintained within the tribe. The group structure of the Gypsies with its inflexible behavior patterns, based on archaic motives, excluded the innocently barren from the group through the social ban. Because of the social isolation, most of the victims developed psychic disturbances.[120]

In connection with reparation demands, the study of pertinent cases showed that "none of the studied victims of forced sterilization were able to work through the damage without considerable psychological weakening."[121] It was acknowledged that victims had suffered a lasting decrease of mental capacity because of the amnesia they suffered as "guinea pigs." The sterilization was (defined) as "a forced intervention into the physical integrity and the necessarily connected reduction of biological, personal, and social advantages."[122] Doctors who were entrusted with these studies explained the psychic disturbances as follows: "The loss of reproductive capacity affects the integrity of the personality in its core; this damage is ideally suited to cause psychological side effects. . . . The feeling to have been struck and damaged in the core of one's personality, and to be seen as inadequate by one's community, intrudes into the consciousness of the victim and preoccupies him. . . . Such inner conflicts also influence the outer conduct . . . seen in its totality— achievement and success of the victim in his 'professional life.' "[123]

Concentration camp inmates who were used for other experiments also complained of delayed reaction. Karl Eberle, a victim of typhoid experiments in Natzweiler, suffered from psychological as well as physical disturbances. Even though he was certified as 70 percent disabled, he was not granted the corresponding financial support. He was allowed early retirement at age fifty-nine.[124]

A majority of the former inmates suffer from consequences of the internment. They returned home ill, never completely recovered, and some died at a young age.[125] Society started only recently to deal with the health damage and the psychological consequences of camp internment and nevertheless continued discriminatory practices: Those with physical injuries were certified to have as high a degree of "work ability" as possible. Psychological suffering was termed "mentally deficient" or "feigning." And to this day forced sterilization is not acknowledged as a permanent injury by the reparations authorities.

8

Concluding Remarks

The Gypsy politics of the National Socialists were effective beyond the Nazi period. Through persecution and extermination they succeeded in destroying the Gypsy group. Entire tribal structures were destroyed; many Gypsies were isolated. [Those values] that had prevented all reeducation attempts during the previous centuries finally were destroyed through the separation of Gypsy families in the concentration camps and the partial or complete dissolution of these families by the end of the war. When the Gypsies were freed in 1945, their sense of values and their group mechanism had been damaged for the first time in their history.

Postwar censuses show that in the Burgenland communities, on the average, only one-half to one-third of the displaced persons returned.[1] In addition to the unsuccessful search for additional survivors, the search for former homes was likewise unsuccessful. They had been levelled.

The Austrian Gypsies soon had to find out that discrimination did not end even after the camp gates opened. Although the Nazi period had torn the Gypsy nation apart, after 1945 they [the Gypsies] found themselves vis-à-vis a bureaucracy that did not constitute a break in continuity.

Fear of renewed registration prevented numerous victims from requesting at least material reparations. Those who took the path of the courts soon had to realize that the humiliation in the concentration camp was followed by that in the court. The testimony of Gypsies, for instance, was strongly questioned; appraisals were issued by doctors who were close to the torturers. Postwar society, at least its majority, had little interest in admitting its guilt toward this persecuted minority and in taking the first step toward understanding. The former Lackenbach inmates had to fight especially hard [to get anything] because this Gypsy camp had not been classified as a concentration camp. Only in 1961 did they receive considerably lower reparations for "limitation of freedom."

The fear of Gypsies to call attention to themselves by their demands as victims of National Socialism was not unfounded. Already in 1948, security agencies and federal police authorities were notified that the "Gypsy vermin already makes itself known again in an unpleasant way" and that "Gypsies, in order to make an impression with the population, often identify themselves as concentration camp victims."[2]

Thereafter, Gypsies tried to assimilate in order to avert aggression against them due to social separation and cultural differences. This resulted in alienation from their own traditions and their original culture. In addition, the changed economic and work structure of postwar society put the former Gypsy ways in sharp relief to their current way of life. The majority has given up the way of life of their forefathers in favor of a socially assimilated way of life.

In Austria, Gypsies today are formally equal to all other citizens in tax, army, and school matters. In contrast to other ethnic minorities, however, they are recognized neither as a separate ethnic group nor as a linguistic minority.[3]

Appendix of Relevant Documents

Note: For actual material, please see German edition: Erika Thurner, *Nationalsozialismus und Zigeuner in Österreich,* vol. 2 in the series *Veröffentlichungen zur Zeitgeschichte,* Erika Weinzierl, Ernst Hanisch, and Karl Stuhlpfarrer, eds. (Wien-Salzburg, 1983).

Index

IX.   Admission of three Gypsies released from prison (Source: DÖW file, No. 12256) and file card of Franziska Reinhart.

X.   Criminal police headquarters, Vienna, to camp administration, February 23, 1945: announcement of three Gypsies from concentration camp Auschwitz.

XI.   Main list (one sheet) of Gypsies deported from Camp Lackenbach to Lodz on November 4, 1941.

XII.   File cards: Angela Held and Regina Weinrich. Both camp inmates were sent to the concentration camp because of escape attempts.

XIII.   1. File cards: Karl Brand and Emily Horvath—Auschwitz deportation (exit stamp).
       2. File cards: Anna Hodos and Katharina Stojka (date stamp).

XIV.   1. Excerpt from death log (coroner's report) of Lackenbach community doctor (two pages).
       2. Fragment of internal death list.

XV.   File cards: Magdalene Bihary and Katharina Brand—contain entries on escape attempts.

XVI.   1. Arrest request to criminal police headquarters, Vienna, July 3, 1942 (Schürwacher, Martin Friedrich).
       2. Camp administration to criminal police headquarters Vienna: "Completed search warrant" (Stefan Horvath and Julius Horvath).
       3. Commissioner, Amstetten, to camp administration, October 31, 1944: notice that two Gypsy boys who had fled from Lackenbach to district Oberdonau had been returned.

XVII.   File cards: Theresia Hodoschi and Ladislaus Weingartner—released as "foreign Gypsies."

XVIII.   File card: Johann Horvath—to demonstrate repeated change of workplace.

XIX.   1. Wage account of Kuschel and Haagen: hours worked and wages from dam construction Oberpullendorf.
       2. Invoice of camp administration to J. Wasinger, Lackenbach, for use of two workers for eleven and nine hours, respectively.

3. Receipt (May 15, 1943): payment of one month wages for camp No. 117 by Franz Wasinger.

XX.   Order of camp leader Eckschlager to employers, dated February 1, 1943 (form).

XXI.   1. Work contract—Hedwig Sarközi (seventeen years old) dated June 3, 1944.

2. "Official entry" dated March 10, 1944, regarding admission of the Gypsy boy Alexander Hodosi (ten years old).

XXII.   1. Camp administration to Lackenbach municipal office, January 20, 1943: regarding forwarding food ration cards of newly admitted Gypsies.

2. "Registration for communal meals" of August 31, 1941 (allows insight into meals and use of foodstuffs).

XXIII.   Passes: Franz Jantschitz and Franz Karall.

XXIV.   Examples of money and package stubs: shipments by relatives and friends.

XXV.   List of file cards.

1. File card collection, yellow, DIN A5.
2. File card collection, grey, DIN A5.
3. File card collection, yellow, small size.
4. File card collection, blue, small size.

XXVI.   Transmission list: twenty-eight Gypsies from concentration camp Mauthausen to Knittelfeld, dated October 8, 1941. Source: Archive of Museum Mauthausen, BMI-Vienna, Zl. E 1a/10.

XXVII.   Criminal police headquarters, Vienna, to camp administration, August 18, 1944: information on inmate Daniel Hubert. Letter by camp administration, dated August 28, 1944: he was deported to Lodz in 1941.

XXVIII. Letter by BMI Vienna to security directorates and federal police authorities, Zl. 84-426-4/48, dated September 20, 1948, regarding "Gypsy vermin."

Note: With the exception of those documents for which the sources have been specifically noted, all documents are from the former Gypsy camp and were located by me there in August of 1981.

Notes

Author's Introduction to the American Edition

1. See Gesellmann, Haslinger, Rieger, and Mayerhofer in the bibliography.

2. Compare chapter 6, "Gypsy Transports from Austria to Lodz and Chelmno" and the "Amended Presentation of the Gypsy Camp(s) Salzburg" in chapter 3.

3. Compare *Gedenkbuch. Die Sinti und Roma im Konzentrationslager Auschwitz-Birkenau* [Memorial Volume. The Sinti and Roma in Concentration Camp Auschwitz-Birkenau] (Munich: Staatliches Museum Auschwitz-Birkenau in Zusammenarbeit mit dem Dokumentations-und Kulturzentrum Deutscher Sinti und Roma, Heidelberg, 1993.)

4. Compare Brigitte Bailer, *Wiedergutmachung kein Thema* [Reparations Are Not a Topic] (Vienna, 1993).

5. See Alan Cowell, "Attack on Austrian Gypsies Deepens Fear of Neo-Nazis," *New York Times*, February 21, 1995, A1 and A5. [Ed.]

6. Just recently, on May 4, 1997, Pope John Paul II beatified a Spanish Gypsy who in 1936 was shot for his faith by forces defending the Republican government during the Spanish Civil War. [Ed.]

Author's Introduction to the First Edition

1. Ernst Tugendhat, preface, in Tilman Zülch, ed., *In Auschwitz vergast, bis heute verfolgt* [Gassed in Auschwitz, and Still Persecuted Today] (Reinbek bei Hamburg, 1979), 11.

2. Selma Steinmetz, *Österreichs Zigeuner im NS-Staat* [Austria's Gypsies in the National Socialist State] (Vienna, 1966).

1. Comments on the State of the Literature and Sources

1. Hermann Arnold, "Anmerkungen zur Geschichtsschreibung der Zigeunerverfolgung" [Notes on the Historiography of Gypsy Persecution], *Mitteilungen zur Zigeunerkunde* [Bulletin for Gypsy Scholarship], Supplement 4 (Mainz, 1977), 5.

2. In this context I would like to point to Hannah Arendt's comments about witness testimony in the Eichmann trial. The survivors had approached the court in droves to serve as witnesses. Most of the testimony revealed noth-

ing new, was secondhand, or was hearsay: "(However), how could the judges justify . . . to refuse to listen to these people? And, who . . . would dare to question their integrity or their memory in matters of detail, when they 'bared on the witness stand what had been locked up in their innermost heart.' " Hannah Arendt, *Eichmann in Jerusalem* (Reinbek bei Hamburg, 1978), 253.

3. "KZ" and "KL" are two abbreviations for concentration camp. Eugen Kogon designates "KZ" as the more severe abbreviation. In this study I used "KL," a form more often used in scholarly discussions. The variant "KZ" was adopted in citations, that is to say, in general formulations.

4. See Lau Mazirel, "Die Verfolgung der 'Zigeuner' im Dritten Reich" [The Persecution of the 'Gypsies' in the Third Reich], *Essays über Naziverbrechen* [Essays on Nazi Crimes], Simon Wiesenthal gewidmet [dedicated to Simon Wiesenthal] (Amsterdam, 1973), 165ff.

5. Response of the Federal Archive in Koblenz, File Az. 9716, Koblenz, June 19, 1980, 1.

6. According to Dr. Sybil Milton, one of seven offices (Office V) of the Central Office for Reich Security (RSHA). Sybil Milton, Milton glossary, 1995.

7. Steinmetz, *Österreichs Zigeuner im NS-Staat,* 5.

8. BMI file (Federal Interior Ministry), Zl. 55.626-18/68. Response to the Dutch Reich Institute, insert, 2.

9. See Zl. 55.626-18/68. Information to Section Commissioner, Dr. Krista, BMI Section 19, 2.

10. The addresses were kindly given to me by Mr. Hermann Langbein, Vienna.

11. The documents include about three hundred file cards, correspondence between the camp command/administration and the criminal police authorities and state authorities, work contracts, pay stubs, fugitive search posters, and much more. A selection is listed in the appendix.

12. In the 1979 report, *Widerstand und Verfolgung im Burgenland 1934–1945* [Resistance and Persecution in Burgenland 1934–1945], by the Archives for Documentation of the Austrian Resistance (DÖW) in Vienna, numerous files on the topic of Gypsy persecution were reproduced. For this study, I frequently used the original files in DÖW.

13. BMI file, Zl. 58.636-2/54. Response BMI, Vienna, to Bavarian State Criminal Authorities, Munich, April 9, 1954, copy, 3.

14. I owe valuable hints and documents to Professor Ernst Hanisch, Salzburg.

2. Ideological Foundations and Legal Ordinances Regarding the Persecution of Gypsies

1. Bernhard Streck, "Die 'Bekämpfung' des Zigeunerunwesens" [The 'Fight against' the Gypsy Vermin], in Zülch, ed., *In Auschwitz vergast,* 73.

2. Joachim S. Hohmann, *Zigeuner und Zigeunerwissenschaft. Ein Beitrag zur*

Grundlagenforschung und Dokumentation des Völkermords im "Dritten Reich" [Gypsies and Gypsy Scholarship. A Contribution to the Foundational Research and Documentation of Genocide in the 'Third Reich']. *Metro* Series, Vol. 6 (Marburg, 1980), 22.

3. "Inclination to prejudice is not typically fascist, but a sign of an authoritarian character. . . . But openly practiced fascism epitomizes the authoritarian character because it needs both, the authoritarian character and the prejudice." Joachim S. Hohmann, *Vorurteile und Mythen in pädagogischen Prozessen* [Prejudices and Myths in Paedagogical Processes] (Lollar, 1978), 71 n. 1.

4. Compare Max Horkheimer, "Über das Vorurteil" [On Prejudice], in Theodor W. Adorno and Walter Dirks, eds., *Frankfurter Beiträge zur Soziologie* [Frankfurt Contributions to Sociology], *Sociologica II, Reden und Vorträge,* 2d ed., Vol. 10 (Frankfurt, 1967), 87–93; also Rudolph M. Loewenstein, *Psychoanalyse des Antisemitismus* [Psychoanalysis of Antisemitism] (Frankfurt, 1968), 26ff.

5. Compare Ben Whitacker, "Zur sozialpsychologischen Analyse von Minderheitenkonflikten" [On the Social-Psychological Analysis of Inferiority Conflicts], in Ruprecht Kurzrock, ed., *Minderheiten* [Minorities], Vol. 17 *Forschung und Information* (Berlin, 1974), 29ff.

6. Patrik von zur Mühlen, *Rassenideologien. Geschichte und Hintergründe* [Racial Ideologies] (Berlin, 1977), 244. While the race ideologist Günther still gloried in exaggerations when describing the nordic human being, Hitler's ideal image of the Aryan is stunted. There was room only for the hate-filled counter ideal. In Rosenberg there were positive as well as negative statements.

7. The value/nonvalue of a human being was judged according to his use for the community. "Racially, politically, or economically 'undesirable' life was at the same time 'nonvaluable' life and could or had to be sacrificed in the interest of 'higher' ideals and purposes." Helmut Erhardt, *Euthanasie und Vernichtung "lebensunwerten" Lebens* [Euthanasia and Extermination of "Life Unworthy of Living"] (Stuttgart, 1965), 24ff.

8. von zur Mühlen, 240ff.

9. Martin Broszat, "Dokumentation. Zur Perversion der Strafjustiz im Dritten Reich" [Documentation. On the Perversion of Penal Justice in the Third Reich], *Vierteljahreshefte für Zeitgeschichte* 6, No. 4 (Stuttgart, 1958), 391.

10. The situation can be compared to the massive Gypsy persecutions that began with the birth of the nation state in the fifteenth century: "In order to strengthen the unity of the nation state, there was an effort to eliminate everything that was different." Mirella Karpati, "Historischer Abriss" [Historical Sketch], in Anno Wilms, *Zigeuner* [Gypsies] (Zürich, 1972), 9.

In order to avert a threat to the *Volks*-community of National Socialism, which rested only on fictional solidarity, aggressive tendencies were consciously ascribed to the outsider groups. The Nazi *Volksgemeinschaft* was incapable of forming a consciousness of its own, collective identity without devaluing other cultural and national identities. "Not lastly, the fascist *Volks*-community owes its satisfactory emotional stability to a collective vindictiveness which it ascribes to other groups." Gerhard Vinnai, "Der Führer war an allem schuld. Zur Sozialpsychologie des 'Dritten Reiches' " [It was All the Führer's Fault. On the Social Psychology of the 'Third Reich'], in Johannes Beck et al., eds., *Terror und Hoffnung in Deutschland 1933–1945* [Terror and Hope in Germany 1933–1945] (Reinbek bei Hamburg, 1980), 473.

11. For instance, it was clear to the lawyers that the concentration camps were not specifically institutions of the *Rechtsstaat,* but "in a state, in which a new idea of state has asserted itself in a revolutionary way, the idea of the *Rechtsstaat* finds its limitations in the demand for an absolute securing of the national way of life." Otto Köllreutter, *Der deutsche Führerstaat* [The German Führer State] (Tübingen, 1934), 21, cited from Ilse Staff, ed., *Justiz im Dritten Reich* [Justice in the Third Reich] (Frankfurt, 1978), 155f.

12. The Nuremberg Laws of September 15, 1935 (*Reichsbürgergesetz* and *Blutschutzgesetz*). In the postwar period, it was often argued that the Gypsies were affected only by the *Reichsbürgergesetz* and not by the *Blutschutzgesetz*. Five of the six paragraphs are directed only against the Jews; in the sixth paragraph, there is the injunction against marriage, "if offspring are expected from the union who will endanger the purity of the German blood." Hans-Joachim Döring, *Die Zigeuner im nationalsozialistischen Staat* [The Gypsies in the National Socialist State], *Kriminologische Schriftenreihe,* Vol. 12 (Hamburg, 1964), 37. This also included marriages with Gypsies. Because, however, a marriage would have been allowed in the case of infertility or inability to produce children, Döring concluded, "From this we may conclude that the *Blutschutzgesetz* and the order to enforce it does not formally constitute a defamation of the Gypsies, while the enactment of the *Reichsbürgergesetz* does constitute a disability." Döring, 39.

13. Wilhelm Stuckart and Hans Globke, *Kommentare zur deutschen Rassengesetzgebung* [Commentaries on German Racial Laws], Vol. 1 (Munich, 1936), 55.

14. Hans F. K. Günther, *Rassenkunde des deutschen Volkes* [Racial Studies of the German People] (Munich, 1922/1937). In this book, mention is made that "blood foreign to Europe" was introduced into the European community by the Gypsies. "They mostly constitute a mixture of different races based on an Oriental-Asia Minor racial mixture" (p. 157).

15. Robert Krämer, "Rassische Untersuchungen an den 'Zigeuner' Kolonien Lause und Altengraben bei Berleburg (Westfalen)" [Racial Investigations in the 'Gypsy' Colonies Lause and Altengraben Near Berleburg (Westphalia)], *Archiv für Rassen-und Gesellschaftsbiologie* [Archive for Racial and Sociological Biology], Vol. 31, No. 1 (Munich, 1937/38), 33f.

16. Eva Justin, "Lebensschicksale artfremd erzogener Zigeunerkinder und ihrer Nachkommen" [Fate of Gypsy Children and Their Descendants Raised Outside Their Tribe], *Veröffentlichungen aus dem Gebiete des Volksgesundheitsdienstes* [Publications of the Public Health Service], Vol. 57, No. 4 (Berlin, 1944), 120.

17. "It was remarkable that the German people considered Gypsy blood to

be more dangerous than Jewish blood. In general, a person who had only one Jewish grandparent was not subject to the Nazi laws. . . . A German, however, whose greatgrandparent was a Gypsy was considered a gypsy half-breed." Donald Kenrick, "Nazi-Deutschland und die Zigeuner" [Nazi Germany and the Gypsies], *Sinti und Roma im ehemaligen KZ Bergen-Belsen* [Sinti and Roma in the Former Concentration Camp Bergen-Belsen] (Göttingen, 1980), 146.

18. Elisabeth Ferst, *Fertilität und Kriminalität der Zigeuner. Eine statistische Untersuchung* [Gypsy Fertility and Criminality. A Statistical Study] (Munich, 1943), 28.

19. Compare A. Würth, "Bemerkungen zur Zigeunerfrage und Zigeunerforschung in Deutschland" [Comments Regarding the Gypsy Question and Gypsy Scholarship in Germany], *Anthropologischer Anzeiger,* Series 9 (Stuttgart, 1938), 96.

20. "The Gypsy problem is not to be compared to the Jewish problem. . . . The Gypsy and Gypsy half-breed question is a part of the asocial problem." Justin, 120. "Beyond that, the Gypsy question also is a problem by itself, whose difficulty beyond the racial [dimension] consists above all in its close association with the question of asocialism." (Source: Regierungsrat Reischauer, Office of the Representative of the Führer, letter to Oberregierungsrat Krüger, Vienna, Minister for Interior and Cultural Affairs, Munich, March 7, 1939, AVA Education). "In the racial-political area, I (see) the dangers of the Gypsy question to be greater than the danger of the actual German [*innerdeutschen*] Jews." (Answer by Krüger to Reischauer, March 11, 1939, 3, both in file AVA, Zl. IV-2a-41906).

21. Heinz Galinski, "Vortrag anlässlich der Gedenkfeier" [Lecture on the Occasion of the Memorial Service], in Mirella Karpati, ed., *Sinti und Roma. Gestern und Heute* [Sinti and Roma. Yesterday and Today] (Bozen o.J., 1993/94), 79.

22. In confidential decree collection "Crime Prevention Measures," series of the Reich Criminal Police, Berlin, No. 15, 1941, Bl. 41ff. Source: IfZ, Munich, Dc. 1702.

23. Hans Buchheim, "Die SS—das Herrschaftsinstrument" [The SS—Instrument of the Ruling Power], in Hans Buchheim, Martin Broszat, Hans Adolf Jacobson, and Helmut Krausnick, eds., *Anatomie des SS-Staates* [Anatomy of the SS State], Vol. 1 (Munich, 1979), 97.

24. Circular of the RKPA (Reich Criminal Police) of April 4, 1938, in "Erlass-Sammlung 'Vorbeugende Verbrechensbekämpfung' " [Decree Collection of Crime Prevention Measures), Bl. 71f.

25. Compare Martin Broszat, "Nationalsozialistische Konzentrationslager 1933–1945" [National Socialist Concentration Camps], in Buchheim et al., *Anatomie,* Vol. 2, p. 76.

26. Steinmetz, *Österreichs Zigeuner,* 13. The Gypsies who were arrested during this campaign were first taken to Dachau but later transferred to other camps. Robert Schneeberger reported: "After three months we (in Dachau)

were loaded onto railroad cars under beatings and taken to Buchenwald like cattle." Eyewitness report by R. Schneeberger in Steinmetz, *Österreichs Zigeuner,* 38. In October 1941, after a short stay in Mauthausen, Schneeberger was taken to Lackenbach.

27. Hans Buchheim, "Die Zigeunerdeportation vom Mai 1940" [The Gypsy Deportation of May 1940], *Gutachten des Instituts für Zeitgeschichte,* Vol. 1 (Munich, 1956), 57.

28. Compare Buchheim, "Die Zigeunerdeportation," *Gutachten,* Vol. 1, p. 57.

29. During such an asocial campaign between June 13 and 18, 1938, at least two hundred male asocials were to be taken from the criminal police district to Buchenwald. Decree collection, No. 15, Bl. 81, cited from Buchheim et al., *Anatomie,* Vol. 2, p. 76. In this decree it was expressed clearly for the first time that forced labor was the main purpose of the concentration camp. Ibid., 77.

30. Gypsy basic decree, "Fighting the Gypsy Plague," RdErl.d.RFSSuChd-Dt.Pol. in RMdI, dated December 8, 1938. The entire decree, as well as the execution instructions, dated March 1, 1939, can be found in Döring, *Die Zigeuner,* appendices 1 and 2, 197–207.

31. Effective October 1, 1938, Himmler incorporated the Gypsy police headquarters Munich into the RKPA Berlin. Circular dated May 16, 1938. Cited according to Streck, in Zülch, 77. "From the police point of view, with this reorganization the preparation for the future fate of the Gypsies—namely arrest of all and deportation as planned—is completed." George von Soest, *Zigeuner zwischen Verfolgung und Integration* [Gypsies between Persecution and Integration] (Weinheim, 1979), 36.

32. The research consisted of the compilation of data of origin and family data; via detailed genealogies the question of the connection between criminality and heredity was to be solved.

33. Compare Robert Ritter, "Die Zigeunerfrage und das Zigeunerbastard-problem" [The Gypsy Question and the Problem of the Gypsy Bastard], *Fortschritte der Erbpathologie* [New Findings in Heredity Pathology], Series 3 (Leipzig, 1939), 1–20.

34. Ritter, 4.

35. Also Robert Ritter, "Zigeuner und Landfahrer" [Gypsies and Travelers], *Der nichtsesshafte Mensch* [Nomadic People]. Ein Beitrag der Neugestaltung der Raum-und Menschenordnung im Grossdeutschen Reich (Munich, 1938), 77.

36. Compare Karl Moravek, *Ein Beitrag zur Rassenkunde der "Burgenländischen Zigeuner"* [A Contribution to the Racial Studies of "Burgenland Gypsies"] (Vienna, 1939), 9 and 90. The successful completion of this research, which had been financed by the "German Research Council, the German school organization Südmark, the Burgenland state organization, and the Reichsnähr-stand Südmark" was made possible "especially through the support of the

teachers in the research area (District Oberwart), who were mostly hired illegally." Moravek, preface, 1.

37. Streck, in Zülch, 78. The approximate goal for the draft of a law, "Measures to end further mixing of Gypsies and Germans, separation of the pure Gypsies from the half-breeds; sterilization and isolation of the asocial half-breeds." Letter by Panke, chief of the [Main Race and Settlement Office], to Himmler, December 19, 1938, Diary No. 299/38. Cited from *Verfahren der Staatsanwaltschaft Köln, Az.,* 24 Js429/61, 10. Source: Central Office of the State Judicial Administration, Ludwigsburg.

38. Hans Buchheim, "Die Verfolgung der Zigeuner aus rassischen Gründen zur Zeit der nationalsozialistischen Herrschaft" [The Persecution of the Gypsies for Racial Reasons during the National Socialist Period], unpublished manuscript, Munich, June 6, 1958, Bl.136f., cited from Streck, in Zülch, 77f. and 310f. n. 55.

39. December 19, 1938, Solution of the Gypsy question, especially in the *Ostmark:* Cooperation by RKPA/RSHA: "The race files of the approximately 7,000 Gypsies of the *Ostmark* will be put at the disposal of the Race and Settlement Office-SS for the creation of a file system of foreign ethnicity within the tribal office and the tribal services office of the *Ostmark.* . . . The Race and Settlement Office is authorized together with the police posts to undertake tribal-biological and heredity-biological examinations using the Gypsies of the *Ostmark* as subjects." Nuremberg Documents: No-1898. Source: IfZ-Munich.

40. At this time, the Gypsy department of the Salzburg Criminal Police station was also established, and shortly thereafter the collection camp Rennbahn was started. Compare "The Founding Phase of Camp Salzburg" section in chapter 3.

41. RKPA decree, Diary No. I A 2d 60001/430.39. Copy in BMI file, Zl. 65-304-2/52. A copy can also be found in Steinmetz, *Österreichs Zigeuner,* Appendix 3, p. 51.

42. Other concentration camp inmates have described the arrival of these Gypsy transports in their memoirs. "If in the first years (in Dachau) the political inmates outnumbered the others . . . the arrests in the years 1937 and 1938 added primarily criminals, asocial people, Gypsies." Benedikt Kautzky, *Teufel und Verdammte* [Devils and Damned People] (Vienna, 1948), 40. But already in the fall of 1939 the Dachau Gypsies were sent to the concentration camp Buchenwald because of the temporary disuse of Dachau as a concentration camp. Hans Marsalek, *Die Geschichte des Konzentrationslagers Mauthausen* [The History of Concentration Camp Mauthausen] (Mauthausen, 1974), 92f.

43. From the temporary timetable of concentration camp Ravensbrück it can be ascertained that on June 29, 1939, 440 Gypsy women from Burgenland, Vienna, and Lower Austria arrived. With this Gypsy transport also the first children arrived in Ravensbrück. From October 1942 on, Gypsy women also were included along with Jewesses in transports from Ravensbrück to Ausch-

witz. DÖW file, No. 2589; this timetable was compiled by the Ravensbrück inmates from different individual reports until April 1, 1945.

44. "The release of numerous 'Gypsy half-breeds' from the concentration
camps at the end of 1940 probably occurred because of the shortage of labor
(due to the war)," Heinz Mode and Siegfried Wölfling, *Zigeuner. Der Weg eines
Volkes in Deutschland* [Gypsies. The Path of a People in Germany] (Leipzig,
1968), 175.

45. Streck, in Zülch, 79.

46. Border district decree dated September 1, 1939 (RGBl. I 1578): Injunction against vagrancy in military assembly areas, cited in Buchheim et al.,
Anatomie, 57.

47. RKPA documents from November 20, 1939, threatened that all fortune-
telling Gypsy women would be taken into preventive detention (this is equal
to deportation to a concentration camp). Buchheim et al., *Anatomie*, 57.

48. Incarceration decree, dated October 17, 1939, Circular RSHA-RKPA
149/19399, cited by Streck in Zülch, 80 and 311 n. 67.

49. These collection points/camps were erected in the vicinity of larger
Gypsy settlements. In addition to the Salzburg camp, there is information about
the collection point Bruckhaufen in Vienna, as well as Hopfgarten/Tyrol. Compare Steinmetz, *Österreichs Zigeuner*, 14. "In Hopfgarten, it was the function of
two shanty towns to house Gypsies on the move and those who lived there
part of the time until their deportation to the East—here especially two families were affected, from whom only one member returned." From the account
of Miriam Wiegele, Vienna, March 24, 1980.

We learn that in February 1943, an adopted child of the Austrian resistance
fighter Johann Beirather was deported there. With the explanation by the
youth office that the mother had been found, the small Gypsy girl Sidonie
Adlersburg was first taken to Hopfgarten and from there deported to Auschwitz. She did not survive Auschwitz. DÖW file, No. 668.

50. The relocation decree dated April 27, 1940, refers to the arrest decree.
Compare Martin Broszat, "Nationalsozialistische KL," in Buchheim et al.,
Anatomie, Vol. 2, p. 93. Comparable with Eichmann's Madagaskar-project for
the Jews, there had been relocation plans for Gypsies among race scholars al-
ready before the beginning of the war. They thought in terms of Polynesia and
Abyssinia. Compare Margret Weiler, *Zur Frage der Integration der Zigeuner in der
Bundesrepublik Deutschland* [On the Question of the Integration of the Gypsies
in the Federal Republic of Germany] (Cologne, 1979), 105f. n. 1.

51. Streck, in Zülch, 81.

52. Point 3 of the decree read, "to deport 'the other 30,000 Gypsies also to
Poland.' " Note dated September 27, 1939, regarding "head officer and Einsatzgruppen leader meeting," cited in Helmut Krausnick, "Judenverfolgung,"
in Buchheim et al., *Anatomie*, Vol. 2, p. 289.

53. DÖW file, No. 2527, Negotiations with the central office for Jewish
emigration, Vienna, October 18, 1939.

54. FS, No. 7743, dated October 16, 1939, SD Danube, Gestapo Section Vienna, to Stapo-district post Mähren-Ostrau, for delivery to SS-officer Nebe. Copied in Simon Wiesenthal, *Doch die Mörder leben* (Munich, 1967), 290f.

55. Wiesenthal, *Doch die Mörder leben*, 290f.

56. DÖW file, No. 2528.

57. Nuremberg Documents PS-2233. *IMG*, Vol. 29, p. 438.

58. Resettlement decree dated April 27, 1940, V B No. 95/40 g, reproduced in Döring, *Die Zigeuner*, Appendix 3, p. 208. Compare also Streck, in Zülch, 81; also Donald Kenrick and Grattan Puxon, *Sinti und Roma—Die Vernichtung eines Volkes im NS-Staat* [Sinti and Roma—The Destruction of a People in the Nazi State] (Göttingen, 1981), 67f. Here one can find details of the fate of these deportees based on eyewitness accounts.

59. Microfilm Dc T 84 R 13 40/255, National Archives Washington, SD Vienna, April 15, 1940. Karl Stadler, *Österreich 1938–1945*. Im Spiegel der NS-Akten (Vienna, 1966), 273.

60. Express letter RMdI to criminal police: Pol. S V B 2 No. 1264, 40 IV, cited in Döring, *Die Zigeuner*, 109.

61. The reordering of the East was to be achieved by the relocation of peoples. These projects fell to Himmler. On October 7, 1939, his title, RFSSu.ChdDt.pol [Reichsführer SS und Chef der deutschen Polizei], was expanded to reflect the new function, RKFDV (Reichs commissioner for the strengthening of German peoplehood).

62. Buchheim et al., *Anatomie*, 54. The author now (1994) sees this assessment by Buchheim differently. Uncertainty about "racial grouping" or, rather, incomplete studies of the racial research, surely had the *least* influence on the delay of the deportations east.

63. These deportations, for which there are no separate decrees, were based on a decision of the January 1940 conference on the clearing of the eastern districts, contained in Eichmann's memo on emigration/evacuation N-B-4 in RSHA. Compare Arendt, *Eichmann in Jerusalem*, 261. See chapter 6, "Gypsy Transports from Austria to Lodz and Chelmno."

64. RSHA-decree V A 2 No. 2551-42, cited by Streck in Zülch, 315 n. 94.

65. Eugen Hodoschi, until the fall of 1942 a seaman with the navy, was to be deported to Buchenwald. Upon his own request, he was then at least allowed to join his family in Lackenbach. Memoirs, in Steinmetz, *Österreichs Zigeuner*, 24f.

66. RSHA decree V A 2 No. 2260/42, dated October 13, 1942, copy. In BMI file, Zl. 65.304-2/52.

67. Compare also Steinmetz, *Österreichs Zigeuner*, 52f. This decree was published almost completely in Appendix 4.

68. Himmler's decision was based on the findings of the "race-biological research office," according to which pure Gypsies were good, but half-breeds were criminally disposed. Since, however, the percentage of pure Gypsies was so low (10 percent), even half-breeds who could be reeducated could be se-

lected. Nine Gypsy spokespersons were to put together lists of those Gypsies who were to be selected. In addition, they were to inform those selected about the measures and instruct them to lead a well-ordered life. Compare Steinmetz, *Österreichs Zigeuner*, Appendix 4, p. 52f.

69. Mazirel considered it a publicity stunt to distract attention from the upcoming Auschwitz campaign. Mazirel, 133. Kenrick and Puxon, *Sinti und Roma*, on the other hand, suspected that "Himmler probably followed only one goal, namely to save a limited number of Roma as study subjects for the SS organization 'Ancestral Heritage' " (p. 77).

70. Compare *Widerstand und Verfolgung im Burgenland*, 252, and *Widerstand und Verfolgung in Wien 1934–1945*, Vol. 3 (Vienna, 1975), 357.

71. RSHA V A 2 No. 59/43 g. Directions for implementation, January 29, 1943, completely printed in Döring, *Die Zigeuner Österreichs*, Appendix 6, pp. 214–18; as well as Steinmetz, *Österreichs Zigeuner*, Appendix 5, pp. 53–55.

For regulation in the "Alp and Danube districts" (Austrian), additional decrees were passed (RSHA V A 2 No. 48/43g dated January 26, 1943, and V A 2 No. 64/43g dated January 28, 1943).

72. Opening date of this part of Camp B IIe, comprising thirty barracks, was March 8, 1943. Compare illegal prisoner calendar of Auschwitz, *Widerstand und Verfolgung im Burgenland*, Doc. 51, 288f.

73. In the instructions for implementation, other groups that were to be given special status are mentioned as well. Compare Döring, *Die Zigeuner Österreichs*, 215f.

74. *Auschwitz Journals*, No. 9 (Cracow, Museum in Auschwitz, 1966), 42.

75. Compare Mazirel, "Die Verfolgung," 132. The Sinti and Lalleri, or rather the good half-breeds among them, were to be the only group who were not to be sterilized even if not imprisoned. However, there are reports—especially by German Sinti—that state that their "racial" purity did not protect them from imprisonment and deportation but from extermination.

76. *Auschwitz Journals*, No. 9, p. 41.

77. *Auschwitz Journals*, No. 9, p. 41.

78. Illegal prisoner calendar in *Widerstand und Verfolgung im Burgenland*, 288f.

79. *Widerstand und Verfolgung im Burgenland*, 288f. and 252.

80. "And so we were all put in cattle cars, 50 people each, on them was written 'Auschwitz.' Almost without stopping we traveled, three days and nights." Memoirs, Kathi Horwath. In Steinmetz, *Österreichs Zigeuner*, 37. The Salzburg resident Karl Eberle also remembered this undignified transport for which they were given not nearly enough food. Conversation with K. Eberle April 30, 1981. For three of these Austria transports the documents on the arrangement of a guard detail have been preserved (March 8, 1943, April 16, 1943, and April 29, 1943). From these documents it can be discerned that ten to fourteen prisoners were watched by one guard. DÖW file, No. 696.

81. Karl Eberle, who first was in the Gypsy camp for one week and then

was sent to the main camp, described that as a civil institution in comparison to the Gypsy camp. Conversation of April 30, 1981.

82. The maximum number of prisoners in camp was 22,696. In this number are included the 1,700 Polish Gypsies from Bialystok who, at the beginning of March 1943, were gassed immediately after their arrival, without registration, because of the suspicion of typhus. On June 1, 1944, there were approximately 6,500—selections for the gas chamber and other concentration camps had already taken place. In the first June days, another 2,300 people were selected and sent to other camps. Compare Tadeusz Szymanski et al., "Über den 'Krankenbau' im Zigeuner-Familienlager in Auschwitz-Birkenau" [On the 'Hospital Wing' in the Gypsy Family Camp Auschwitz-Birkenau), *"Auschwitz"-Anthologie,* Vol. 2, Part 2 (Warsaw, 1970), 3 and 34.

83. In February 1944, there were only sixty-four Gypsies left in Buchenwald. Their number increased only in August 1944 by the referrals of those who could work from Camp Birkenau. Nuremberg document No. 1187. Source: State Archives Nuremberg, Rep. 502 IV, Bl. 770. Compare also Gerald Reitlinger, *Die Endlösung* [The Final Solution] (Berlin, 1956), 210f. Continuation, 28. About the arrival of women in Ravensbrück, Berta Fröhlich reported, "When, in the summer of 1944, a large train with our people arrived from Auschwitz, we ran there and searched for our families." Memoirs, Steinmetz, *Österreichs Zigeuner,* 39. A group of female Gypsies was executed in the forest near Ravensbrück in February of 1945. Chronology of Ravensbrück, in DÖW file, No. 2589.

84. *Auschwitz Journals,* No. 8, 1965, p. 55. Compare also report by Steinmetz, *Österreichs Zigeuner,* 251f., also ibid., Document 54 and 55, 290f.

85. Testimony by Major Josef Piwko, officer from Chorczow, January 1943 to end of 1944 in Auschwitz. Inge Deutschkron, *Denn ihrer war die Hölle* [For Theirs Was Hell] (Cologne, 1965), 129.

86. RSHA-decree V No. 591-Al-A 2, dated March 28, 1942, copy. In BMI file, Zl. 65.304-2/52. This regulation was already valid for the Poles and some months later also for the Jews. Compare Kenrick and Puxon, *Sinti und Roma,* 71.

87. "Special treatment," this cynical "terminus technicus," appears for the first time as a symbol for execution in a decree by Heydrich, dated September 3, 1939, "on the principles of internal state security during the war." It became infamous later as a pseudonym for extermination. Compare Broszat, *Dokumentation,* 399.

88. Discussion between Reich justice minister Thierack and Himmler on September 18, 1942: Those concerned were Poles with more than three years of prison, and Czechs and Germans with more than eight years; in contrast lumped together were all those, independent of the length of their imprisonment, designated as "security risks": Jews, Gypsies, Russians, and Ukrainians. Nuremberg Document, PS 654. *IMG,* Vol. 26, p. 200; compare also Buchheim et al., *Anatomie,* Vol. 2, p. 320.

89. This remarkably candid language can be found in a letter by Thierack to the leader of the party office, Martin Bormann, dated October 1942. Nuremberg Document, NG-558, microfilm IfZ-Munich. Cited according to Buchheim et al., *Anatomie,* Vol. 2, p. 320.

90. DÖW file No. 2570: Verdict of state court Salzburg, April 3, 1944, against Gypsy J. Walter (E 1699). Walter, employed by the RAB *[Reichsauto-bahn]* in Tyrol until 1939, was sent to the Salzburg Gypsy camp after his deportation from Tyrol. After a successful escape, he was sentenced to a year of severe imprisonment because of thefts and consequently sent to Mauthausen. After he also succeeded in fleeing from there, he committed those crimes that brought with them the death penalty in January (pp. 1–3).

91. DÖW file No. 2570, 5.

92. RGBl. 268, dated April 25, 1943. Cited according to Döring, *Die Zigeuner,* 169.

93. A document on the Gypsy deportations from Burgenland confirms that the number of those left behind was minimal: "On Thursday, April 15, 1943, there will be a new deportation of Gypsies. Presumably only a few families will be left, so that most of the Gypsy camps will become completely empty." DÖW file No. 11293.

94. "In as far as the Jews and Gypsies are concerned, the evacuation which was carried out by the chief of security and the SD, and the isolation of these groups, has removed them from being singled out publicly in ways hitherto used with regard to the voluminous prohibitions in many areas of life." SPo IV D2 c 927/44 g.24. Cited according to Kenrick and Puxon, *Sinti und Roma,* 78.

3. The Situation of the Gypsies in Salzburg before 1939 and Gypsy Camp Salzburg (1939–1943)

1. Compare Loewenstein, 59ff.

2. Compare Hohmann, *Zigeuner und Zigeunerwissenschaft,* 15: "If anthropology, study of folklore, and ethnology see the Gypsy in his primarily Gypsy-specific qualities and modes of behavior, this anthropological picture changes when seen from a socio-political and police perspective and turns the Gypsy into a counter-myth, by demythologizing him, and he becomes the crafty criminal who forever escapes."

3. Report BH-Hallein, Zl. 12.167/2, to state leadership, Salzburg, December 31, 1937.

4. Police report from the years 1937–1940 to the state leadership, that is, the state representatives. Information and documents were made available to me by Professor Ernst Hanisch, Salzburg.

5. In the summer, these Gypsies, who had primarily settled at the edge of Vienna, traveled in all of Austria. In addition there were Sinti from Lower Austria, Upper Austria, and also from Southern Germany.

6. Police inspector Hallein, E. No. 2279, Zl. 310/4-R. D. to BH Hallein, December 24, 1938, 1.

7. Police station Mitterberghütten, E. No. 4, dated January 2, 1939, 1.

8. Police station Saalfelden, E. No. 1473, dated May 31, 1939, to police inspector Zell am See, 2. The undifferentiated measures of the Tyrolian authorities are also proven by the case of Johann Walter. He was working for Reich highway construction when he was told to leave Tyrol. DÖW file No. 2570, verdict state court Salzburg, E 1699, dated April 3, 1944.

9. Police station Saalfelden, 1.

10. Police station Saalfelden, 1. The Gypsies were sent to Saalfelden with the last passenger train so that they could not be sent back toward Tyrol on the same day.

11. Police report Weissbach/Lofer, Ex. No. 477, May 29, 1939, to police inspector Zell am See, 1.

12. Compare district council Markt Pongau, Diary No. 5600a/24 dated October 12, 1939, to minister president in Salzburg, 1.

13. In addition to the radical suggestions for solutions, the understanding that in one case was extended to the victims was an exception worth mentioning: "It can be well understood and goes without saying that the Gypsies were extremely agitated with that much back and forth and . . . react to the police who interfere with all the resistance they can muster. This can easily lead to harsh measures by the police or even the use of weapons." Report by the police station Weissbach, dated March 29, 1939, 2.

14. Tobias Portschy, *Die Zigeunerfrage* [The Gypsy Question] (Eisenstadt, 1938). Source: DÖW-Library 8085. Portschy was at first state captain for Burgenland, then deputy district leader for Steiermark. See chapter 4.

15. Police inspector St. Johann/Pg., E. No. 113, dated January 12, 1939, to district council St. Johann, 3.

16. Police Inspector, St. Johann/Pg., E. No. 113, 3.

17. Police district Salzburg, Diary No. 2215, dated October 13, 1939, to district council, Salzburg, 1.

18. Here they have in mind the consequences of the arrest decree of October 1939.

19. Police station Neumarkt-Köstendorf, Diary No. 1, dated January 2, 1940, to district council, Salzburg, 1.

20. In recent years, additional source material was discovered that allows a more detailed reconstruction of the camp conditions. At the end of chapter 3 a short, more recent discussion will provide this information. The first attempted reconstruction is essentially correct; but I would like to point out in advance, for the sake of clarity, that "Salzburg" contains two locales: (a) Camp Salzburg-Maxglan (synonyms: Leopoldskron, Leopoldskron-Moos, Kräutlerweg, Marienbad). This camp resulted from a former collection point and was enlarged and turned into a strictly guarded Nazi Gypsy camp in the course of the changed nature of persecution. (b) In addition, Camp Rennbahn existed.

In the fall of 1940, the horse stalls of the Salzburg race track became the collection area of the planned and then cancelled deportations east.

21. BMI file, Zl. 178.401-2/56: Testimony Lambert Brandner, copy, 1.

22. Steinmetz, *Österreichs Zigeuner,* 14.

23. DÖW file, No. 2570: Verdict-LG Sbg. dated April 3, 1944 against Gypsy Johann Walter.

24. BMI file, Zl. 99.851-2/53: Letter of prosecutor Stuttgart, Bl.2. The position of the plaintiff, the Reinhardt family: "The incarceration in Salzburg and Lackenbach equalled concentration camp conditions." BMI file, Zl. 119.843-2/53.

25. BMI file, Zl. 178.401-2/52, cover sheet.

26. BMI file, Zl. 99.851-2/53: Information of the federal police directorate Salzburg to the BMI (I/1-34869/52), dated December 8, 1952. "In June 1939, they established a collection camp for Gypsies in the area Salzburg Rennbahn as a temporary measure. Shortly thereafter a collection camp for Gypsies was established in Moos Street in Salzburg, called 'Marienbad.' " However, the installation Rennbahn seems to still have existed in the summer of 1940, in addition to the camp in Leopoldskron. Thereafter, the *Areal* [racetrack] had to be cleared for the fall races. According to information by K. Eberle, conversation April 30, 1981.

27. Basis for the camp establishment was the arrest decree of October 1939 and the related impending transport of Gypsies to the East.

28. BMI file, Zl. 178.401-2/56: Witness testimony Ludwig Nessl, copy, 1. The file on the establishment of this camp can no longer be located in the Salzburg city council. Information according to BMI file, Zl. 119.843-2/53 and Zl. 95.353-2/57.

29. BMI file, Zl. 119.843-2/53: Entry in operations book of police station Dorfgastein, dated October 27, 1939, No. 233.

30. BMI file, Zl. 119.843-2/53. Entry in operations book, dated August 13, 1940, No. 138. The dates given by Konrad Reinhardt—January 1939 arrest in Dorfgastein/June 1939 transfer to Camp Salzburg—show a difference of approximately one year from the entry in the operations book. The arrest date in Salzburg given by K. Reinhardt cannot be correct because the camp did not yet exist at that time.

31. On the basis of an inquiry with the state police command post in Salzburg on January 4, 1980, Col. Altrichter issued an order to all seventy-two police posts in the province of Salzburg to check their chronicles and possible other documents (operations books, etc.) from the time in question regarding entries on Gypsy detentions and to send copies to the LGK. Col. Altrichter's pessimism about the success of this action was correct—the histories were kept, but the entries were too sparse. The police station in Schwarzach was the only one that responded to the order and supplied two entries from the history.

32. This statute deals with the arrest decree dated October 17, 1939. The text stated: "Arrest and counting of all Gypsies and Gypsy half-breeds in the

time period from 10/25 to 10/27/39 and establishment of appropriate collection points."

33. Copies from the police history Schwarzach, October 25, 1939, and August 13, 1940, in connection with the LGK-order, E. No. 2106/1-3c/80, dated January 8, 1980. The Gypsies detained in Schwarzach were housed partly in Kloster Schernberg, partly on Glocklehenbauer's property until their transfer to Salzburg. Ibid., note of October 25, 1939, and conversation with A. Rauter, Schwarzach, March 5, 1982.

34. According to information K. Eberle, conversation April 30, 1981.

35. BMI file, Zl, 58.636-2/54: Information BMI to Bavarian LKA, Munich (Zl. 55.390-13/54), dated April 9, 1954.

36. Photos of the camp area allow the conclusion that the actual space used for the camp must have been much smaller. Individuals familiar with the camp conditions could not give precise information.

37. BMI file, Zl. 178.401-2/56: Testimony G. Widl, copy, 3, and testimony A. Laventin, copy, 1.

38. Conversation with Karl Eberle, Salzburg, 4/30/81. Karl Eberle's family—the father was Sinto from the south German area, the mother non-Gypsy from South Tyrol—had lived primarily in Austria since the mid-1920s. Before he was sent to Camp Rennbahn, he was employed by a construction firm in Glasenbach and housed in the Marienheim there.

39. Note in file of LGK, Salzburg, regarding conversation between Col. Altrichter and the retired official, in February, 1980. In the sources the camp is mentioned as "Kräutlerweg," "Leopoldskron," "Leopoldskron-Moos," but also "Marienbad." Investigations showed that these different names refer to one and the same place.

40. Personal information from Nina Gladitz and Gerhard Dietrich, Kirchzarten, March 25, 1981, and letter dated April 10, 1981, as well as conversation with Karl Eberle on April 30, 1981, and June 17, 1981. The oldest daughter of Eberle's wife, 10-year-old Angela, also was chosen for the filming. He remembers that the girl was enthusiastic and in return received a larger amount of money and a pair of boots. Others, who knew of this event through relatives and others, did not know anything of payment. It may, however, be assumed that the film company had to pay money to the camp treasury, especially since guard personnel had to be assigned for this purpose. Ms. Gladitz and Mr. Dietrich, who are working on a film project that also has as its theme the activities of the Riefenstahl film company during the Nazi period, received their information from Mr. Josef Reinhardt. As a child, he also participated in the film in the Tyrol; later the Reinhardt family was sent to Lackenbach. A number of Reinhardt's details agree to the greatest extent with the experiences reported by Karl Eberle.

41. Conversation with Ernst Pilz, Salzburg, on June 16, 1981. From 1940 to 1955 he was employed by the criminal police and frequently had business in camp but did not belong to the guard detail there.

42. BMI file, Zl. 178.401-2/56: Testimony A. Laventin, 1.

43. BMI file, Zl. 178.401-2/56. Testimony L. Nessl, copy, 3: "They were given civilian clothing, linens, shoes from camp supply."

44. Karl Eberle remembers only one case of illness. He was in the camp for three and one-half years.

45. According to available information, all illnesses, even light ones, were treated in the hospital.

46. BMI file, Zl. 178.401-2/56: Testimony K. Eberle, 2.

47. Karl Eberle, who reported this, was himself assigned to the construction detail Maria Plain-Liefering Bridge. During this project the laborers were housed outside the camp. Conversation of April 30, 1981.

48. According to information by residents of the Kendler settlement in September 1980 and testimony of Therese Wolf, copy, 5. In BMI file, Zl. 178.401-2/56.

49. BMI file, Zl. 79.899-2/56: Review of information on the former Gypsy camp Salzburg, file 13 (Zl. 75.731-13/56).

50. BMI file, Zl. 79.899-2/56, file 13.

51. BMI file, Zl. 178.401-2/56: Testimony L. Nessl, 3.

52. BMI file, Zl. 178.401-2/56: Testimony L. Brandner, 1. "This was forced labor in arrest-like conditions." Contrary to this, the report to the Bavarian state criminal office stated (Zl. 55.390-13/54, in BMI file, Zl. 58.636-2/54), 2: "Gypsies were not used for forced labor. If they volunteered for any kind of work, they were compensated accordingly."

53. Escape attempts were numerous, but only very few escapees managed to go underground for a longer period of time. Former inmates also reported that it was possible to leave the camp at night. Most were caught again a short time later and returned to camp.

54. BMI file, Zl. 178.401-2/56. Testimony L. Nessl, 1–3. Ludwig Nessl's description was at first given the most weight in the evaluation because he was the representative of the criminal police. A few years after these proceedings there was apparently another trial in Bad Reichenhall, during which Nessl had to repudiate a large part of his original testimony. According to information by N. Gladitz/G. Dietrich, conversation on March 25, 1981.

55. BMI file Zl. 178.401-2/56. Testimony of K. Eberle, 1.

56. A large number of the Salzburg police were drafted for Poland, hence numerous assistant policemen came as guards. In their civilian life they were conductors, gardeners, butchers, etc.

57. BMI file, Zl. 178.401-2/56: Witness testimony L. Nessl, 1–3.

58. BMI file Zl. 178.401-2/56. Testimony G. Widl, 2 and 4.

59. BMI file Zl. 178.401-2/56. Testimony L. Brandner, 1.

60. One can assume that this change in camp activities came about as a result of the cancellation of deportations east to the *Ostmark*. (Compare chapter 2.) Even though the collection camps were at first meant only as temporary solutions, they now had to be adapted to a longer duration. According to infor-

mation from Karl Eberle, camp inmates had been informed that they were to be resettled in the East. There they had been promised living quarters and work. When this transport did not materialize, they were told that the destination in question was already full due to other evacuations. Conversation, June 17, 1981.

61. Both reported in their testimony that the camp was fenced in with barbed wire and that armed policemen stood 40 to 50 meters apart. In addition, there are said to have been watch towers with floodlights and a machine gun. The camp door is said to have always been locked and under guard.

62. K. Eberle told in this connection that all assistant policemen were alright and behaved fairly.

63. BMI file, Zl. 178.401-2/56: Testimony L. Nessl, 2.

64. BMI file, Zl. 178.401-2/56. Testimony A. Netbal, 1.

65. BMI file, Zl. 58.636-2/54, insert 55.390-13/54, 3.

66. The notation "Laxenburg near Vienna" means Lackenbach in Burgenland.

67. Note in file LGK, Salzburg, 2.

68. Here the testimony varies between one and three families.

69. BMI file, Zl. 178.401-2/56. Testimony A. Laventin, 2: "When I was sent to Auschwitz on April 1, the Reinhardt family still remained in Salzburg." Ibid., testimony L. Brandner, 2: "I was in camp until the largest number of the inmates, except for two or three families, was sent to Auschwitz. In any case, only a few remained, who were then sent to Camp Lackenbach." Brandner was in the Salzburg camp until April 1943.

70. BMI file, Zl. 168.538-2/52: State office for reparations, Tübingen, to police authorities in Lackenbach. Here seven names are mentioned: Reinhardt: Konrad, Anna, Josef, Maria, Elisabeth, Erika and Josefa. In addition, Johann Bocdech, manager of the Stoob ceramics factory, confirmed that a part of the Reinhardt family was employed there after their settlement in Lackenbach. In BMI file, Zl. 178.401-2/56, 1.

71. Of the file cards that were found in the Lackenbach headquarters building, only two could be identified as admissions from Salzburg. This again concerns members of the Reinhardt family; there is a card for Anna Reinhardt, camp No. 3057, as well as a notice about and a card for the child Josefa Reinhardt, camp No. 3074. Both bear an admission date of April 6, 1943. The first part of the camp diary, copy, DÖW file, No. 11340, comprises the period January 4, 1941, to February 4, 1941.

72. *Auschwitz Journals*, Nos. 1 (1959) to 15 (1975): From the end of March 1943, there were altogether ten transports with Austrian Gypsies (eight only with Austrians, two together with other nationalities).

73. BMI file, Zl. 79.899-2/56: Investigations of the Bavarian state reparations office in the matter of Josef Krems. According to this testimony, the transport to Auschwitz is to have taken place in March or April 1943.

74. Conversation with K. Eberle, April 30, 1981. After a short stint building

barracks in Auschwitz, he was sent as a guinea pig to the typhoid projects in Natzweiler. Thereafter he had to work building tunnels in two small camps—Neckarelz and Neckargerau. On a transport from there to Dachau in January of 1945, he managed to escape.

Amended Presentation of Gypsy Camp(s) Salzburg: Salzburg-Maxglan/Leopoldskron or Salzburg-Rennbahn

1. Erika Thurner, "Die Verfolgung von Minderheiten: Zigeuner" [The Persecution of Minorities: Gypsies], *Widerstand und Verfolgung in Salzburg 1934–1945* [Resistance and Persecution in Salzburg 1934–1945] (Vienna, 1991). Compare also Barbara Rieger, " 'Zigeunerleben' in Salzburg 1930–1943" ["Gypsy Lives" in Salzburg 1930–1943] (master's thesis, University of Vienna, 1990).

2. Nina Gladitz, "Zeit des Schweigens und der Dunkelheit" [Time of Silence and Darkness] (Video Westdeutscher Rundfunk, 1983).

3. The Salzburg Gypsy camp was located between Moosstrasse and Kendlerstrasse-Kräutlerweg-am Schwarzgrabenweg an der Glan (today the section Leopoldskron-Moos). In the sources it appears as "Leopoldskron," "Maxglan," "Kräutlerweg," "Leopoldskron-Moos" and "Marienbad." In this chapter, the term "Maxglan/Leopoldskron" or "Maxglan" is used.

4. BMI file, Zl. 58.636-2/54.

5. SLA (Salzburger Landesarchiv [Salzburg District Archive]) RSTH I/3 45/1943 Kripo Salzburg/SS-Obersturmführer and Criminal Police Commissioner Huber to district leader Salzburg.

6. Compare in bibliography the publications by Selma Steinmetz, Herbert Michael Burggasser, Claudia Mayerhofer, and Erika Thurner.

7. BMI file, Zl. 99.851-2/53. Letter by district attorney Stuttgart to Federal Ministry of the Interior, Vienna, June 18, 1953, compare *Widerstand und Verfolgung in Salzburg* (WuVS/DÖW, Document/Doc. 32).

8. Compare Kenrick and Puxon, *Sinti und Roma,* 66.

9. SLA, K45, NS: Letter of criminal police station Salzburg to RSHA Berlin, February 16, 1940 (WuVS, Doc. 15).

10. SLA, K45, NS: In a later deposition, Anton Böhmer, the former leader of the criminal police station in Salzburg, stated that none of those imprisoned in Camp Salzburg were in danger of being sent to the concentration camp and that those who had already been sent to concentration camps before the establishment of the camp [Salzburg] were innocent victims of a misunderstanding (WuVS, Doc. 23).

11. SLA, K45, NS: Letter by the district farmers' organization Alpenland to the Reich governor in Salzburg, September 7, 1940 (WuVS, Doc. 23).

12. SLA, K45, NS: Letter by the criminal police station Salzburg to RSHA, February 16, 1940 (WuVS, Doc. 15).

13. SLA, K45, NS: Letter by the Kripo station Salzburg to Reich governor, July 5, 1940, and July 8, 1940 (WuVS, Doc. 20, 18, 19).

14. SLA, K45, NS: Letter by Kripo station Salzburg to Reich criminal director Nebe in RKPA, Berlin, September 6, 1940 (WuVS, Doc. 22).

15. According to different witnesses, the guard unit consisted of one officer and six assistant policemen. They were armed with a carbine and gun. Later two watch towers were erected (WuVS, Doc. 34, 36).

16. SLA, K45, NS: camp order dated October 28, 1940 (WuVS, Doc. 28, 34).

17. BMI file, Zl. 178.401-2/56. Eyewitness testimony by Lambert Brandner (Doc. 34/36).

18. Original plans to use Salzburg Gypsies in the Hermann-Göring-Works in Linz, in the work education camp St. Pantaleon, or in Ibmer-Moos were discarded because of spatial distance due to low efficiency. Male and female Gypsies of the labor-education camp/Gypsy camp Weyer were used to drain the Ibmer marsh. This camp, which was established for more than three hundred Sinti and Roma arrested in Upper Austria, existed only a few months: from January 19, 1941, to, at the latest, October 29, 1941. For these Gypsies, Lackenbach, Lodz, or Chelmno became the next, often "final," stations. See also the chronicle of the police station Wildshut, January 19, 1941 and October 29, 1941 (Gendarmeriepostenkommando Wildshut = DÖW 15.061/7). [Also] Andreas Maislinger, "Gypsy holding camp" and "labor education camp" Weyer. "Amendment of a Local Chronicle," in *Pogrom* 137/18, Vol. 1987, 33f. (WuVS, Doc. 27).

19. Compare Rieger, 97f; Gladitz, "Zeit des Schweigens und der Dunkelheit."

20. DÖW file E 18.518. Verdict of district court Munich in private suit of Leni Riefenstahl vs. Helmut Kindler because of defamation of character, November 30, 1949 (DÖW E 18.518). The hopes of the participants that Mrs. Riefenstahl might speak out on their behalf to help their cause were not fulfilled. Compare also WuVS, Doc. 25, 27, and Rieger, 97f.

21. Express letter from January 29, 1943, RSHA V A 2 No. 59/43g, or Decree of RSHA V A 2 No. 48/43g dated January 26, 1943, and V A 2 No. 64/43g dated January 28, 1943, for the Alps and Danube districts. Source: Döring, *Die Zigeuner,* 156 and 214f; compare also Michael Zimmermann, "Die nationalsozialistische Vernichtungspolitik gegen Sinti und Roma" [National Socialist Politics of Destruction of Sinti and Roma], in *Politik und Zeitgeschichte,* supplement to the daily paper *Das Parlament,* B16–17 (Bonn, 1987), 36f.; Erika Thurner, " 'Ortsfremde, asoziale Gemeinschaftsschädlinge'—die Konsequenzen des 'Anschlusses' für Sinti und Roma (Zigeuner)" ["Alien, Asocial Community Enemies"—the Consequences of the "Anschluss" for Sinti and Roma], in Rudolf G. Ardelt and Hans Hautmann, eds., *Arbeiterschaft und Nationalsozialismus in Österreich* [Workers and National Socialism in Austria] (Vienna, 1990), 542ff.

22. On the basis of more recent sources, we know that at least two-thirds of the Austrian Roma-Sinti did not survive the Holocaust.

4. Discrimination and Persecution
of the Burgenland Gypsies

1. This reorganization (Regulations from 1761, 1767, and 1783), which, after apportionment of property, gave the Gypsies the status of "new farmers" or "new citizens," contained prohibitions that would have meant not only a loss of the Gypsy culture but also the loss of their children. Also in the older Gypsy literature, which often emphasized the humanity of the Habsburg rulers, these measures were described as extremely harsh. Compare Johann H. Schwicker, *Die Zigeuner in Ungarn und Siebenbürgen* [The Gypsies in Hungary and Siebenbürgen] (Vienna, 1883), 54.

2. According to a survey by the police in 1933, at that time 7,153 Gypsies lived in Burgenland (see Steinmetz, *Österreichs Zigeuner,* Appendix 1, p. 49f.); according to a 1938 NS estimate, 8,000 lived there. Compare also "Camp Population—Gypsy Classifications" section in chapter 5.

3. In 1674, for the first time, a Gypsy clan is documented as having received permission to settle in Vas (Eisenburg). Josef Bertha, "Die Schwierigkeit der Zigeuner-Integration" [The Difficulty of Gypsy Integration], *Das Menschenrecht,* Series 32, Vol. 168, No. 1 (Vienna, 1977), 8.

From 1879 on, there existed in Unterwart demonstrably permanent residences of Gypsies. Compare Bertha, 8. For approximately 150 years, Gypsies have lived in Lafnitztal. The Hungarian communities had to provide soldiers for a twelve-year-long military service. For this purpose they bought three Gypsies who, in return, received residency. Compare Helga Thiel, "Die Zigeuner in Neustift an der Lafnitz" [The Gypsies in Neustift on Lafnitz], *Österreichische Zeitschrift für Volkskunde,* Vol. 28 (Vienna, 1974), 269f.

4. Of the 10,000 Gypsies who were picked up during this census, 761 were musicians, 4,229 [black]smiths, 5,309 day laborers, 79 horse dealers, and 131 beggars. This round-up campaign also includes other areas of the monarchy. Compare Walter Dostal, "Zigeunerleben und Gegenwart" [Gypsy Life and Now], in Walter Starkie, *Auf Zigeunerspuren* [On Gypsy Tracks] (Munich, 1957), 280f.

5. Compare Dostal in Starkie, 276.

6. "Gedanken zur Zigeunerfrage" [Thoughts on the Gypsy Question], *Burgenländische Heimat,* August 6, 1932, p. 5. See also in *Burgenländische Heimat,* October 2, 1931, p. 5: "Die Zigeunerfrage im Burgenland" [The Burgenland Gypsy Question]; also *Der freie Burgenländer,* Vol. 10, No. 462, May 11, 1930, 7f; No. 463, May 18, 1930, 5f; and No. 464, May 25, 1930, 5f. *Burgenlandwacht,* No. 2, May 18, 1930, 2f., and No. 3, May 25, 1930, 4; *Ödenburger Zeitung,* Vol. 58, No. 262, November 18, 1926, 2.

7. Personal communication from RA [advocate] Dr. Emil Szymanski, Vienna, October 26, 1980, 1.

8. *Tagespost Graz,* No. 185, July 6, 1940. Cited from Zentrales Staatsarchiv Potsdam (Central State Archives Potsdam), R1B No. 9368, Bl. 77.

9. DÖW file, No. 11293. Letter of representative Dr. Hinterlechner, Oberwart, to the mayor of Unterwart, April 13, 1943. Cited from *Widerstand und Verfolgung im Burgenland,* 287.

10. Portschy, *Die Zigeunerfrage.* In March of 1938 Portschy, who had been sentenced several times because of illegal activities for the NSDAP, became district leader and state captain of the Burgenland. After the dissolution of the Burgenland as an independent region, October 1, 1938, he was assistant district leader of Steiermark.

11. Portschy, 8f. This "behavior" entails the prohibition to employ Gypsies or to give them gifts, as well as the prohibition to make music.

12. *Der Freie Burgenländer,* Vol. 10, No. 463. Eisenstadt, May 18, 1930, 6.

13. The central registration office in Austria began in 1936, following the opening of an "International Central Office to Combat the Gypsy Vermin" by the federal police directorate in Vienna on December 17, 1935. A central registration office had already been planned from 1931 on. BKA, Zl. C/165670 GD2 I.K.P.K. 140/5/36. In BMI file, Zl. 55.626-18/68.

14. "It is also noteworthy that there exists a Gypsy file from an earlier Burgenland period which now has been confiscated by the state police in Vienna." BKA Directorate, box 551 o.Z., Fol. 15f., Point 32/Gypsies, 23. AVA, Vienna.

15. BMI file, Zl. 55.626-18/68. This file contained the draft for the Gypsy law of 1931; see copy: Appendix I.

16. *Der Freie Burgenländer,* F.464, May 25, 1930, 5.

17. Portschy, 33.

18. Portschy, 36.

19. Portschy, 19.

20. Portschy, 22.

21. Compare the more recently published studies by Georg Gesellmann and Michaela Haslinger (see bibliography).

22. Border district Burgenland, September 4, 1938. Cited from *Widerstand und Verfolgung im Burgenland,* 259.

23. DÖW file, No. 11151.

24. For instance, Franz Horvath from Redlschlag who, together with other Gypsies, complained to the Reich government because of the discrimination on May 12, 1938, was taken to Dachau that same summer. DÖW file, No. 12543. Cited from *Widerstand und Verfolgung im Burgenland,* Dok. 3, 4, and 5, 254f. Also already on June 22, 1938, Adolf Gussak was sent to Dachau together with a group of Stegersbach Gypsies. DÖW file, No. 1371.

25. "Ordnung in der Zigeunerfrage" [Order Regarding the Gypsy Question]. *Grenzmark Burgenland,* August 4, 1938, 1. A ten-hour work day for groups of workers was planned.

26. AVA-Lessons, Zl. IV-3a-327994-1939. Report State School Director ND, dated July 6, 1939, 2.

27. "During the weekend detention the Gypsies are to be given merely water and bread. The monies for this are to be advanced by the community,

which amount they can then turn in to the employer for deduction from the Gypsies' wages." DÖW file, No. 11293, cited from *Widerstand und Verfolgung im Burgenland,* 264.

28. Instructions for deportation, dated January 29, 1943.

29. State office bulletin, Vol. 18, No. 39, September 15, 1938. Source: DÖW, Gypsy file IIIc/1.

30. AVA Lessons, Zl. IV-2a-41906-a-1938. Queries of the LSR OÖ, the STSRS Vienna, the district school director Baden.

31. AVA Lessons, Zl. IV-2a-313.026-a, Ministry for Interior and Cultural Matters, Vienna, March 23, 1939, 1.

32. Compare AVA lessons, Zl. IV-2a-313026-a, 1939. District school director Fürstenfeld, May 19, 1939, 1.

AVA lessons, Zl. IV-2a-313026-a, 1939. City school director Vienna, May 22, 1939, 2: "For teaching we would consider teachers who have a bad reputation politically and professionally. The use of other teachers could only become possible if additional monies . . . were provided."

33. AVA lessons, Zl. IV-2a-313026-a, 1939, circular of the Reich Ministry for Science, Education, and Public Education, E II e 624/39, Berlin, dated 6/15/39.

34. AVA lessons, Zl. IV-2a-313026-a, 1939, 1. This decree merely considered "the dangers which Gypsy children might pose for German children"; the problem of education of Gypsies as such, as Portschy saw it, was not discussed.

35. AVA Bürckel/2473,Zl. II-9193-a-1939. State Administration of the Reich District Vienna, Department II, Education and Public Education (formerly Office of the City School Director in Vienna), to the Reich Commissioner for the Reunification of Austria with the German Reich, dated November 13, 1939, 2.

36. Economic-Political Office, 199, dated August 31, 1939, cited from Zentrales Staatsarchiv Potsdam, RlB 9368, Bl. 76.

37. Circular by RMfWEuV. dated March 22, 1941, E II e 703, not published, communicated to Sipo and SD via circular of RSHA, dated November 21, 1941, Zl. V A 2 No. 981/41, cited from Döring, *Die Zigeuner,* 130.

5. Camp Lackenbach

1. Neues Wiener Tageblatt, No. 336, dated December 5, 1940. Cited according to Zentrales Staatsarchiv Potsdam, RlB 9368, Bl. 77.

2. On the basis of the 1938 measures against asocial persons and the 1939 measures against the Burgenland Gypsies, more than three thousand Gypsies had already been taken to concentration camps.

3. Terms such as "temporary detention" and "final deportation" at that time not only were products of Nazi linguistics but also had a basis in reality. For one, they were based on the planned deportation to the East, and, in addition, the completion of the final Gypsy statutes was expected.

4. Heinz Boberach, *Meldungen aus dem Reich* [News from the Reich] (Munich, 1968), 36.

5. Portschy, 33. In January of 1939, Portschy sent "his proposal for a solution" to the party secretary, to the attention of Heinrich Lammers. Nuremberg Document NG-845. Source: IfZ Munich.

6. Special delivery letter Pol. S V B 2 No. 1264, 40 IV.

7. BMI file, Zl. 47.558-2/52, BH Oberpullendorf, regarding Voluntary Association for Gypsy camp Lackenbach, agreement, Zl. KV-3/5-1945, 1.

8. Compare sworn testimony of Julius Brunner to the Compensation Authorities, Cologne, March 23, 1957. Source: DÖW, six pages typescript, 2f.

9. BMI file, Zl. 119.843-2/53. Document of the Security Office, Eisenstadt, to BMI, Vienna, August 20, 1953, 1.

10. See Appendix II/1, 2, and 3: these documents tell about reputation, established work relationships, and ownership of property.

11. Rudolf Weinrich, Memoir. Steinmetz, *Österreichs Zigeuner,* 24.

12. Compare BMI file, Zl. 47.558. Information Camp Lkb. (Lackenbach), 5f. and sworn testimony J. Brunner, DÖW, 2 (see note 8 above).

13. Cited according to Lackenbach original documents, discovered August 1981.

14. Here the individuals in question are police administration officials Josef Hajek, Nikolaus Reinprecht, and Roman Neugebauer.

15. Lackenbach original document; see also excerpts in appendix.

16. DÖW file, No. 11340, copy (hereafter cited as TB [diary]).

17. The name Kollross is spelled in different ways in the sources and in the diary. The variant chosen corresponds to his own signature; in letter from Camp Lackenbach to sugar manufacturer Hirm, August 7, 1941. In the death notice we read "Kollroß." Source private property of Leo Banny, Lackenbach.

18. Whether Langmüller had SS status is not quite clear. He himself only signed his name and the title "camp commander." The former police chief in Lackenbach, Ingenieur Karpischek, spoke of "Obersturmführer Langmüller." In DÖW file, No. 82. Cited in *Widerstand und Verfolgung im Burgenland*, doc. 31, 277.

19. Compare "Camp Living Conditions—Punitive Measures" section in chapter 5.

20. Letter by Professor Johann Knobloch, Bonn, January 7, 1980, 1. Details about Professor Knobloch's stay in Lackenbach in the spring of 1943 are in the "Camp Living Conditions—Daily Routine" section of chapter 5.

21. Sworn testimony, J. Brunner, DÖW, 4 (See note 8 above).

22. A reduction in terroristic methods occurred in the large concentration camps as early as 1941–42. "The painful drills, often dragged out for hours, exercises, senseless harassment and punishment, were limited or completely abolished. On December 2, 1942, Himmler gave orders via a circular to camp commanders to use beatings 'in the future only as a last resort.' " Buchheim et al., *Anatomie*, Vol. 2, 105f.

23. Sworn testimony, J. Brunner, DÖW (see note 8 above).

24. Brunner was already camp commander in Lackenbach from January 6, 1941, to March 10, 1941. Diary entry regarding replacement by Hans Kollross: "Begin of office by SS major Kollross and transfer of camp leadership by K. O. S. Brunner." In DÖW file, No. 11340, entry March 10, 1941.

25. Compare Steinmetz, *Österreichs Zigeuner,* 20, and the same in *Widerstand und Verfolgung im Burgenland,* 248, as well as ibid., document 30, 276: "Our situation in the camp only improved when Langmüller was replaced by . . . Eckschlager and . . . Brunner." Testimony by F. Eidler, Lackenbach, and innkeeper Ferdinand Wegscheider, Lackenbach, conversation August 19, 1981.

26. In spite of this, there always were attempts at escape.

27. The Burgenland Roma had found out that their houses and sheds had been destroyed after their internment. The camp became their home of necessity. Letter, J. Knobloch, 2. Confidential decree Zl. 14-Zi-1/64-1942 to all mayors of the district of Oberwart. Order to tear down Gypsy shacks. Cited according to special insert Vol. 1, No. 1, Vienna, September 1977, 25.

28. BMI file, Zl. 47.558-2/52, 2.

29. Testimony of Nikolaus Reinprecht, Eisenstadt, October 8, 1954. DÖW file, No. 9626. Verdict of the LG [Landgericht = state court]. Vienna against the police officer Franz Langmüller because of war crimes, LG Vienna. Vg l c V r 4594/47, August 15, 1948, 2.

30. BMI file, Zl. 178.401-2/56. Witness testimony Raimund Frost, 9 Hc 141/56, in legal case of Konrad Reinhardt, April 26, 1956, 2: "The fence was seamless. Within a very short distance from the camp gate, but outside the camp, the camp command was located."

31. Interview with Mr. Weinreich. In *teleobjektiv* of May 23, 1979, manuscript 9/122/223, 6.

32. Testimony Franz Langmüller, October 15, 1948. DÖW file, No. 9626, 3.

33. Diary entry, June 19, 1941. In DÖW file, No. 11340.

34. Diary entry, April 1, 1941: the Gypsies fled while lunch was being distributed.

35. Sworn testimony by J. Brunner, DÖW, 5 (see note 8 above).

36. BMI file, Zl. 119.843-2/53, witness testimony J. Bocdech, copy, 2f.

37. Personal communication by Professor Knobloch, Bonn, November 26, 1981, 2.

38. January 4, 1941, to February 4, 1942.

39. DÖW file, No. 11340, for instance, entry of January 23, 1941.

40. Diary entry, February 16, 1941.

41. Diary entry, March 21, 1941.

42. Diary entry, April 21, 1941.

43. The terms "camp elder" and "Kapo" were used interchangeably. In Lackenbach, the title "Kapo" was not connected with the job of overseeing a work detail.

44. Diary entry, February 16, 1941.

45. Diary entry, July 7, 1941.

46. Lackenbach original documents, discovered August 1981.

47. The following names of camp orderlies were noted in the diary on April 20, 1941: Horvath, Stefan, No. 180; Horvath, Matthias, No. 351; Horvath, Josef, No. 256; Horvath, Georg, No. 10 and Horvath, Johann, No. 443. In DÖW file, No. 11340.

48. Diary entry, April 21, 1941.

49. In the Langmüller trial, Sarközi called himself "deputy to the camp elder." Testimony A. Sarközi. DÖW file, No. 9626, 12f. In diary entry of February 16, 1941, Sarközi appears as "Kapo"; on April 13, 1941, he appears as "camp elder."

50. BMI file, Zl. 178.401-2/56, testimony R. Frost, 2. Raimund Frost was imprisoned in Lackenbach from the beginning of the camp until its dissolution in April 1945.

51. DÖW file, No. 9626, testimony A. Sarközi, 12. From August 1938 on, Gypsies were also imprisoned in concentration camp Mauthausen. Precise figures about Austrians cannot be given because they were not mentioned separately in the statistics. As of September 29, 1939, 1,087 AZR-DR (i.e., Austrian, German, and Sudeten-German asocial individuals, among them Gypsies) were listed. H. Marsalek, 93. In April of 1940, three hundred Burgenland Gypsies arrived from concentration camp Buchenwald; in June 1941, another sixty Austrian Gypsies were transferred from Buchenwald to Mauthausen. Compare Marsalek, 94f. In October 1941, a transport of eighty Gypsies arrived in Lackenbach from Mauthausen.

52. According to Professor Knobloch, letter dated January 7, 1980, 3. The advocate (Gypsy king) is the highest instance of an autonomous Gypsy group. His influence extends only over that group that chose him as a spokesman. His most important task is to watch that the taboo laws are kept. If one measures his position according to traditional standards, there were several points of conflict regarding the performance of his job in a camp. His influence in this constellation was shaken, if not shattered, on the one hand by the presence of other authorities outside the group. On the other hand, with the lesser importance of the traditional taboo laws, which only function well within an integral clan, the advocate loses his importance. This was also true with the changed family structures in Lackenbach. Compare H. Arnold, *Die Zigeuner. Herkunft und Leben der Stämme im deutschen Sprachgebiet* [The Gypsies. Origin and life of the Tribes in the German-speaking Areas] (Olten/Freiburg i.Br., 1965), 186ff; and Weiler, 17.

53. DÖW file, No. 9626, criminal file Langmüller, 2.

54. DÖW file, No. 9626, testimony R. Frost, 2. Whether there was a strict separation of foreman and Kapo in Lackenbach—that is to say, Kapos who did not themselves work and only watched the work details as supervisory personnel—is not clear.

55. All three of them—Hajek, Reinprecht, and Neugebauer—were police administration officials.

56. They signed food ration cards as "administrative officials." Lackenbach original document.

57. DÖW file, No. 9626, testimony N. Reinprecht, 3. Together with other personnel, E. Pekovits had to begin a ten-day quarantine.

58. Diary entry, September 13, 1941. In DÖW file, No. 11340.

59. For example, camp elders had to confirm ration distribution on the ration cards with their signature; in addition, they had to carry out the distribution of packages and money shipments and perhaps sign as witnesses.

60. According to information from Professor Knobloch, who shared a room with this Gypsy during his stay in the camp. Letter of January 7, 1980, 1.

61. Diary entry, January 25, 1941. "Franz Hodosi was in possession of a paper regarding his genealogy from the Reich Office for Genealogical Inquiries, branch office Vienna, issued on April 4, 1940 (Zl. o 4215 e/Le), according to which he is a Gypsy half-breed, first degree." In DÖW file, No. 11340.

62. Sworn testimony J. Brunner, DÖW, 6 (see note 8 above).

63. See Appendix III/1: Prescriptions of the doctors in question. Lackenbach original document.

64. Appendix III/2: In such cases the firms requested replacement of labor.

65. Details of the epidemic in chapter 5, "Camp Population—Deaths."

66. Diary entry, March 12, 1941.

67. This is the name that the residents gave to the part of town located on a hill that today is partly built up. There are no street names here.

68. Sworn testimony J. Brunner, DÖW, 4 (see note 8 above).

69. Compare Steinmetz, *Österreichs Zigeuner,* 18.

70. Entry in diary, February 8, 1941: "Today the Gypsies refused to go to their sleeping quarters at the appointed time, since their straw beds and bedding were completely soaked due to the prevailing thawing and rain." DÖW file, No. 11340.

71. Steinmetz, *Österreichs Zigeuner,* 18.

72. The Lackenbach temple also fell victim to the attacks during *Kristallnacht* [Night of Broken Glass].

73. Memoirs of Franz Karall. Steinmetz, *Österreichs Zigeuner,* 25.

74. Memoirs of Rosalia Karoly. Steinmetz, *Österreichs Zigeuner,* 22f.

75. DÖW file, No. 11340.

76. According to diary entries.

77. Diary entries, July 2, 1941, May 21, 1941, and June 9, 1941. DÖW file, No. 11340.

78. Diary entries, August 11 and 12, 1941.

79. Letter from January 7, 1980, 2.

80. Diary entry, January 23, 1941: "Dr. Zieglauer . . . inspected the Gypsy camp on the orders of the Reich representative. He also inspected the fountains that had been installed. He commented that the location was not suitable."

81. Sworn testimony by J. Brunner, DÖW, 4 (see note 8).

82. Diary entry, August 5, 1941. DÖW file, No. 11340.

83. Lackenbach original document. Notices of the camp administration/command about trial drilling to the commissioner in Oberpullendorf, Zl. 461/42 and 493/495-1942, as well as correspondence on well construction, Zl. 521/18/42. Similar to the large concentration camps, in Lackenbach the water shortage also contributed decisively to the increasing deterioration of living conditions. Temporary solutions sufficed for a long time before the problem was tackled. Eugen Kogon, *Der SS-Staat. Das System der deutschen Konzentrationslager* [The SS-State. The German Concentration Camp System], 10th edition (Munich, 1981), 75: "Not even water supply played the usual role in the planning. Temporary water lines, sufficient for the SS, were quickly installed. . . . The inmates could wait."

84. Lackenbach original document, bill for camp lighting, from June 18, 1942.

85. BMI file, Zl. 47.558-2/52. Information Gypsy camp Lackenbach, 7.

86. Selma Steinmetz interviewed numerous victims and published the reports of their experiences in a monograph.

87. Rudolf Weinrich, Memoir. In Steinmetz, *Österreichs Zigeuner,* 24.

88. Steinmetz, *Österreichs Zigeuner,* Eugen Hodoschi memoirs, 24f. RA Dr. Szymanski wrote in his letter of October 26, 1980: "When now, after 1945, scholars and lawyers often assert that the deprivation of freedom in Camp Lackenbach was less than in the real concentration camps, this is only partially true; in any case, we must point out that early on the hygienic conditions in Camp Lackenbach were horrendous, so that horrible epidemics broke out there and a large part of the camp population died because of lack of treatment and care."

89. List of all those inmates who died in the one-time collection camp Lackenbach, survey department of police headquarters for Burgenland, Eisenstadt 1954 (E. No. 1003/54), taken in its entirety from the death records of the registrar in Lackenbach. In DÖW file, No. 9626, criminal file Langmüller.

90. BMI file, Zl. 47.558-2/52. Statutes of the Voluntary Association, 3. See also Appendix IV: Admissions agreement Franz Papai, Ternitz, as well as entry of August 21, 1941: "Police president Graz and criminal police chief Graz arrived . . . in camp, regarding negotiations, or rather admission, of Steiermark Gypsies."

91. A majority of those unable to work were deported to death camps anyway.

92. Compare chapter 2.

93. BMI file, Zl. 65.304-2/52, copy: "Auswertung der rassenbiologischen Gutachten über zigeunerische Personen" ["Assessment of race-biological evaluations of Gypsies"], 3. Compare also Döring, *Die Zigeuner,* 120. There the individual categories are described in even more detail, for example, "ZM, I. degree" and "ZM, II degree."

94. Compare Miriam Wiegele, "Die Zigeuner in Oesterreich" [The Gypsies

in Austria], in Zülch, 264. According to the 1934 census, the number was six thousand Roma. This census for the first time categorized the Gypsies according to their ethnicity. For this census, a part of the Roma probably also was categorized according to the old method of linguistic typology. Compare *Die Bevölkerungsentwicklung im Burgenland zwischen 1923 und 1971* [The Development of the Populations in Burgenland between 1923 and 1971], published by the Office of the Burgenland state government, Dept. IV. (Eisenstadt, 1976).

95. Compare Walter Dostal, "Die Zigeuner in Österreich" [The Gypsies in Austria], *Archiv für Völkerkunde,* Vol. 10 (Vienna, 1955), 1f.

96. Lackenbach original document, grey file card collection, DIN A5: of the twenty-eight cards, twenty-four show a notation in the column "race."

97. See Appendix XXV/2: listing of the grey file cards, which contain the appropriate information.

98. The half-breed and the non-Gypsy were, according to the file card entry, released again.

99. Document about the persecution of Gypsies in the district Niederdonau, printed in *Jahrbuch 1990 des Dokumentationsarchivs des österreichischen Widerstandes* [1990 Yearbook of the Documentation Archive of the Austrian Resistance] (Vienna, 1990), 34–39.

100. This information was to be obtained together with fingerprints and possible photo. Form RKP No. 172 for Christine Sarközi, see Appendix V/1. In the headquarters building, a complete personal file on Christine Sarközi was found, including correspondence carried on in connection with her arrest; all in Appendix V 1/2.

101. Appendix VI: Confirmation "Franz Karoly." Source DÖW-folder IIIc/1.

102. Sworn testimony by J. Brunner, DÖW, 2 (see note 8 above). The command post in Vienna also had to agree to voluntary admissions to the camp.

103. DÖW file, No. 12486. From report of the police command Grosswarasdorf to the state police command for Burgenland for the "red-white-red-book," May 21, 1946, cited according to *Widerstand und Verfolgung im Burgenland,* 274.

104. DÖW file, No. 9626. Testimony A. Sarközi, 12.

105. The camp numbers 71, 85, 96, 97, 98, 122, 135, 148, 155, and 158 were given to women. Determined on the basis of file card entries and other documents found in camp. See also Appendix XXVI/1, 2, 3, and 4, lists of file cards.

In addition A. Sarközi had reported that his own wife was among the first admissions. DÖW file, No. 2606, "Zigeuner erzählen über ihre Verfolgungen" [Gypsies Tell about Their Persecutions], June 1965, Conversation with A. Sarközi.

106. No. 74: five years; No. 62: nine years; No. 103: ten years; No. 117: thirteen years; and No. 123: fourteen years.

107. As can be seen from the Mauthausen-documentation, Marsalek, *Die Geschichte des Konzentrationslagers Mauthausen,* on October 8 and October

9, 1941, eighty Gypsies (according to diary 79) were transferred from Mauthausen to Lackenbach and "28 to a Gypsy camp near Knittelfeld (Steiermark)," 223.

On the subject "Gypsy Camp Knittelfeld," Mr. Marsalek could not give any further information. Letter of April 9, 1980. Inquiries on my part with Knittelfeld authorities did not bring any results. In Appendix XXVI, the list of the Gypsies who were sent to Knittelfeld, was printed. Zl. E 1a/10 Archive Museum Mauthausen in BMI, Vienna.

108. Appendix VII, admissions list: on the basis of diary entries, all new admissions of more than ten individuals for 1941 were entered in a column.

109. Here also the card files were an important source. However, only in 115 cases was the date of admission entered. The following summary results: six admissions for 1940, ninety-three for 1941, three for 1942, nine for 1943, and, for 1944 and 1945, two admissions each.

110. Diary entry, February 1, 1942. In DÖW file, No. 11340.

111. DÖW file, No. 10501 C. List of children born in Gypsy camp Lackenbach, 1941–1945.

112. Diary entry, January 6, 1942.

113. Among the original documents found in Camp Lackenbach were a bulletin and the file card of Josefa Reinhardt, camp No. 3074, as well as the file card of Anna Reinhardt, No. 3057. Both show as date of admission April 6, 1943. In addition, camp No. 3068 for Konrad Reinhardt could be established from a wage stub. In the reparations claim, seven names were given for the Reinhardt family: Reinhardt, Konrad, born 1895; Anna, born 1904; Josef, born 1927; Maria, born 1929; Elisabeth, born 1932; Erika, born 1943; and Josefa, born 1939. In BMI file, Zl. 168.538-2/52, 1. Johann Bocdech, manager of the Stoob ceramics factory, additionally testified that the parents Konrad and Anna Reinhardt, as well as the two oldest children, Josef and Maria, were sent to work there. In BMI file, Zl. 178.401-2/56 testimony of J. Bocdech, 1. See Appendix VIII: file card of Anna Reinhardt. Different documents were in such bad condition (dirty, faded, and torn) that they could still be used as a source but no longer as a copy for the appendix; this was also true for the leaflet of Josefa Reinhardt. On it was noted: "lived in Gypsy camp Maxglan."

114. Appendix IX: file card Franziska Reinhart and "notification of the arrival of three Gypsies, criminal police headquarters Vienna to Gypsy camp Lackenbach." Source: DÖW file, No. 12256. *Widerstand und Verfolgung im Burgenland,* Document 24, 273.

115. Lackenbach original document, Appendix V: personal file Christine Sarközi. When admitted on May 30, 1944, she received the camp number 3158.

116. Appendix X: criminal police headquarters Vienna informs camp leader of arrival of Helmut Hoff, Paul Klein, and Anton Winter.

117. This refers to the decree of June 5, 1939, "Combat of the Gypsy Plague in Burgenland."

118. A member of the Floridsdorf family, Weinrich, was sent to Lackenbach at the age of 10 while his parents were sent to Auschwitz. In Lackenbach he also found out about the death of his mother. In *teleobjektiv* interview, 3f.

119. The corresponding text in the decree reads: "It seems to make sense to hand them (the children) over to private religious welfare. Since there can be no costs involved, it will be a matter of clever negotiations." Cited in DÖW file, No. 2607 (footnote 2).

120. Correspondence of criminal police headquarters Vienna to Camp Lackenbach regarding admission on August 15, 1944. In DÖW file, No. 12256, *Widerstand und Verfolgung im Burgenland,* Document 25, 274. The file card of Peter Horvath, camp No. 3168, date of admission August 22, 1944, showed as place of admission: "Children's Absorption Center Vienna."

121. DÖW file, No. 11293, decree of the commissioner in Oberwart, regarding regulation of the Gypsy question, November 11, 1941, 2. The following passage there is worth mentioning: "If, for instance, the material of the shacks, namely the wood, is usable, the communities can sell it. However, the wood may not become part of the household of a comrade [Nazi], since there is the danger of the spreading of epidemics. . . . It is beneath the dignity of a German comrade (*Volksgenosse*) to enrich himself with the property of Gypsies."

122. Diary entry, May 13, 1941, and May 30, 1941.

123. Memoir Rosalia Karoly, 22.

124. Interview with Julius Hodosi, Vienna. Recorded by Emmi Moravitz, in September 1957, copy: private property of Hermann Langbein, Vienna, 1.

125. Memoir E. Hodoschi, in Steinmetz, *Österreichs Zigeuner,* 24. In connection with the exclusion of Gypsies from the army in summer of 1942 it seems worth mentioning that—according to an entry in the camp diary—still in 1941 some Lackenbach prisoners were given a medical and drafted; for instance entry April 3, 1941.

126. Diary entries, May 13, 1941: "Today the following Gypsy family came to camp voluntarily, since the husband who was here had gotten melancholy." Or, "October 14, 1941: Marksman Johann Rosch voluntarily surrendered for admission to camp, since his family is here in camp; he was given the camp number 2080."

127. This testimony corresponds to the interrogation record of witness Johann Bocdech. In BMI file, No. 178.401-2/56, 3.

128. See Appendix IX, Admission Franziska Reinhart, especially the passages: "released from the local prison on the morning of 3/31/44 and received permission to go to Lackenbach at their own expense. . . . It is noted, that (they) . . . of their own . . . requested admission to the camp." In DÖW file, No. 12256.

129. Compare admissions list, Appendix VII, as well as entries in diary. In DÖW file, No. 11340.

130. Sworn testimony J. Brunner, DÖW, 5 (see note 8 above).

131. At the beginning of November 1941, approximately three hundred

Sinti arrived from Weyer/Inn. There the criminal police stations had run a Gypsy camp for a few months. We can assume that these Gypsies who were sent from Oberösterreich to Lackenbach were from there deported to Lodz (Litzmannstadt) and murdered.

132. These twenty Italians came to Lackenbach on November 1, 1941, via the Criminal Police in Innsbruck.

133. Some of the Hungarian prisoners were able to effect their release from Lackenbach by regaining their Hungarian citizenship.

134. Johann Knobloch gave the information that "in the third (row of barracks) Sinti from Württemberg were living." Letter dated January 7, 1980, 2.

135. The compilation of the Lackenbach population is derived from the admissions (Admissions list, Appendix VII), as well as from the available file cards.

136. See Appendix XXVI/1, 2, 3, and 4.

137. The camp population only fell below this number in the first months after the opening of the camp; from November 1940 to April 1941 there were fewer than two hundred Gypsies in Lackenbach.

138. Based on collection of file cards, Lackenbach original documents and entries in camp diary. In DÖW file, No. 11340.

139. Compare chapter 5, "Camp Population—Deaths" section.

140. Josef Bertha (Official of Unterwart), *Die Zigeuner in Unterwart* [The Gypsies in Unterwart], 4. Source: DÖW-folder IIIc/1; also published abridged, in *Das Menschenrecht,* Vol. 168, 1977, 8–12.

141. The grey file cards, which go into great detail in some cases, also listed job information.

142. Bertha, *Die Zigeuner,* 5.

143. In 1933, Karl Berger was the Gypsy mayor of the settlement Sulzriegel, Burgenland. The Gypsy mayor was spokesman of his clan; at the time he was the confidante of the mayor, the municipal authority, and the police.

144. "Die 'zahmen' Zigeuner von Sulzriegel" [The 'Tame' Gypsies of Sulzriegel), *Arbeiter-Zeitung,* Vienna, February 16, 1933, 6.

145. Johann Galatsai had been employed as a stoker by the Walbersdorf brick works since 1904. Shortly after he had been admitted to the camp in the spring of 1941, he was again sent to work there. See also chapter 5, "Internal and External Forced Labor—Compensation" section.

146. This was confirmed by different diary entries and a letter (Appendix XX/2—advance payment to Gypsies) by the administration of Estate Harrch, dated December 10, 1941.

147. "Many of us believed to be able to escape this fate (the racial persecutions), if they [we] voluntarily entered military service." Interview with J. Hodosi, 1.

148. DÖW file, No. 82b, *Widerstand und Dokumentation im Burgenland,* Document 30, p. 276. Here they speak of approximately three hundred dead. Compare ibid., 266 n. 1.

149. Diary entry, October 29, 1941: "199 returned to camp from Alland and Klausen-Leopoldsdorf."

150. Diary entry, August 6, 1941: "Camp Number 950 Karoline Held was handed over to district court Wr. Neustadt for the punishment of two months imprisonment." Compare also August 14 and August 26, 1941.

151. These transports from November 4, 1941, and November 7, 1941, are mentioned in the camp diary (DÖW file, No. 11340) as well as in the police history of Lackenbach (DÖW file, No. 11278).

152. See chapter 6 for details.

153. For the second transport, the deportees were loaded into railroad cars in Lackenbach. Diary entry, November 7, 1941.

154. DÖW file, No. 9626. Written testimony of Josef Hajek, state court Vienna Vg 1 c Vr. 4597/47, from October 17, 1954, 1.

155. Diary entry, 11/4/41. Admissions via other criminal police posts occurred in agreement with criminal police headquarters in Vienna.

156. Testimony of Franz Karall, Wiesen. Vg. Vienna, November 15, 1954. In DÖW file, No. 9626 and memoir of same. Steinmetz, *Österreichs Zigeuner,* 25.

157. See Appendix XI, "Main list of the Gypsies evacuated on November 4, 1941, from collection camp Lackenbach."

158. The available thirty-six cases of age information only account for 1.8 percent of the two thousand deported.

159. DÖW file, No. 9626. Testimony of Jakob Schneeberger, main trial Langmüller, October 15, 1948, 17.

160. A majority of the Gypsies interviewed by Dr. Steinmetz in the 1960s lost family members in Lodz. In DÖW file, No. 2606.

161. See Appendix XII: two examples for concentration camp admissions because of escape attempts.

162. See Appendix XIII/1.

163. These examples were taken from the grey file cards; see Appendix XIII/2.

164. See Appendix XIII/2. Source: yellow file card collection, small size; these cards did not show an admissions date.

165. Due to new information, after the publication of the Auschwitz decree, also in Lackenbach two larger transports were compiled in the spring of 1943 with the destination Auschwitz-Birkenau.

166. DÖW file, 9626. Testimony of Franz Langmüller, 6.

167. "Because of the lack of sanitary facilities, typhus broke out in the camp in 1941, and approximately 300 of us died from it." DÖW file, No. 82b, *Widerstand und Verfolgung im Burgenland,* Document 30, p. 276.

168. *Widerstand und Verfolgung im Burgenland,* 248.

169. The Lackenbach death register begins in 1939; at the time of my visit to the Lackenbach village doctor, Dr. Tschida, on December 14, 1979, it was still in his use. Until 1972 all deaths of Lackenbach citizens were recorded in

it; since the institution of a new ordinance, only those who die in the village have their names recorded in it. The death register for the time period of March 1941 to January 12, 1942, was available as a source.

170. Diary entry, January 6, 1942.

171. Figures calculated on the basis of the death register.

172. Information of the son, O. Belihart. In Leopold Banny, "Das Anhaltelager Lackenbach" (typescript). Lackenbach, o.J., 7.

173. "Influenza" was, for the first time, mentioned as a cause of death on December 6, 1941.

174. DÖW file, No. 9626. Testimony of Dr. Georg Belihart, 8. Dr. Belihart was village doctor in Lackenbach until 1965. He retired on March 6, 1966; he died on October 24, 1967. According to information by Dr. Tschida, December 14, 1979.

175. According to information by Dr. Tschida, December 14, 1979.

176. A comparison with the handwriting in the camp diary lets one assume that the death register was at times kept by the police administration official Josef Hajek. The other handwriting examples partly agree with those in the camp files. See also Appendix XIV: Excerpt from the death register.

177. Diary entry, January 6, 1942.

178. Only on January 30, 1942, another visit by Dr. Zieglauer and Dr. Brenner took place. Diary entry, January 30, 1942.

179. Diary entry, January 6, 1942.

180. Memoir of Rosalia Karoly, in Steinmetz, *Österreichs Zigeuner,* 23.

181. *Teleobjektiv* interview, 4f.

182. *Teleobjektiv,* 5.

183. DÖW file, No. 9626. Testimony of N. Reinprecht, cited according to: *Widerstand und Verfolgung im Burgenland,* 248. Some relatives of those who died in Lackenbach took care of graves in the Jewish cemetery there and placed headstones. Today some of the Gypsy graves remind of the many victims: for instance, Johann Fojn—died 1942, Johann Held—died 1943 in camp, Schoschoni Held—died 1941, Josef and Theresia Hodosi—died 1942, Johann Papai—died 1942. F. Eidler, retiree, who keeps the keys to the Jewish cemetery, reported that relatives still come to visit the graves. Conversation August 19, 1981.

184. Calculated on the basis of entries in death register.

185. List of camp inmates who died in the Gypsy camp. In DÖW file, No. 9626.

186. Status according to diary: November 7, 1941: camp population 628, 54 deaths; December 1, 1941: population 631, 60 deaths; and January 1, 1942: population 572, 44 deaths.

187. In DÖW file, No. 9626.

188. Compare Appendix XIV/2.

189. Here only sixty-three of the seventy-two deaths could be included, since not all appear with birth dates.

190. Omission: beginning months of 1945.

191. DÖW file, No. 10501 C. List of births in Gypsy camp Lackenbach.

192. Compare listing, "Time Period 3/12/41–1/12/42."

193. Thus, all the camp inmates who died in 1944 were babies.

194. All figures were derived from the birth and death register of the Lackenbach registrar. DÖW file, No. 9626 and 10501 C.

195. Compare testimony of Franz Langmüller, 3. DÖW file, No. 9626. Escape attempts were the only crimes for which Langmüller admits having ordered beatings. Compare also chapter 5, "Camp Living Conditions—Punitive Measures" section.

196. Interview J. Hodosi, 4. Julius Hodosi was again arrested by the Gestapo and, together with his wife and two children, deported to Auschwitz. He survived Auschwitz by serving at the front in April 1945 in a so-called probationary battalion.

197. Compare Steinmetz, *Österreichs Zigeuner,* 19.

198. Only with the increasing length and expansion of the war did some of the population get up the courage to help escapees with their flight. See also Langbein, Hermann: . . . *nicht wie die Schafe zur Schlachtbank* [. . . Not Like Sheep to Slaughter] (Frankfurt, 1980), 274.

199. Diary entry, December 17, 1941, and January 2, 1942.

200. Diary entry, Saturday, June 7, 1941: "In the late evening hours Amalie Horvath, camp No. 98, surrendered willingly."

201. See Appendix XII. Notations in the files confirm deportations to death camps as a response to escapes.

202. Interview with Alois Fröhlich. DÖW file, No. 2606, spring 1965.

203. Two such examples are printed in the Appendix, No. XV.

204. Diary entry, May 27, 1941.

205. Diary entry, April 3, 1941: "In addition, lunch was withheld from all Gypsies who were weaving baskets, because they discussed escape while they worked." This punishment of fellow inmates is reminiscent of the punitive methods of the concentration camps. Höss practiced the following method in Auschwitz: comrades of the escapee were imprisoned and left to die of starvation. Compare Langbein, 272.

206. Sworn testimony by J. Brunner, DÖW, 5 (see note 8 above).

207. See Appendix XVI/1, arrest order.

208. Letter of criminal police headquarters Vienna to Gypsy camp Lackenbach, KPL, IB 308/H/42 of August 27, 1942. Source: Lackenbach original documents.

209. Diary entry, May 2, 1941: "The police stations Oberwart and Markt Allhau were today notified by telephone, since it is assumed that they (the Gypsies) fled to their hometown."

210. See Appendix XVI/2: postcard preprint "Completed search."

211. Appendix XVI/3: In this case the commissioner in Amstetten informed the camp administration that he had been notified by the criminal police in

Linz that two Gypsy boys from Camp Lackenbach had been caught in district Oberdonau. They were returned to Lackenbach.

212. Grouping of Gypsies and Gypsy half-breeds by the RKPA on the basis of expert evaluations from the "race-biological research office": ZM- or ZM(-) means "Gypsy half-breed" with primarily German blood. Compare also chapter 5, "Camp Population—Gypsy Classifications" section.

213. After the establishment of the Gypsy statutes of December 8, 1938, which made a distinction between domestic and foreign Gypsies, all those were foreigners who could not prove German citizenship. From the start, they were to be prevented from entering onto German soil, that is to say, be returned to the other side of the border. Compare Döring, *Die Zigeuner,* 197f.

214. Sworn testimony J. Brunner, DÖW, 5 (see note 8 above).

215. Here it must again be noted that not all file cards contain sufficient information. On one kind—yellow file cards, DIN A5, for example—only the following information was noted: number, name, birth date and birth place.

216. In these cases the discharge was noted on the file cards with the stamp "foreign Gypsies." See also Appendix XVII.

217. Corresponding information can be obtained from her file.

218. Lackenbach original document, file cards, as well as diary entry, October 15, 1941: "Since she could document her Aryan descent, Josefa Horvath, Camp No. 1599, with her four children, Nos. 1600–1603, was released from camp."

219. Diary entries, May 6, 1941, and May 16, 1941.

220. Diary entries, June 14, 1941; June 16, 1941; June 29, 1941; and October 31, 1941.

221. Sworn testimony by J. Brunner, DÖW, 3 (see note 8 above).

222. BMI file, No. 47.558-2/52. Information on the Gypsy camp, 5.

223. In the diary, the two cooks Hodosy and Nikolaus Horvath are named. In DÖW file, No. 11340.

224. Compare Steinmetz, *Österreichs Zigeuner,* 18f.

225. Diary entry, February 16, 1942.

226. Diary entry, September 3, 1941.

227. Diary entry, September 3, 1941: On the basis of this complaint, the district leader of Oberpullendorf received the notification "that the recall (of the labor forces) occurred on order of criminal police headquarters in Vienna and that he should turn to them regarding the complaint."

228. All names are taken from Lackenbach original documents, as, for example, wage statements, work contracts, different kinds of correspondence. It was possible to double-check them on the basis of the diverse diary entries.

229. Diary entry, September 5, 1941: "Shipment of 93 men and 100 women (Gypsies) by rail to Baden near Vienna for building of national expressway . . . Via Mayor Neureiter from Forchtenau, the RAB [*Reichsautobahn*] requests another 10 women (Gypsies) for cleanup; due to lack of suitable laborers, these cannot be supplied."

September 21, 1941: "Today 33 Gypsies (7 men and 26 women) were sent to Alland for RAB construction to replace Gypsies who had returned [to camp]."

September 25, 1941: "141 Gypsies (101 men and 40 women) to RAB Alland." Almost as many women as men were sent to the RAB construction, that is, 201 men and 176 women.

230. Numbers were determined on the basis of diary and Lackenbach original documents.

231. The allotments were noted on the file cards; see Appendix XVIII.

232. Appendix XIX/1: Balance sheet of company Kuschel & Haagen. On the basis of this information, a fifty-three-hour week can be ascertained; in the Walbersdorf brick works the work week even consisted of fifty-five.

233. BMI file, Zl. 178.401-2/56. Testimony by J. Bocdech, 2.

234. This testimony is based on different pay stubs found in the headquarters building. See also Appendix XIX/2: from the bill for Josef Wasinger one can ascertain that on April 19 a Gypsy worked eleven hours.

235. For the inmate laborers in the large concentration camps, work hours in the first work years were nine to ten hours. In 1943, the eleven-hour work day was instituted, from Monday through Saturday. "When extraordinary urgency exists, the inmates are also to be put to work on Sunday, but only in the morning." From Circular Pohl to camp commanders, November 22, 1943, Nuremberg Document No. 1290. Cited according to Buchheim et al., *Anatomie*, Vol. 2, p. 118.

236. BMI file, Zl. 178.401-2/56. Testimony Anton Schneeberger, 2.

237. Memoir of Rudolf Weinrich. In Steinmetz, *Österreichs Zigeuner*, 24.

238. DÖW file, No. 82b, report of former inmates, *Widerstand und Verfolgung im Burgenland*, Document 30, p. 276.

239. Diary entry, April 22, 1941: "On Sunday, April 19, 1941, at 2 p.m., Franz Ranz, born in Frauenhaid in 1911, and employed by the Warda Bakery, was taken from his home by criminal police secretary Kollross and criminal police assistant Franz Langmüller because he had left the bakery without continuing to work for his employer, whose husband was called up for the military. When he left his place of employment, he remarked that he didn't want to work (he refused). He was threatened with deportation to a concentration camp."

240. Diary entry, April 5, 1941: Extent of punishment—six hours detention in solitary and withholding of lunch.

241. Compare Steinmetz, *Österreichs Zigeuner*, 19.

242. BMI file, Zl. 178.401-2/56. Testimony R. Frost, 2f.

243. Diary entry, February 3, 1941.

244. Compare diary entry, April 23, 1941.

245. Diary entry, September 5, 1941.

246. Diary entry, April 18, 1941: "Head guard officer Auerl went to gather wood with 80 Gypsies."

247. Diary entry. On April 20, 1941, four camp orderlies (inmates who

maintain order) accompanied twenty women to the forest administration Lackenbach. Thirty women with five orderlies went to the Ritzing forest administration.

248. Sworn testimony by J. Brunner, DÖW, 5 (see note 8 above).

249. Compare sworn testimony of J. Brunner, ibid., 1.

250. Diary entry, June 30, 1941: "District secretary Kollross inspected the work places."

251. BMI file, Zl. 178.401-2/56. Testimony of A. Schneeberger, 2 and R. Frost, 2f.

252. BMI file, Zl. 178.401-2/56. Testimony of J. Bocdech, 2: "They were merely supervised by one of their co-workers . . . and also could . . . go to the village."

253. BMI file, Zl. 178.401-2/56. Testimony of R. Frost, 3.

254. Lackenbach original document. Letter by camp administration to Alfred Schmidt, regarding exchange of labor. Letter of Kuschel and Haagen: Return of workers, request for replacement. See Appendix III/2.

255. Diary entries. In DÖW file, No. 11340.

256. The description covers the period August 1, 1942, until the middle of November 1942. Testimony J. Bocdech, 1f.

257. Appendix XX: Orders of camp leader Eckschlager, February 1, 1943, form. Source: Lackenbach original document.

258. Sworn testimony of J. Brunner, DÖW, 1 (see note 8 above).

259. Policeman Hajek mentioned sums between 10 and 20 RM.

260. But in a BMI statement one reads: "For these outside laborers the pay was by the hour, which was somewhat lower than normal hourly wages." BMI file, Zl. 47.558-2/52. 5.

261. Diary entry, March 23, 1941.

262. DÖW file, No. 82 b, report by former inmates, *Widerstand und Verfolgung im Burgenland*, Document 30, p. 276.

263. Lackenbach original document: see Appendix XIX/1,2,3. From many wage stubs one cannot ascertain the monthly hours. There were monthly account settlements of between 10 and 44 RM, but neither hours worked nor number of workers were explicitly mentioned. With an eleven-hour work day, the armament industry had to pay between 4 RM (for unskilled labor) and 6 RM (for skilled labor) for concentration camp inmates. Compare Buchheim et al., *Anatomie*, Vol. 2, 113.

264. Diary entry, June 11, 1941.

265. See Appendix XXI/1.

266. DÖW file, No. 82, work confirmation by the Walbersdorf brick works in Mattersburg for the Gypsy Johann Galatsai, January 16, 1943, and March 20, 1955. *Widerstand und Verfolgung im Burgenland*, Document 33, p. 278.

267. The admissions date can be ascertained from his camp number in the diary. Galatsai's number was 248, diary April 6, 1941: "Today 398 Gypsies

from the villages of Mattersburg and surroundings were brought in. They were assigned to rooms 9 and 12. Camp numbers 214–612."

268. Diary entry, May 26, 1941.

269. DÖW file, No. 82.

270. Diary entry, January 24, 1941.

271. Compare Appendix XI: One page of the main list of the Gypsies deported from the collection camp Lackenbach to Lodz on November 4, 1941; and Franz Karall memoir, in Steinmetz, *Österreichs Zigeuner,* 25.

272. Calculated on the basis of the blue and gray file cards; Appendix: XXV/2 and 4.

273. Diary entry, May 12, 1941: "A 12-year old Gypsy girl, Anna Horvath, camp no. 645, was assigned to farmer Wilhelm Radha in Neudorf 6 for guarding cattle." July 1, 1941: "Today 10 children were taken to Unterpullendorf to work in the silk worm culture." In addition, work contracts and file card entries confirm the use of children, for example, camp no. 1131, Emilie Horvath, born 1930, for river regulation and camp no. 3176, Berta Karoly, ten years old, to building firm Kuschel and Haagen.

274. See Appendix XXI/2.

275. R. Karoly memoirs, in Steinmetz, *Österreichs Zigeuner,* 22f. Rosalia Karoly arrived in camp in August 1941.

276. BMI file, Zl. 178.401-2/56. Testimony by Anton Schneeberger, 2.

277. See Appendix XXI/1: Hedwig Sarközi, hired out in this "work contract," was already seventeen years old. In other contracts that were also found in the headquarters building, twelve- to fourteen-year-olds were hired out; for example, Johann Horvath, twelve (contract date June 14, 1944); Rudolf Karoly, twelve (August 20, 1942); Adolf Amberger, fourteen (August 28, 1943).

278. For example, it can no longer be determined how old the children were who were used for the silk worm culture.

279. Diary entry, April 15, 1941: "Christine Horvath, camp no. 189, punished for noncompliance on April 13, 1941, wanted to commit suicide." June 15, 1941: "During the night, camp no. 435, Elisabeth Horvath, attempted to commit suicide."

280. Sworn testimony by J. Brunner, DÖW, 4 and 5 (see note 8 above).

281. Information from Professor Knobloch, November 26, 1981, 1.

282. Diary entry, March 26, 1941.

283. Letter, J. Knobloch. Bonn, January 7, 1980, 1.

284. Diary entry, March 29, 1941.

285. Letter, J. Knobloch, 2. Gypsy bands also existed in other camps. For instance, the first orchestra in Buchenwald in 1938 consisted of Gypsies. Kogon, 152.

286. Diary entry, July 8, 1941: "Children's matron Helene Steiner . . . exchanged because of incompetence, she was replaced by . . . Maria Weinrich."

287. Letter, J. Knobloch, January 7, 1980, 3.

288. Legacy, Berlin-Dahlem to criminal police headquarters Vienna. Nuremberg Document, No. 1725, Himmler, September 16, 1942, to "Legacy," diary A41/90/42. Source: IfZ-Munich.

289. Kater, Michael H. *Das "Ahnenerbe" der SS 1935–1945. Ein Beitrag zur Kulturpolitik des Dritten Reiches* [The "Legacy" of the SS 1935–1945. A Contribution to the Cultural Politics of the Third Reich] (Stuttgart, 1974), 207.

290. Personal communication, Johann Knobloch, Bonn: January 7, 1980, 1f.; see also November 26, 1981, 1f.

291. Diary entry, April 7, 1941: "The shoemaker was given a cubicle of boards in front of the kitchen (room 2) as a work room."

292. Diary entry, April 6, 1941: "Today 398 Gypsies . . . were assigned to rooms 9 and 12."

293. Compare sworn testimony by J. Brunner, DÖW, 3 (see note 8 above).

294. Letter, J. Knobloch, November 26, 1981, 1.

295. Lackenbach original document: Letter by camp director Eckschlager to the municipal authority January 20, 1943; see Appendix XXII/1. The sending of ration cards probably did not occur without interruption, for some cards were still found in the headquarters building: one card for eggs for Helene Hodosi, Vienna (valid until July 1942); clothes cards for Elisabeth Papai, Liebing (valid to August 31, 1941), Antonia Reinhardt, Kobersdorf (to June 30, 1944), and Rosa Schneeberger, Klostermarienburg (to December 31, 1945).

296. Appendix XXII/2: registration (almost the same form was used for cancellation of communal meals); and Appendix XXII/3: cancellation confirmation.

297. Diary entry, May 28, 1941, and August 9, 1941.

298. Compare BMI file, Zl. 47.558-2/52. Information on the Gypsy camp, previously cited, 7.

299. Ration cards. Lackenbach original document, see also Appendix XXII/4: ration card from August 31, 1941.

300. Since the column in the ration confirmation book was not filled in, the number of inmates is determined on the basis of the diary entries. Grocery usage, however, was listed in detail on the form.

301. Whether these grocery amounts actually reached the inmates for distribution cannot be ascertained because the usage for the [camp] personnel was not mentioned separately.

302. Compare Kogon, 137.

303. There is plenty of literature about the fact that the amounts prescribed for concentration camps were never actually distributed.

304. *Auschwitz. Faschistisches Vernichtungslager* [Auschwitz. Fascist Extermination Camp] (Warsaw, 1978), 78.

305. Diary entry, March 3, 1941.

306. BMI file, Zl. 178.401-2/56. Compare testimony by J. Bocdech, 2.

307. Compare BMI file, Zl. 178.401-2/56, testimony of Anton Schneeberger, 2.

308. Testimony by F. Eidler, Lackenbach. Walter Göhring/Werner Pfeifenberger, *60 Jahre Burgenland. Eine Dokumentation* [60 Years Burgenland. A Documentation] (Mattersburg, 1981), 30.

309. Sworn testimony of J. Brunner, DÖW, 5 (see note 8 above).

310. Rudolf Weinrich memoir, 24, and testimony by R. Frost, 3, as well as A. Schneeberger, 2, both in BMI file, Zl. 178.401-2/56.

311. Diary entry, May 31, 1941: "A portion of these vacationers still have clothes and linens in their former homes, which they get and bring to the camp."

312. Diary entry, July 11, 1941: "Arrival of a shipment of old clothes from NSV (National Socialist People's Welfare) from Vienna." April 18, 1941: "Today 1,500 kg of linens and clothes arrived from the NSV." September 4, 1941: "Dr. Ehrenberg . . . let us know that the commissioner of Oberpullendorf . . . will give out ration cards for work clothes . . . for the local camp inmates."

313. Letter dated November 26, 1981, 1.

314. Diary entry, March 29, 1941.

315. Compare H. Langbein, "Holocaust," in Anita Geigges and Bernhard W. Wette, *Zigeuner heute. Verfolgung und Diskriminierung in der BDR* [Gypsies Today. Persecution and Discrimination in the Federal Republic of Germany] (Bornheim-Merten, 1979), 298. For instance, the families were also together in the "star camp" in concentration camp Bergen-Belsen and wore civilian clothing. (As a sign of recognition, they wore the Star of David, hence the designation.) If this section of the camp initially had a special character—it was intended as an exchange camp—this was less and less true as time passed and in the last stage was completely lost. Compare Eike Geisel, ed., *Vielleicht war alles erst der Anfang* [Maybe It All Was Only the Beginning] (Berlin, 1979), 108ff., and Langbein, 24.

316. Sworn testimony by J. Brunner, DÖW, 3 and 5 (see note 8 above). Testimony by N. Reinprecht confirms that Brunner was generous in granting vacations and that he even went against orders. "Brunner told me himself once that he gives the Gypsies time off and could be punished because of it." Witness testimony N. Reinprecht, 3. DÖW file, No. 9626.

317. Numerous testimonies of former Lackenbach residents confirm Brunner's information as credible.

318. See Appendix XXIII.

319. Diary entry, April 15, 1941, May 24, 1941, and April 14, 1941.

320. Diary entry, May 31, 1941: "75 people who were especially diligent when working outside the camp . . . were sent on vacation."

321. Diary entry, March 8, 1941.

322. At this time Fritz Eckschlager was camp commander and Julius Brunner his deputy.

323. Diary entry, February 8, 1941.

324. Compare sworn testimony by J. Brunner, DÖW, 3f. (see note 8 above).

325. Diary entry, September 7, 1941.

326. Diary entry, September 9, 1941.

327. Diary entry, March 23, 1941.

328. Lackenbach original documents: in the administration building nine postal orders were found from 1941, 1943, and 1944, as well as the following package receipts: twenty-nine from 1941; eighteen from 1942; five from 1943, and two from 1944. For instance, shipments came from Deutschkreutz or Oberpullendorf by mail. See also Appendix XXIV. To what extent the fear of attracting attention influenced the decision to refrain from visits to the camp cannot be estimated.

329. We know from Camp Buchenwald that the receipt of money was limited to 30 RM per inmate each month. Compare Kogon, 142ff. As can be documented, the amounts of money received in Lackenbach usually were below 30 RM. One time the amount of 30 RM was transmitted; the highest amount was around 50 RM.

330. On October 21, 1941, and on October 28, 1941—receipts, Lackenbach original document.

331. Compare sworn testimony by J. Brunner, 3, and testimony by R. Frost, 3. In BMI file, Zl. 178.401-2/56.

332. In Buchenwald, receiving packages was not allowed until the fall of 1941. After the lifting of the restriction, SS men stole the majority of the contents.

333. The name of camp elder Sepp Brandner (Brantner) appears in the various sources—as do other Gypsy names—in different spellings. The variant here mentioned is in his own hand.

334. A stub from January 11, 1941, is signed by Brunner. The date falls in the period when Brunner was camp leader for a short time before Kollross. See also Appendix XXIV.

335. Diary entry, July 27, 1941: "When searched today, Camp No. 856, Georg Fröhlich, was in possession of 300 RM." Compare ibid., October 5, 1941.

336. Sworn testimony by J. Brunner, DÖW, 6 (see note 8 above).

337. Compare Kogon, 144f.

338. DÖW file, No. 82b. Notes of former inmates, previously mentioned, cited according to *Widerstand und Verfolgung im Burgenland,* Document 30, p. 276.

339. Diary entry, March 29, 1941.

340. For instance, a money shipment of 10 RM to Anton Schneeberger was returned. One may assume that the use of the number was necessary because of the frequently similar names of inmates.

341. For the concentration camps there were strict formal regulations. In most camps a letter was allowed every two weeks and occasionally a post card with a prescribed number of lines. From March 1942 on, there was an additional restriction in Auschwitz for Jews and inmates from the eastern territories to one letter in two months. Compare *Auschwitz. Faschistisches,* 84f., and Kogon, 148ff.

342. Since the beginning of the registration of minorities in 1875, compulsory school attendance existed for the children of these minorities as well as for all others. Thus it was not only the Gypsies who tried to get around this law. The communities themselves effected the exclusion of the Gypsy children from instruction with the argument: "For financial reasons it is impossible to comply with the government's orders." The statutes, however differed in the individual communities. If the Stegersbach [Gypsies] already had regular classes since 1924, the Unterwart Gypsies had to wait till 1952. Compare Bertha, 9.

343. In many cases, three crosses replaced the signature on package receipts as well as on documents.

344. Compare chapter 4, "Legal and Administrative Measures against the Burgenland Gypsies during the National Socialist Regime" section. The decree for the *Ostmark* was issued only on June 15, 1939. In the *Altreich,* this directive took effect only on November 21, 1941.

345. Diary entry, April 19, 1941.

346. Diary entry, April 19, 1941. The description in the diary is as follows: "He was grasped with the clasp in the courtyard for 15 minutes."

347. DÖW file, No. 9626. Testimony F. Langmüller, 3.

348. In Auschwitz the following prescriptions existed for implementation: "The number of lashes—which, according to regulations were to be carried out quickly, one after the other—was not to exceed 25 for one beating." However, the actual extent of the punishment depended on the SS man who supervised the execution [of the order]. "The beatings were administered with a stick, less frequently with a whip, as prescribed." *Auschwitz. Faschistisches,* 104.

349. LG Vienna Vg 1 c V r 4594/47. Verdict of the LG Vienna as VG against Franz Langmüller, policeman from Vienna, because of war crimes, main trial August 15, 1948. In DÖW file, No. 9626.

350. LG Vienna Vg 1 c V r 4594/47, cited according to *Widerstand und Verfolgung im Burgenland,* Document 29, p. 275f.

351. LG Vienna Vg 1 c V r 4594/47, witness testimony Margarethe Papai, 9.

352. LG Vienna Vg 1 c V r 4594/47, witness testimony Martin Horwath, 11. M. Horwath was in Lackenbach from November 1941. He came from Mauthausen with a larger transport.

353. The horse—a specially fashioned and equipped table-like wooden structure on which the delinquent was tied down, lying on his stomach, his head lower than his body, the derriere up in the air, and the legs pulled towards the front—was a familiar instrument for beatings in all the camps. Compare Kogon, 128.

354. DÖW file, No. 9626. Testimony by N. Reinprecht before the Security Directorate for Burgenland, Eisenstadt, October 8, 1954, 1.

355. DÖW file, No. 9626, testimony of Josef Hajek to the Department of Victims' Compensation of the Ministry for Social Affairs, October 27, 1954, 1.

356. Compare DÖW file, No. 9626, testimony of A. Sarközi: In the case of escape, the camp leader gave the order to the camp elders to administer five to twenty-five blows with the stick to the escapees.

357. DÖW file, No. 9626, testimony of Ludwig Horwath, 15.

358. DÖW file, No. 9626, testimony of Mathias Hlavin, 16.

359. Testimony of Ingenieur Karpischek, summer 1954. In Steinmetz, *Österreichs Zigeuner,* 25.

360. Verdict against Langmüller, cited according to *Widerstand und Verfolgung im Burgenland,* Document 29, p. 275.

361. This recent discrimination against the Gypsies in doubting their credibility runs through all the trials of the postwar period. Compare also chapter 7, "Medical Experiments—Desalination Experiments" section.

362. DÖW file, No. 9626, main trial, October 15, 1948, protocol, 4.

363. Here, above all, the report of Jakob Schneeberger, who had been Kapo of a work detail, found credence. *Widerstand und Verfolgung im Burgenland,* Document 29, p. 276. Raimund Frost and Anton Schneeberger also reported on these incidents in the proceedings against "Reinhardt" in 1956. BMI file, Zl. 178.401-2/56. Such harassment and punishments were meant to contribute to the demoralization of and to break the willpower of the inmates.

364. Testimony of Martin Horwath: "Beatings were given especially to those who attempted escape," DÖW file, No. 9626, 11. Joseph Hodosi: "I (couldn't) stand it anymore and ran away. . . . They caught me and . . . 25 lashes with the rubber hose was the punishment." Steinmetz, *Österreichs Zigeuner,* 23.

365. Lackenbach did not have specific penal companies, as in the concentration camps, but some heavy labor was categorized as punishment, for instance, building of the camp road. Diary entry, February 16, 1941.

366. Diary entry, January 23 and 24, 1941.

367. Diary entry, April 23, 1941: "Because of suspected theft of a key for a suitcase [inmate was given] 9 hours of solitary detention, and lunch was withheld."

368. Diary entry, June 18, 1941: "Three foremen, who watched (the three escapees), were punished with detention in a single room and their lunch was withheld."

369. Diary entry, April 19, 1941.

370. Escape attempts were also a reason for punishment in such cases. Diary entry, June 15 and September 1, 1941.

371. Sworn testimony by J. Brunner, DÖW, 4 (see note 8 above).

372. *Teleobjectiv,* interview, 6.

373. Sworn testimony by J. Brunner, DÖW, 6 (see note 8 above).

374. From winter 1944–45 on, when the Allied armies advanced further, the SS deported the inmates from concentration camps near the front to the interior of the Reich. At the beginning of 1945, the Buchenwald and Ra-

vensbrück inmates arrived in Mauthausen. (These transports also included Gypsy children. Marsalek, 85f.) From Mauthausen, they continued to Bergen-Belsen. These transports often were en route for weeks, during icy cold weather, without food and on foot or in open freight cars. The SS did not stop to drive the prisoners from one camp to the other, for a central order directed that no inmate was to reach the Allies alive. (Compare Geisel, 108f., and Langbein, 29f.) Thus many died still during the last marches or later in the completely overcrowded concentration camp Bergen-Belsen by freezing, starving to death, or exhaustion.

375. Banny, "Das Anhaltelager," 6.

376. Compare Martin Broszat, "National Socialist Concentration Camps 1933–1945," in Buchheim et al., *Anatomie*, Vol. 2, 97ff.

377. Collection of decrees "Vorbeugende . . . " ["Preventive . . . "], cited according Buchheim et al., *Anatomie*, Vol. 2, 77.

378. Broszat, *Nationalsozialistische KL*, 110.

379. "Extermination through work" did not only concern those people who were handed over from the judicial system to the concentration camps for this purpose, but all prisoners. In cost calculations of the SS, the average life span of a concentration camp inmate was figured to be nine months. Compare Heinz Kühnrich, *Der KZ-Staat. Rolle und Entwicklung der faschistischen KL 1933–1945* [The Concentration Camp State. Role and Development of Fascist Concentration Camps 1933–1945] (Berlin, 1960), 86.

380. Compare Langbein, 23f.

381. Compare chapter 5, "Camp Administration—Supervisory Personnel."

382. Langbein, 28.

383. Compare Kogon, 75, as well as *Auschwitz. Faschistisches,* 13ff.

384. DÖW file, No. 9626: Testimony A. Sarközi, 12. On December 14, 1940, six Gypsies from concentration camp Mauthausen were transferred to Lackenbach.

385. Compare Geisel, 108.

386. Apart from the fact that, for instance, also in the Auschwitz Gypsy camp prisoners wore civilian clothing, a shortage of supplies led to non-Gypsy inmates also being allowed to wear civilian clothes. In Auschwitz, two circulars of February 1943 stipulated that inmates who were employed in the camp were to be given civilian clothing. Compare *Auschwitz. Faschistisches,* 75: APMO, Archives of the State Museum in Oswiecim, "Collection of Decrees," identification D-RF-9/WVHA/8/, 20, 23, and 24.

387. Compare Buchheim, "Die SS," in Buchheim et al., *Anatomie*, Vol. 1, 101ff.

388. Buchheim et al., *Anatomie*, Vol. 1, 103: The acceptance of policemen into the SS occurred in two stages. The first stage was the acceptance into the SS; the second was the subsequent promotion to SS ranks, which corresponded to their police ranks (parallelization of official rank).

6. Gypsy Transports from Austria to Lodz and Chelmno

1. Like many other Polish places during the time of the Nazi rule, "Lodz" was made German. Except in quotes, I chose to use the Polish version.

2. DÖW file, No. 2606. "Gypsies tell about their persecutions during the period 1938–1945."

3. Jerzy Ficowski, *Cyganie na polskich drogach,* 2d edition (Krakow, 1965). (Working translation: *Zigeuner auf polnischen Strassen* [Gypsies in Polish Streets], by Martin Pollak, Warszawa. Source: DÖW file IIIc/1.) Jerzy Ficowski, "Vernichtung" [Extermination], *Polnische Zigeuner* [Polish Gypsies]. Historie und Sittenskizzen (Warsaw, 1953). (Translation by a Warsaw lawyer.) Source: IfZ Munich, Akz. 2694/61/Ms-89.

4. Letter by Martin Pollak, Warsaw, to DÖW, Vienna, January 18, 1976, 2. DÖW file IIIc/1.

5. Compare Arendt, *Eichmann in Jerusalem,* 261.

6. Compared to 1983, knowledge about Gypsy transports to Lodz has expanded. Documents can be found in the Jewish Museum in Frankfurt, binder Ghetto Lodz 1940–1944, documents "Non-Jews in the ghetto," "Gypsy camp," "Polish youth detention camp (document 11/13/41)."

7. Since numerous Gypsies of other nationalities had come to Austria already before the beginning of the war, it cannot be estimated how many persons actually were Austrian Gypsies.

8. Compare DÖW file, No. 11340 and 11278.

9. DÖW file, No. 1978.

10. Ficowski, *Polish Gypsies,* 8.

11. Josef Wulf, "Lodz—Das letzte Ghetto auf polnischem Boden" [Lodz— The Last Ghetto on Polish Soil], *Schriftenreihe der Bundes-Zentrale für Heimatdienst* 59 (Bonn, 1962), 40.

12. A. Eisenbach, " 'Dokumenty i materialy' Ghetto Lodskie" [Documents and Materials from Ghetto Lodz] (Warszawa, 1946). Cited from Miriam Novitch, *Contribution a l'etude du genocide des Tziganes sous le regime nazi* [Contribution to the Study of the Gypsy Genocide under the Nazi Regime] (Prague, 1963), 30. This document, regarding the "admission of 20,000 Jews and 5,000 Gypsies into ghetto Lodz [Litzmannstadt]" is dated September 24, 1941.

13. These spatial relationships—three hundred square meters for five thousand people—ought to be questioned, but Josef Wulf mentions them twice in his report. (Compare note 11.)

14. These facts are supported by Ficowski's work ("Archive of the Elder of the *Judenrat* [Jewish Council]," "Bulletin of Daily Events") and the reports by Wulf, which agree in the decisive testimony. Wulf also refers to Polish documents or to other works that are based on such, for example, Nachman Blumental, "Obozy" (Polish) (Lodz, 1946) (documents); A. Eisenbach, Ghetto

Lodz (Polish) (Warsaw, 1946) (documents); Bendet Hershkovitch, "Ghetto Litzmannstadt," *Yivo Bleter* 30 (fall 1947), Memories; Bulletin of the Jewish Historical Institute in Warsaw.

15. Compare DÖW file, No. 11477.

16. Compare DÖW file, No. 11293.

17. See Appendix XI.

18. Lackenbach Original Document, copy, see Appendix XXVII.

19. Diary entry, November 4, 1941. In DÖW file, No. 11340.

20. Adalbert Rückerl, ed., *NS-Vernichtungslager im Spiegel deutscher Straf-prozesse* [Nazi Extermination Camp Seen through German Penal Proceedings], 2d ed. (Munich, 1978), 280.

21. Compare Rückerl, 268f.

22. Rückerl, 289.

23. Compare Novitch, 10–12. This study named SS Obersturmführer Joseph W. Rauff ("specialiste des chambres a gaz ambulantes") as one of the men responsible for the genocide of these five thousand Gypsies.

24. Arendt, *Eichmann in Jerusalem,* 129.

25. Arendt, *Eichmann in Jerusalem,* 129. The trial took place in 1961–1962.

26. Arendt, *Eichmann in Jerusalem,* 129.

7. Gypsies as Subjects of Medical Experiments

1. Alexander Bein, "Der moderne Antisemitismus und seine Bedeutung für die Judenfrage" [Modern Antisemitism and Its Significance for the Jewish Question], *Vierteljahreshefte für Zeitgeschichte* 6 (Stuttgart, 1958), 353.

2. Alexander Mitscherlich and Fred Mielke, *Medizin ohne Menschlichkeit. Dokumente des Nürnberger Ärzteprozesses* [Medicine without Humanity] (Frankfurt, 1978), 14.

3. Ino Arndt, "Das Frauenkonzentrationslager Ravensbrück" [The Women's Concentration Camp Ravensbrück], *Studien zur Geschichte der Konzentrationslager. Schriftenreihe der Vierteljahreshefte für Zeitgeschichte* 21 (Stuttgart, 1970), 124.

4. Mitscherlich and Mielke, 237f. Defense arguments of the defendant Pokorny, No. 035.

5. Concluding remarks, Dr. Beiglboeck, 2: "In my experiments no life was sacrificed, no permanent damage to the health [of the victim]." Cited from *Kriegsverbrecher-Prozesse* [War Crimes Trials] (KV Prozess), doctors' trial, case 1, LXIII B, No. 1. Source: State Archive Nuremberg, Rep. 501.

6. W. Birkmayer, "Charakter und Vererbung" [Character and Heredity], *Wiener klinische Wochenschrift* 51 (Vienna, 1938), 1245.

7. W. Birkmayer, "Über die Vererbung der Nervenkrankheiten" [On the Heredity of Nervous Disorders], *Wiener klinische Wochenschrift* 51 (Vienna, 1938), 1150.

8. Victor von Weizsaecker, " 'Euthanasie' und Menschenversuche"

[Euthanasia and Human Experiments], *Psyche* 1 (1947). Cited from Gerhard Baader and Ulrich Schultz, eds., *Medizin und Nationalsozialismus. Tabuisierte Vergangenheit—ungebrochene Tradition?* [Medicine and National Socialism. Taboo Past—Unbroken Tradition?], Vol. 1 (Berlin, 1980), 196.

9. *Auschwitz. Faschistisches,* 139. From this preserved correspondence between the company and the camp commander we can also ascertain that all persons died. "Shortly we will get in touch with you regarding further shipments." Nuremberg Document NI-7184. Source: Jan Sehn, *Konzentrationslager Auschwitz-Birkenau* [Concentration Camp Auschwitz-Birkenau] (Warszawa, 1964), 80–84.

10. Compare Kogon, 193, and Mitscherlich and Mielke, 96ff.

11. Not all doctors who committed provable medical crimes were tried by the court. However, we can ascertain that there existed broad-based Nazi medicine from the fact that among the doctors of the German Reich, 45 percent belonged to the Nazi Party, 26 percent of all doctors were members of the Brown Shirts, and, in comparison to the male work force, doctors were represented in the SS seven times as often as others. Compare Baader and Schultz, 185.

12. Mitscherlich and Mielke, 122 (Nuremberg Protocols 1376 and 1767). Dr. Gräfe was assistant to Professor Haagen, chief of the typhoid experiments in Natzweiler.

13. U. Schultz, *Soziale und biographische Bedingungen medizinischen Verbrechens* [Social and Biographical Conditions of Medical Crimes], in Baader and Schultz, 186.

14. Baader and Schultz, 184.

15. Klaus Dörner, "Nationalsozialismus und Lebensvernichtung" [National Socialism and the Destruction of Life], in Härlin Dörner et al., eds., *Der Krieg gegen die Psychisch Kranken* [The War against the Mentally Ill] (Rehburg-Loccum, 1980), 104.

16. Kautzky, 63.

17. Ota Kraus and Erich Kulka, *Massenmord und Profit* [Mass Murder and Profit] (Berlin, 1963), 228.

18. Document No. 216, letter dated July 1942 from the headquarters of the Führer: "The Reichsführer-SS approved brigade commander Prof. Clauberg's request to use concentration camp Auschwitz for his human and animal experiments." Cited from Mitscherlich and Mielke, 248.

19. Compare H. Langbein, *Menschen in Auschwitz* [People in Auschwitz] (Vienna, 1972), 381; also, Szymanski et al., *Auschwitz-Anthology,* Vol. 2, 32.

20. Compare Kogon, 188.

21. Szymanski et al., 35.

22. O. Kraus and E. Kulka, *Die Todesfabrik* [The Death Factory] (Berlin, 1957), 15.

23. Compare *IG Farben. Auschwitz-Massenmord* [IG Farben. Auschwitz Mass Murder], published by the study group of former inmates of concentration camp Auschwitz (Berlin, 1964), 61.

24. *IG Farben*, 61.

25. Testimony, Arthur Dietzsch. Do. No. NI-12184 Office of Chief Counsel for War Crimes. *IG Farben*, Document 40, p. 62.

26. Dr. Conti was state secretary in the Reich Interior Ministry and chief of the Reich doctors.

27. Mitscherlich and Mielke, 95.

28. Mitscherlich and Mielke, Doc. No. 1188, p. 100.

29. Mitscherlich and Mielke, Doc. No. 179, p. 80.

30. Mitscherlich and Mielke, Doc. No. 179, opinion of Nebe: "I suggest to use the asocial 'Gypsy half-breeds' in concentration camp Auschwitz for that purpose."

31. Mitscherlich and Mielke, 124.

32. Compare Mitscherlich and Mielke, 85.

33. Witness testimony of Gypsy Laubinger in Nuremberg doctors' trial; final report against Oskar Schröder (June 16, 1947). In KV Prozess, L XIII, Case 1, No. 6; 47f. Source: State Archives Nuremberg, Rep. 501.

34. KV Prozess, L XIII, Case 1, No. 6; 48.

35. Compare Kraus and Kulka, *Die Todesfabrik*, 93.

36. Mitscherlich and Mielke, 285 n. 8.

37. Kogon, 191.

38. Kogon, 192.

39. Mitscherlich and Mielke, Doc. No. 1188, p. 100.

40. Mitscherlich and Mielke, Doc. No. 1188.

41. Mitscherlich and Mielke, Doc. No. 265, p. 101.

42. Bernhard Streck, "Zigeuner unter dem Nationalsozialismus" [Gypsies during National Socialism], in Edith Gerth et al., *Projekt Tsiganology* [Project Gypsiology] (Giessen, 1978), 25.

43. Mitscherlich and Mielke, Prot. 9769, p. 100.

44. Mitscherlich and Mielke, Doc. No. 121, p. 123.

45. Mitscherlich and Mielke, Doc. No. 121.

46. Udo Dietmar, *Häftling X in der Hölle auf Erden!* [Inmate X in Hell on Earth!] (Mainz, 1946), 53f.

47. Mitscherlich and Mielke, Prot. 9616f, p. 124.

48. Mitscherlich and Mielke, Prot. 10588ff. and 10622ff, p. 124.

49. Conversation with K. Eberle, April 30, 1981.

50. Mitscherlich and Mielke, Prot. 8504f, p. 72.

51. No. 177, Prosecution testimony 133, R. 479. Prosecution against Hermann Becker-Freyseng, 18f. KV-Prozess, Case 1, D 10.

52. Precondition was that the "guinea pigs' " physical condition corresponded to that of the members of the air force.

53. We have to mention here that the first efforts (with *Berkatit*) did not last the necessary length of time. For this reason there was no lasting damage.

54. Mitscherlich and Mielke, Doc. No. 184, p. 73.

55. Mitscherlich and Mielke, Prot. 8130f, p. 76.

56. Mitscherlich and Mielke, Prot. 8309f, p. 79: Undoubtedly forty volunteers could have been found, but they knew "that in Berlin in the summer of 1944 there surely were no 40 healthy young men . . . whose time was at their disposal."

57. Prosecution against Beiglböck, 9. KV Prozess, Case 1, E 6.

58. Mitscherlich and Mielke, 80.

59. Mitscherlich and Mielke: Letter from Schröder to Himmler, 78.

60. From the testimony of witness Laubinger, who was "guinea pig" No. 7, we know that he and other inmates in Buchenwald were asked whether they would volunteer for a cleaning detail in Dachau. "The inmates were under the impression that conditions in Dachau were better and agreed." Final report against Professor Schröder, 48. KV Prozess, Case 1, X No. 6.

61. In addition to better food, they were promised a better work detail for later. "These promises were, however, not kept. After the experiments, these Gypsies in their weakened condition were immediately sent to hard outside details. Others were sent to overcrowded blocks where they did not receive any food rations." No. 3282, sworn testimony Joseph Vorlicek, 3. Source: State archives Nuremberg, Rep. 502 I.

62. "On the whole approximately 60 Gypsies were used, these were chosen from a group of 80 or 90. Volunteers they surely were not, since all tried to get out of it." No. 3342, sworn testimony Josef Tschofenig, April 15, 1947, 1, KV Prozess.

63. No. 3282, sworn testimony J. Vorlicek, 2.

64. "Laubinger, who was in the Schäfer group, received Schäfer water for 12 days and fasted at least nine days." Prosecution against Schröder, 48, KV Prozess. The intolerability of these experiments is also reflected in incidents in which the "guinea pigs" tried to disobey the orders. Thus, they took advantage of unguarded moments to obtain fluids from buckets and cleaning rags.

65. DÖW file, No. 2573. Report of the State Police Vienna, February 16, 1946, 1. In these notes we also read that in 1944 Beiglböck's wife supposedly stated that "her husband frequently was in danger through the experiments which he carried out in Dachau, because the inmates . . . suffered from fits of rage and madness."

66. DÖW file, No. 2573, 2.

67. DÖW file, No. 2573, testimony of Josef Tschofenig, February 7, 1946, 1f.

68. No. 3342, testimony of J. Tschofenig, 2. After the conclusion of the experiments those unable to work were sent to disabled stations. "On the basis of my general camp experience I assume that approximately 30 percent . . . did not survive the disabled block and other strains."

69. Mitscherlich and Mielke, Doc. No. 912/Fritz Pillwein, 87.

70. Mitscherlich and Mielke, 90.

71. Dr. Gustav Steinbauer, Vienna, defender of Dr. Beiglböck.

72. "It is his (Steinbauer's) duty as defense attorney to check the credibility

of the witnesses, and one can ascertain from the literature that especially the asocial person has no compunctions about lying." Defense response, Steinbauer, 7a. KV Prozess, Case 1.

73. Comment of Steinbauer to the witness Höllenreiner during cross examination: "Don't sidestep my question according to Gypsy practices." Prosecution against W. Beiglböck, 10. KV Prozess, Case 1.

74. In this context it is suitable to point to a lecture by Joachim Hohmann, "Failure of German (Gypsy) Scholarship," on the occasion of the Third International Roma-Congress in Göttingen, May 20, 1981: "It seems incredible to me that even in questions of reparations the tone is so often set by envy, elitism, and an especially base form of structural force. . . . For 35 years we have had authentic testimony which documents the Gypsy genocide, file material enough to be able to call this testimony genuine and true." (7f.).

75. After declaring his unfitness for future service at the front, he was able to achieve his transfer to Auschwitz, a place where there "was enough human material at his disposal."

76. Noma is a rare form of cancer from which especially children in the concentration camp suffered.

77. These writings can today be found in the State Museum in Auschwitz. Compare Szymanski et al., 215.

78. Testimony, T. Joachimowski. "Protokoll einer Zigeunervernehmung" [Protocol of a Gypsy Interrogation] (unpublished typescript, Krakau, July 2, 1968). Cited from Geigges and Wette, 286.

79. Szymanski et al., 37f.

80. Elisabeth Guttenberger, "Das Zigeunerlager" [The Gypsy Camp], in H. Langbein and E. Lingens-Reiner, eds., *Auschwitz. Zeugnisse und Berichte* [Auschwitz. Testimony and Reports] (Frankfurt, 1962), 161.

81. Institute for Eugenics and Race Research in Frankfurt.

82. Langbein, *Menschen in Auschwitz*, 384.

83. Compare Langbein, *Menschen in Auschwitz*, 381.

84. Szymanski et al., *Auschwitz-Anthology*, Vol. 2, Part 2, p. 29.

85. No. 411, KV-Prozess, Bl. 311. Source: State Archives, Nuremberg, Rep. 502 I.

86. Compare No. 411, KV-Prozess, Bl. 309; Kater, 206; and Raul Hilberg, *The Destruction of the European Jews* (Chicago, 1961), 608.

87. von zur Mühlen, 239.

88. Hans-Günter Zmarlik, "Der Sozialdarwinismus in Deutschland als geschichtliches Problem" [Social Darwinism in Germany as a Historical Problem], *Vierteljahresheft für Zeitgeschichte* 11 (Stuttgart, 1963), 267.

89. Sworn testimony by R. Brandt, June 16, 1947, 10. In KV-Prozess, Case 1, No. I/4, Pkt. II, A. If the Gypsies are not mentioned here among those to be murdered, there is, on the one hand, a quantitative reason; on the other hand, one must think of the schizophrenic attitude with which the Nazis persecuted

the Gypsies. The thoroughness with which they were persecuted—measured by Nazi standards—could not be compared to their importance within society; on the other hand, their unimportance—and corresponding inferiority—was so great that it seemed superfluous to mention them separately.

90. Mitscherlich and Mielke, Doc. No. 035, 237.

91. Mitscherlich and Mielke, Prot. 10291, testimony of Dr. Koch, Madaus-works, 240.

92. KV-Prozesse, Case 1, against R. Brandt, Pkt. II, A, 14.

93. Mitscherlich and Mielke, Doc. No. 036, p. 240.

94. Mitscherlich and Mielke, Doc. No. 241, p. 203.

95. Mitscherlich and Mielke, Doc. No. 205, p. 242.

96. Mitscherlich and Mielke, Doc. No. 602, p. 245.

97. Testimony, G. Winkowska before Major A. K. Mant, R.A.M.C., War Crimes Investigation Unit, Headquarters British Army, Stockholm, September 18, 1946. Source: State Archives Nuremberg, Rep. 502 I/Bl. 926.

98. Mitscherlich and Mielke, Doc. No. 212, p. 246.

99. Langbein and Lingens-Reiner, 373.

100. DÖW file, No. 2589.

101. Friedrich Karl Kaul, *Ärzte in Auschwitz* [Doctors in Auschwitz] (Berlin, 1968), 280.

102. *Auschwitz. Faschistisches,* 137.

103. Erika Buchmann, *Die Frauen von Ravensbrück* [The Women of Ravensbrück] (Berlin, 1961), 78f.

104. Interview, J. Hodosi, 3.

105. Witness testimony, Gerber, in Hermann Langbein, *Der Auschwitz-Prozeß. Eine Dokumentation* [The Auschwitz Trial. A Documentation] (Vienna, 1965), 618.

106. Testimony, Suhren, Nuremberg Doc. No. 3647, dated December 30, 1945. Cited from Arndt, 124.

107. Szymanski et al., *Auschwitz-Anthology,* Vol. 2, Part 2, 39.

108. Deutschkron, 123.

109. Hohmann, *Zigeuner und Zigeunerwissenschaft,* 44.

110. Hohmann, *Zigeuner und Zigeunerwissenschaft,* 46.

111. BKA-Interior, 551 o.Z. Activities report, Ethnic and Border Land Office, 1938/39, Pkt. 32/Gypsies, 22. AVA, Vienna.

112. Walter von Baeyer, Heinz Häfner, and Karl Peter Kisker, *Psychiatrie der Verfolgten* [Psychiatry of the Persecuted] (Berlin, 1964), 253.

113. Taped protocol of lecture by Theresia Seible, "Widerstand von Frauen im Dritten Reich" [Women's Resistance in the Third Reich], in *Courage* 5 (Berlin, 1981), 21.

114. This regulation occurred in connection with the Auschwitz decree. "It is up to the Reich criminal police office to select those important to the war industry, those who earned special honors in the war and their spouses, and

economically dependent children; the police should also 'stress their agreement to be sterilized.' " The campaign was to be carried out between March 1 and 31, 1943. Mazirel, 132.

115. An example is the fate of the Gypsy Lucia Strasdinsch, who was allowed to continue living in Libau after her sterilization: In the first letter the police inform the city magistrate of the decision that the Gypsy woman could only continue to live in the city if she would agree to the procedure. Second document: The notification of the magistrate to the police that the sterilization has been completed. The confirmation from the hospital was enclosed with the letter. *IMG* [*Internationaler Militärgerichtshof*], Vol. 8, p. 345.

116. Marta Adler, *Mein Schicksal waren die Zigeuner* [My Fate Were the Gypsies] (Bremen, 1957), 383.

117. Kogon, 207.

118. The parents, who knew of the intended sterilization of their children, were prohibited by the sexual taboo of the Gypsies to prepare their children. The sexual taboo is part of the established ethical code of the Gypsies. The customs that are anchored in a taboo system include the three major life cycles of pregnancy, birth, and naming; courting and marriage; and death and burial. Also included are certain rules that have to do with clothing, food, living quarters, and especially religious ritual. Compare Arnold, *Die Zigeuner,* 4ff.

119. Selma Steinmetz, "Die 'deutsche Rassenforschung' ist mitverantwortlich für die NS-Zigeunerverfolgung" [German 'Racial Research' is Co-responsible for the Nazi Persecution of Gypsies], *Mitteilungen zur Zigeunerkunde* 9 (1978), 3.

120. Compare P. Petersen and U. Liedtke, "Zur Entschädigung zwangssterilisierter Zigeuner" [On Reparations for Forcibly Sterilized Gypsies], *Der Nervenarzt* 42 (Berlin, 1971), 204.

121. Baeyer et al., 258.

122. Baeyer et al., 253.

123. Baeyer et al., 259.

124. Conversation with Karl Eberle, April 30, 1981. The corresponding evaluation regarding his disability was written by Dr. Hesse, State Psychological Clinic, Salzburg.

125. Many of Dr. Steinmetz's conversation partners had complained to her about poor health.

8. Concluding Remarks

1. Of the eleven thousand Gypsies before 1938, only about one-third survived the National Socialist genocide. The correction of the total victim count against 1983, when we thought that about half of Austria's Sinti had been murdered, resulted primarily from the new documents on the Lodz deportations.

2. BMI Zl. 84.426-4/48 dated September 20, 1948; see Appendix XXVIII.

3. See author's introduction to the American edition.

Bibliography

Published Sources

Adam, Walter. *Nacht über Deutschland* [Night over Germany]. Vienna: 1947.

Adelsberger, Lucie. *Auschwitz. Ein Tatsachenbericht* [Auschwitz. A Factual Report]. Berlin: 1965.

Adler, Hans-Günther. *Die Erfahrung der Ohnmacht* [The Experience of Impotence]. Slg. "Res novae," 29. Frankfurt: 1964.

Adler, Marta. *Mein Schicksal waren die Zigeuner* [My Fate Were the Gypsies]. Bremen: 1957.

Arendt, Hannah. *Eichmann in Jerusalem. Ein Bericht von der Banalität des Bösen* [Eichmann in Jerusalem. A Report on the Banality of Evil]. Reinbek bei Hamburg: 1978.

Arndt, Ino. "Das Frauenkonzentrationslager Ravensbrück" [The Women's Concentration Camp Ravensbrueck]. *Studien zur Geschichte der Konzentrationslager.* Schriftenreihe der Vierteljahreshefte für Zeitgeschichte (VfZG), 21. Stuttgart: 1970, 93–130.

Arnold, Hermann. "Anmerkungen zur Geschichtsschreibung der Zigeunerverfolgung" [Notes on the Historiography of Gypsy Persecution]. *Mitteilungen zur Zigeunerkunde,* Supplement 4. Mainz: 1977.

———. *Randgruppen des Zigeunervolkes* [Marginal Groups of Gypsies]. Neustadt: 1975.

———. Die Zigeuner. Herkunft und Leben der Stämme im deutschen Sprachgebiet [The Gypsies. Origin and Life of the Tribes in the German Language Realm]. Olten/Freiburg i.Br.: 1965.

Auschwitz. Faschistisches Vernichtungslager [Auschwitz. Fascist Death Camp]. Warsaw: Staatliches Museum in Auschwitz, 1978.

Auschwitz: Hefte [Journals] 1 bis 15. Cracow: Museum in Auschwitz, 1960–1975.

Baader, Gerhard, and Ulrich Schultz, eds. *Medizin und Nationalsozialismus. Tabuisierte Vergangenheit—ungebrochene Tradition?* [Medicine and National Socialism. Taboo Past—Unbroken Tradition?] Vol. 1. Berlin: 1980.

Baeyer, Walter von. *Über die Auswirkungen rassischer Verfolgung und Konzentrationslagerhaft vom Standpunkt des Psychiaters* [On the Consequences of Racial Persecution and Concentration Camp Imprisonment from the Psychiatrist's Point of View]. Emuna-Horizonte, Series V, No. 1. Frankfurt: 1970, 65–68.

Baeyer, Walter von, Heinz Häfner, and Karl Peter Kisker. *Psychiatrie der Verfolgten* [Psychiatry of the Persecuted]. Berlin: 1964.

Bailer, Brigitte. *Wiedergutmachung Kein Thema. Österreich und die Opfer des Nationalsozialismus* [Reparations Are Not a Topic. Austria and the Victims of National Socialism]. Vienna: 1993.

Bauer, Yehuda. "Gypsies." *Encyclopedia of the Holocaust.* Vol. 2. New York: Macmillan, 1990, 634–38.

———. "Holocaust and Genocide: Some Comparisons." In Peter Hayes, ed. *Lessons and Legacies: The Meaning of the Holocaust in a Changing World.* Evanston, Ill.: Northwestern University Press, 1991.

———. "Jews, Gypsies, Slavs: Policies of the Third Reich." *UNESCO Yearbook on Peace and Conflict Studies 1985.* Paris: 1987, 73–100.

Beck, Johannes, et al., eds. *Terror und Hoffnung in Deutschland 1933–1945* [Terror and Hope in Germany 1933–1945]. Reinbek bei Hamburg: 1980.

Bein, Alexander. "Der moderne Antisemitismus und seine Bedeutung für die Judenfrage" [Modern Antisemitism and Its Meaning for the Jewish Question]. *VfZG* 6, No. 4. Stuttgart: 1958, 353–60.

Benkö, Joska. *Zigeuner—ihre Welt—ihr Schicksal* [Gypsies—Their World—Their Fate]. Pinkafeld: 1979.

Bercovici, Konrad. *The Story of the Gypsies.* New York: Cosmopolitan Book Corporation, 1931.

Bertha, Josef. "Die Schwierigkeit der Zigeuner-Integration" [The Difficulty of Gypsy Integration]. *Das Menschenrecht,* Ser. 32, Vol. 168, No. 1. Vienna: 1977, 8–11.

———. "Die Zigeuner in Unterwart" [The Gypsies in Unterwart], in *Das Menschenrecht,* Vol. 168, 1977, 8–12.

Bettelheim, Bruno. *Aufstand gegen die Masse. Die Chance des Individuums in der modernen Gesellschaft* [Revolt Against the Masses. The Individuum in Modern Society]. Munich: 1964.

Die Bevölkerungsentwicklung im Burgenland zwischen 1923 und 1971 [Population Development in Burgenland between 1923 and 1971]. Eisenstadt: Amt der Burgenländischen Landesregierung, Abt. 4, 1976.

Birkmayer, W. "Charakter und Vererbung/Über die Vererbung von Nervenkrankheiten" [Character and Heredity/On the Hereditary Nature of Nervous Disorders]. *Wiener klinische Wochenschrift,* Ser. 51. Vienna: 1938, 1245 bzw. 1150.

Block, Martin. *Zigeuner, ihr Leben und ihre Seele* [Gypsies, Their Life and Soul]. Leipzig: 1936.

Boberach, Heinz. *Meldungen aus dem Reich* [News from the Reich]. Munich: 1968.

Bock, Gisela. *Zwangssterilisierungen im Nationalsozialismus. Studien zu Rassenpolitik und Frauenpolitik* [Forced Sterilization during National Socialism. Studies on Race Politics and Women's Politics]. Opladen: 1986.

Brandis, Ernst. *Die Ehegesetze von 1935* [The Marriage Laws of 1935]. Berlin: 1936.

Breitling, Rupert. *Die nationalsozialistische Rassenlehre. Entstehung, Ausbreitung, Nutzen und Schaden einer politischen Ideologisierung* [National Socialist Racial Theory. Origin, Expansion, Use and Damage of a Political Ideologization]. Meisenheim am Glan: 1971.

Broszat, Martin. "Dokumentation. Zur Perversion der Strafjustiz im Dritten Reich" [Documentation. On the Perversion of Penal Justice in the Third Reich]. *VfZG* 6, No. 4. Stuttgart: 1958, 390–405.

Buchenwald. *Mahnung und Verpflichtung* [Warning and Duty]. Dokumente und Berichte. Frankfurt: 1960.

Buchheim, Hans. "Die Zigeunerdeportation vom Mai 1940" [The Gypsy Deportation of May 1940]. *Gutachten des Instituts für Zeitgeschichte,* Vol. 1. Munich: 1956, 51–60.

Buchheim, Hans, Martin Broszat, Hans Adolf Jacobson, and Helmut Krausnick. *Anatomie des SS-Staates* [Anatomy of the SS State]. Vols. 1 and 2, 2d edition. Munich: 1979.

Buchmann, Erika. *Die Frauen von Ravensbrück* [The Women of Ravensbrück]. Berlin: 1961.

Clebert, Jean-Paul. *Das Volk der Zigeuner* [The Gypsy Nation]. Vienna: 1964.

Cowell, Alan. "Attack on Austrian Gypsies Deepens Fear of Neo-Nazis," *New York Times,* February 21, 1995, A1 and A5.

Crowe, David, and John Kolsti, eds. *The Gypsies of Eastern Europe.* Armonk, N.Y.: M. E. Sharpe, 1991.

———. *A History of the Gypsies of Eastern Europe and Russia.* New York: St. Martin's Press, 1995.

Deutschkron, Inge. *Denn ihrer war die Hölle. Kinder in Gettos und Lagern* [For Theirs Was Hell. Children in Ghettoes and Camps]. Cologne: 1965.

Dietmar, Udo. *Häftling X in der Hölle auf Erden!* [Inmate X in Hell on Earth]. Mainz: 1946.

Döring, Hans-Joachim. "Die Motive der Zigeunerdeportation vom Mai 1940" [The Reasons for the Gypsy Deportation of May 1940]. *VfZG* 7, No. 4. Stuttgart: 1959, 418–28.

———. *Die Zigeuner im nationalsozialistischen Staat* [The Gypsies in the National Socialist State]. *Kriminologische Schriftenreihe,* Vol. 12. Hamburg: 1964.

Dörner, Klaus, Christiane Haerlin, Veronika Rau, Renate Schernus, and Arnd Schwendy. *Der Krieg gegen die psychisch Kranken* [The War against the Mentally Ill]. Rehburg-Loccum: 1980.

Dostal, Walter. "Die Zigeuner in Österreich" [The Gypsies in Austria]. *Archiv für Völkerkunde.* Vienna: 1955, 1–14.

———. "Zigeunerleben und Gegenwart" [Gypsy Life and the Present]. In Walter Starkie, ed., *Auf Zigeunerspuren.* Munich: 1957, 175–301.

Erhardt, Helmut. *Euthanasie und Vernichtung 'lebensunwerten' Lebens* [Euthanasia and Extermination of Life 'Unworthy of Living']. Stuttgart: 1965.

Faschismus—Getto—Massenmord [Fascism—Ghetto—Mass Murder]. 2d edition. Berlin: Jüdisches Historisches Institut in Warschau, 1960.

Feher, Gyorgy. *Struggling for Ethnic Identity. The Gypsies of Hungary.* New York: Human Rights Watch, 1993.

Feldscher, Werner. "Rassen und Erbpflege im deutschen Recht" [Race and Heritage Cultivation in German Law]. *Rechtspflege und Verwaltung,* 3. Berlin: 1943.

Ferst, Elisabeth. *Fertilität und Kriminalität der Zigeuner. Eine statistische Untersuchung* [Fertility and Criminality of the Gypsies. A Statistical Study]. Munich: 1943.

Ficowski, Jerzy. *Cyganie na polskich drogach.* Working translation by Martin Pollak, Warsaw (DÖW). Cracow: 1965.

——. *The Gypsies in Poland. History and Customs.* Warsaw: Interpress Publishers, 1989.

Friedman, Philip. *Roads to Extinction. Essays on the Holocaust.* Ada June Friedman, ed. New York: Conference on Jewish Social Studies, 1980.

——. *Their Brother's Keepers.* New York: Holocaust Library, 1978.

Gedenkbuch. Die Sinti und Roma im Konzentrationslager Auschwitz-Birkenau [Memorial Volume. The Sinti and Roma in Concentration Camp Auschwitz-Birkenau]. 2 Vols. Munich: Staatliches Museum Auschwitz-Birkenau in Zusammenarbeit mit dem Dokumentations-und Kulturzentrum Deutscher Sinti und Roma, Heidelberg, 1993.

Geigges, Anita, and Bernhard W. Wette. Zigeuner heute. Verfolgung und Diskriminierung in der BDR [Gypsies Today. Persecution and Discrimination in the Federal Republic of Germany]. Bornheim-Merten: Lamuv-Verlag, 1979.

Geisel, Eike, ed. *Vielleicht war das alles erst der Anfang* [Maybe It All Was Only the Beginning]. Hanna Lévy-Hass. Tagebuch aus dem KZ Bergen-Belsen 1944–1945. Berlin: 1979.

Gesellmann, Georg. "Die Zigeuner im Burgenland in der Zwischenkriegszeit" [The Gypsies in Burgenland in the Interwar Years]. Die Geschichte einer Diskriminierung. Phil. Diss. Vienna: 1989.

Gmelin, Walter. "Zur Sterilisierungsfrage! Soll nur bei Einwilligung sterilisiert werden?" [On the Sterilization Issue! Shall Sterilization Occur Only by Consent?]. *Ziel und Weg,* Ser. 3, No. 6. Munich: 1933, 116–18.

Göbbels, Hans. *Die Asozialen. Über Wesen und Begriff der Asozialität* [The Asocials. On the Essence and Concept of Asocialism]. Hamburg: 1947.

Göhring, Walter, and Werner Pfeifenberger. *60 Jahre Burgenland.* Eine Dokumentation. Mattersburg: 1981.

Gotovitch, José. "Quelques données rélatives à l'éxtermination des Tsiganes de Belgique" [Some Reasons/Causes for Gypsy Extermination in Belgium]. *Cahiers d'Histoire de la Seconde Guerre Mondiale,* No. 4. Brussels: 1976.

Grellmann, Heinrich M. G. *Historischer Versuch über die Zigeuner* [A Historical Study of the Gypsies]. 2d edition. Göttingen: 1987.

Günther, Hans F. K. *Rassenkunde des deutschen Volkes* [Racial Studies of the German People]. München: 1937.

Günther, Wolfgang. *"Ach, Schwester, ich kann nicht mehr tanzen. . . . " Sinti und Roma im KZ Bergen-Belsen* [Sister, I Cannot Dance Any Longer. Sinti and Roma in Concentration Camp Bergen-Belsen]. Hannover: 1990.

Hancock, Ian F. *Land of Pain: Five Centuries of Gypsy Slavery and Persecution.* Buda, Tex.: World Romani Union, 1986.

——. *The Pariah Syndrome: An Account of Gypsy Slavery and Persecution.* Ann Arbor, Mich.: Karoma Publishers, 1987.

Haslinger, Michaela. "Rom heißt Mensch. Zur Geschichte des 'geschichtslosen Zigeunervolkes' in der Steiermark (1850–1938)" [To Be a Rom is to be Human. Regarding the 'Gypsy People Without History' in Steiermark (1850–1938)]. Phil. Diss. Graz: 1985.

Heinschink, Mozes F., and Ursula Hemetek, eds. *Roma. Das unbekannte Volk. Schicksal und Kultur* [Roma. The Unknown People. Fate and Culture]. Vienna: 1994.

Herbermann, Nanda. *Der gesegnete Abgrund* [The Blessed Abyss]. Nuremberg: 1948.

Hilberg, Raul. *The Destruction of the European Jews.* Chicago: Harper and Row, 1961.

Hoehne, Werner Kurt. *Die Vereinbarkeit der deutschen Zigeunergesetze und verordnungen mit dem Reichsrecht, insbesondere der Reichsverfassung* [The Integration of German Gypsy Laws and Ordinances with the Law of the Reich, Especially the Constitution]. Heidelberg: 1929.

Hohmann, Joachim S. *Geschichte der Zigeunerverfolgung in Deutschland* [History of Gypsy Persecution in Germany]. Frankfurt: Campus Verlag, 1988.

——. *Robert Ritter und die Erben der Kriminologie. Zigeunerforschung im Nationalsozialismus und in Westdeutschland im Zeichen des Rassismus* [Robert Ritter and the Heirs of Criminology. Gypsy Research during the National Socialist Period and West Germany from the Perspective of Racism]. Frankfurt: 1991.

——. *Vorurteile und Mythen in pädagogischen Prozessen* [Prejudices and Myths in Pedagogical Processes]. Lollar: 1978.

——. *Zigeuner und Zigeunerwissenschaft. Ein Beitrag zur Grundlagenforschung und Dokumentation des Völkermords im 'Dritten Reich'* [Gypsies and Gypsy Scholarship. A Contribution to the Foundational Research and Documentation of Genocide in the 'Third Reich']. Marburg: 1980.

Hohmann, Joachim S., and Roland Schoff, eds. *Zigeunerleben. Beiträge zur Sozialgeschichte einer Verfolgung* [Gypsy Lives. Contributions to the Social History of a Persecution]. Darmstadt: 1979.

Horkheimer, Max. "Über das Vorurteil" [On Prejudice]. *Frankfurter Beiträge zur Soziologie* [Frankfurt Contributions to Sociology]. In Theodor W. Adorno and Walter Dirks, eds., *Sociologica II. Reden und Vorträge,* Vol. 10, 2d edition. Frankfurt: 1967, 87–93.

IG-Farben. Auschwitz-Massenmord [IG-Farben. Auschwitz Mass Murder]. Berlin: Arbeitsgruppe ehemaliger Häftlinge des KZ Auschwitz, 1964.

In der Maur, Wolf. *Die Zigeuner. Wanderer zwischen den Welten* [The Gypsies. Wanderers between the Worlds]. Vienna: 1978.

Internationaler Militärgerichtshof [International Military Court]. 42 Vols. Nuremberg: 1947–1949.

Jahrbuch 1990 des Dokumentationsarchivs des österreichischen Widerstandes [1990 Yearbook of DÖW]. Vienna: 1990.

Jochimsen, Lucretia. *Zigeuner heute. Untersuchung einer Außenseitergruppe in einer deutschen Mittelstadt* [Gypsies Today. Studies of an Outsider Group in a Middle-Size German City]. Stuttgart: 1963.

Justin, Eva. "Lebensschicksale artfremd erzogener Zigeunerkinder und ihrer Nachkommen" [Fate of Gypsy Children and Their Descendants Raised Outside Their Tribe]. *Veröffentlichungen aus dem Gebiete des Volksgesundheitsdienstes,* Vol. 57, No. 4. Berlin: 1944.

Kaniak, Gustav, ed. *Das österreichische Strafgesetz mit den wichtigsten strafrechtlichen Nebengesetzen* [Austrian Penal Law and the Most Important Secondary Laws]. *Österreichische Gesetze,* Vol. 4, 4th edition. Vienna: 1956.

Karpati, Mirella, ed. *Sinti und Roma. Gestern und heute* [Sinti and Roma. Yesterday and Today]. Bozen o.J.: 1993/94.

Kater, Michael H. *Das 'Ahnenerbe' der SS 1935–1945. Ein Beitrag zur Kulturpolitik des Dritten Reiches* [The 'Legacy' of the SS 1935–1945. A Contribution to the Cultural Politics of the Third Reich]. Stuttgart: 1974.

Kaul, Friedrich Karl. *Ärzte in Auschwitz* [Auschwitz Doctors]. Berlin: 1968.

Kautzky, Benedikt. *Teufel und Verdammte* [Devils and Damned People]. Vienna: 1968.

Kenrick, Donald. *Nazi-Deutschland und die Zigeuner. Sinti und Roma im ehemaligen KZ Bergen-Belsen* [Nazi Germany and the Gypsies. Sinti and Roma in Former Concentration Camp Bergen-Belsen]. Göttingen: 1980.

Kenrick, Donald, and Grattan Puxon. *Sinti and Roma. The Destiny of Europe's Gypsies.* London: Chatto; Heinemann Educational for Sussex University Press, 1972.

———. *Sinti und Roma—die Vernichtung eines Volkes im NS-Staat* [Sinti and Roma—The Destruction of a People in the National Socialist State]. Göttingen: 1981.

Khonig, Ulrich. *Sinti und Roma unter dem Nationalsozialismus. Verfolgung und Widerstand* [Sinti and Roma during National Socialism. Persecution and Resistance]. Bochum: N. Brockmeyer, 1989.

Klamper, Elisabeth. "Persecution and Annihilation of Roma and Sinti, 1938–1945." *Journal of the Gypsy Lore Society,* Ser. 5, Vol. 3, No. 2 (Aug. 1993): 55–65.

Knobloch, Johann. *Romani-Texte aus dem Burgenland* [Romani Texts from Burgenland]. *Burgenländische Forschungen,* 24. Eisenstadt: 1953.

Knobloch, Johann, and Inge Sudbrack, eds. "Zigeunerkundliche Forschungen" [Gypsy Research]. *Innsbrucker Beiträge zur Kulturwissenschaft,* Sonderheft 42. Innsbruck: 1977.

Kogon, Eugen. *Der SS-Staat. Das System der deutschen Konzentrationslager* [The SS State. The System of German Concentration Camps]. 10th edition. Munich: 1981.

Körner, Erich. "Die Zigeuner im Spiegel der Stegersbacher Ortschronik" [The Gypsies in Stegersbach History]. *Das Menschenrecht,* Ser. 22, Vol. 118, No. 1. Vienna: 1967, 3–7.

Krämer, Robert. "Rassische Untersuchungen an den 'Zigeuner'-Kolonien Lause und Altengraben bei Berleburg (Westf.) [Racial Research in the 'Gypsy' Colonies Lause and Altengraben Near Berleburg (Westphalia). *Archiv für Rassen-und Gesellschaftsbiologie,* Vol. 31, No. 1. Munich: 1937/38, 33–56.

Kranz, H. W. *Die Gemeinschaftsunfähigen* [The Asocials]. Ein Beitrag zur wissenschaftlichen und praktischen Lösung des sogenannten Asozialenproblems. Gießen: 1939/41.

——. "Zigeuner, wie sie wirklich sind" [Gypsies, As They Really Are]. *Neues Volk.* Supplement to *Deutsches Ärzteblatt.* Berlin: 1957, 21–27.

Kraus, Ota, and Erich Kulka. *Massenmord und Profit* [Mass Murder and Profit]. Berlin: 1963.

——. *Die Todesfabrik* [The Death Factory]. Berlin: 1957.

Kühnrich, Heinz. *Der KZ-Staat. Rolle und Entwicklung der faschistischen Konzentrationslager 1933–1945* [The Concentration Camp State. Role and Development of Fascist Concentration Camps 1933–1945]. Berlin: 1960.

Langbein, Hermann. *Der Auschwitz-Prozeß. Eine Dokumentation* [The Auschwitz Trial. A Documentation]. Vienna: 1965.

——. *. . . nicht wie die Schafe zur Schlachtbank. Widerstand in den nationalsozialistischen Konzentrationslagern* [. . . Not Like Sheep to Slaughter. Resistance in National Socialist Concentration Camps]. Frankfurt: 1980.

——. *Die Stärkeren. Ein Bericht* [The Stronger Ones. A Report]. Vienna: 1949.

Langbein, H., and E. Lingens-Reiner, eds. *Auschwitz. Zeugnisse und Berichte* [Auschwitz. Testimony and Reports]. Frankfurt: 1962.

Liebich, Richard. *Die Zigeuner in ihrem Wesen und in ihrer Sprache* [Gypsy Essence and Language]. Wiesbaden: 1863/1968.

Loewenstein, Rudolph M. *Psychoanalyse des Antisemitismus* [Psychoanalysis of Antisemitism]. Frankfurt: 1968.

Marsalek, Hans. *Die Geschichte des Konzentrationslagers Mauthausen* [The History of Concentration Camp Mauthausen]. Mauthausen: 1974.

Mayerhofer, Claudia. *Dorfzigeuner. Kultur und Gesellschaft der Burgenland-Roma von der ersten Republik bis zur Gegenwart* [Village Gypsies. Culture and Society of Burgenland-Roma from the First Republic to the Present]. Vienna: 1987.

Mazirel, Lau. "Die Verfolgung der 'Zigeuner' im Dritten Reich" [The Persecution of the 'Gypsies' in the Third Reich]. *Essays über Naziverbrechen* [Essays on Nazi Crimes]. Simon Wiesenthal gewidmet [Dedicated to Simon Wiesenthal]. Amsterdam: 1973, 123–76.

Memorial Book. The Gypsies at Auschwitz-Birkenau. Published by State Museum

Auschwitz-Birkenau, in cooperation with the Documentary and Cultural Center of German Sintis and Roms, Heidelberg. Munich: Saur, 1993.

Milton, Sybil. "Antechamber to Birkenau: The Zigeunerlager after 1933." In Helge Grabitz, Klaus Bästlein, Johannes Tuchel, et al., eds., *Die Normalität des Verbrechens: Bilanz und Perspektiven der Forschung zu den nationalsozialistischen Gewaltverbrechen; Festschrift für Wolfgang Scheffler zum 65. Geburtstag.* Berlin: Hentrich, 1994, 241–59.

——. "The Context of the Holocaust." *German Studies Review* 13, no. 2 (May 1990): 269–83.

——. Correspondence. *The History Teacher* 25, no. 4 (Aug. 1992): 515–21.

——. "Gypsies and the Holocaust." *The History Teacher* 24, no. 4 (Aug. 1991): 375–87.

——. "Holocaust: The Gypsies." In William S. Parsons, Israel W. Charny, and Samuel Totten, eds., *Genocide in the Twentieth Century: Critical Essays and Eyewitness Accounts.* New York: Garland Publishing, 1995, 209–64.

——. "Nazi Policies toward Roma and Sinti, 1933–1945," *Journal of the Gypsy Lore Society,* ser. 5, vol. 2, no. 1 (Feb. 1992): 1–18.

——. "The Racial Context of the Holocaust." *Social Education* 55, no. 2 (Feb. 1991): 106–10.

——. "Sinti und Roma als 'vergessene Opfergruppe' in der Gedenkstättenarbeit" [Sinti and Roma as 'Forgotten Victim Group' in Memorial Site Work]. In Edgar Bamberger, ed., *Der Völkermord an den Sinti und Roma in der Gedenkstättenarbeit* [Genocide of Sinti and Roma in Memorial Site Work]. Heidelberg: Dokumentations-und Kulturzentrum Deutscher Sinti und Roma, 1994, 53–60.

——. *The Story of Karl Stojka. A Childhood in Birkenau.* Washington, D.C.: U.S. Holocaust Memorial Museum, 1992.

——. "Vorstufe zur Vernichtung: Die Zigeunerlager nach 1933" [Prelude to Destruction: The Gypsy Camps after 1933]. *Vierteljahreshefte für Zeitgeschichte* 43, no. 1 (Jan. 1995): 115–30.

Milton, Sybil, and David Lübke. "Locating the Victim: An Overview of Census-taking, Tabulation Technology, and Persecution in Nazi Germany." *IEEE Annals of the History of Computing* 16, no. 3 (fall 1994): 25–39.

Mitscherlich, Alexander, and Fred Mielke. *Medizin ohne Menschlichkeit. Dokumente des Nürnberger Ärzteprozesses* [Medicine Without Humanity. Documents of the Nuremberg Doctors' Trial]. Frankfurt: 1948/1978.

Mode, Heinz, and Siegfried Wölfling. *Zigeuner. Der Weg einen Volkes in Deutschland* [Gypsies. The Path of a People in Germany]. Leipzig: 1968.

Moravek, Karl. *Ein Beitrag zur Rassenkunde der 'Burgenländischen Zigeuner'* [A Contribution to the Racial Studies of 'Burgenland Gypsies']. Vienna: 1939.

Müller-Hill, Benno. *Murderous Science. Elimination by Scientific Selection of Jews, Gypsies, and Others, Germany 1933–1945.* Translated by George R. Fraser. Oxford: Oxford University Press, 1988.

Novitch, Miriam. *Contribution à l'étude du génocide des Tziganes sous le régime nazi*

[Contribution to the Study of the Gypsy Genocide under the Nazi Regime].
Prague: 1963.

Peterson, P., and U. Liedtke. "Zur Entschädigung zwangssterilisierter Zigeuner"
[On Reparations for Forcibly Sterilized Gypsies]. *Der Nervenarzt,* Vol. 42,
No. 4. Berlin: 1971, 197–205.

Pischel, Richard. *Beitrag zur Kenntnis der deutschen Zigeuner* [Contribution to the
Understanding of German Gypsies]. Halle: 1894.

Poller, Walter. *Arztschreiber in Buchenwald* [Medical Recorder in Buchenwald].
Hamburg: 1946.

Porter, Jack N., ed. *Confronting History and Holocaust. Collected Essays, 1972–1982.*
Lanham, Md.: University Press of America, 1983.

——. *Genocide and Human Rights.* Lanham, Md.: University Press of America,
1982.

Portschy, Tobias. *Die Zigeunerfrage* [The Gypsy Question]. Denkschrift des Burgenländischen Landeshauptmannes. Eisenstadt: 1938.

Pott, A. F. *Die Zigeuner in Europa und Asien* [The Gypsies in Europe and Asia].
2 Vols. (Erstauflage, Halle 1844–45). Leipzig: 1964.

Pross, Christian. *Wiedergutmachung. Der Kleinkrieg gegen die Opfer* [Reparations.
The Petty War against the Victims]. Frankfurt: 1988.

Puxon, Grattan. "Forgotten Victims. Plight of the Gypsies." *Patterns of Prejudice,*
Institute of Jewish Affairs, Vol. 11, No. 2. London: 1977, 23–29.

Ramati, Alexander. *And the Violins Stopped Playing. A Story of the Gypsy Holocaust.*
London: Hodder and Staughton, 1985.

Reinbeck, Emil. *Die Zigeuner. Eine wissenschaftliche Monographie nach historischen
Quellen bearbeitet* [The Gypsies. A Scholarly Monograph from Historical
Sources]. Salzkotten: 1861.

Reitlinger, Gerald. *Die Endlösung. Hitlers Versuch der Ausrottung der Juden Europas
1939–1945* [The Final Solution. Hitler's Attempt to Exterminate the Jews
of Europe 1939–1945]. Berlin: 1956.

Rieger, Barbara. " 'Zigeunerleben' in Salzburg 1930–1943. Die regionale Zigeu-
nerfolgung als Vorstufe zur planmäßigen Vernichtung in Auschwitz"
["Gypsy Life" in Salzburg 1930–1943. The Regional Gypsy Persecution as
a Preliminary Step to Systematic Destruction in Auschwitz]. Dipl. Arb. Vienna: 1990.

Ritter, Robert. "Die Bestandsaufnahme der Zigeuner und Zigeunermischlinge
in Deutschland" [Taking Account of Gypsies and 'Half-Breeds' in Ger-
many]. *Der öffentliche Gesundheitsdienst,* Sonderdruck, Vol. 6, No. 21.
Leipzig: 1941, 477–89.

——. "Die Zigeunerfrage und das Zigeunerbastardproblem" [The Gypsy
Question and the Problem of the Gypsy Bastard]. *Fortschritte der Erbpathologie,* Ser. 3. Leipzig: 1939, 1–20.

——. *"Zigeuner und Landfahrer." Der nichtseßhafte Mensch* [Gypsies and Travel-
ers. The Nomadic Person]. Ein Beitrag zur Neugestaltung der Raum- und
Menschenordnung im Großdeutschen Reich. Munich: 1938, 71–88.

Rose, Romani. *Bürgerrechte für Sinti und Roma. Das Buch zum Rassismus in Deutschland* [Civil Rights for Sinti and Roma. The Book on Racism in Germany]. Heidelberg: Zentralrat Deutscher Sinti und Roma, 1987.

Rose, Romani, and Walter Weiss. *Sinti und Roma im "Dritten Reich". Das Programm der Vernichtung durch Arbeit* [Sinti and Roma in the Third Reich. The Program of Extermination through Work]. Göttingen: Zentralrat Deutscher Sinti und Roma, 1991.

Rosenkranz, Herbert. *Verfolgung und Selbstbehauptung der Juden in Österreich 1938–1945* [Persecution and Self-Assertion of Jews in Austria 1938–1945]. Vienna: 1978.

Rückerl, Adalbert, ed. *NS-Vernichtungslager im Spiegel deutscher Strafprozesse* [National Socialist Death Camps Seen through German Penal Proceedings]. 2d edition. Munich: 1978.

Sacher, Hermann, ed. *Staatslexikon* [State Dictionary]. Vol. 5: Stichwort Zigeuner, 5. Rev. edition. Freiburg i. Br.: 1932, 1594–1600.

Saller, Karl. *Die Rassenlehre des Nationalsozialismus in Wissenschaft und Propaganda* [National Socialist Racial Theory in Science and Propaganda]. Darmstadt: 1961.

Schmitt-Egner, Peter. *Kolonialismus und Faschismus* [Colonialism and Fascism]. Eine Studie zur historischen und begrifflichen Genesis faschistischer Bewußtseinsformen am deutschen Beispiel. Gießen: 1975.

Schwicker, Johann H. *Die Zigeuner in Ungarn und Siebenbürgen* [The Gypsies in Hungary and Siebenbürgen]. Vienna: 1883.

Seible, Theresia. "Widerstand von Frauen im Dritten Reich. Tonbandprotokoll eines Vortrags" [Women's Resistance in the Third Reich. Tape Recording of a Lecture]. *Courage*, No. 5. Berlin: 1981.

Sinti und Roma im ehemaligen KZ Bergen-Belsen am 27. Okt. 1979 [Sinti and Roma in Former Concentration Camp Bergen-Belsen on October 27, 1979]. Eine Dokumentation der "Gesellschaft für bedrohte Völker" und des "Verbands deutscher Sinti." Göttingen: Gesellschaft für bedrohte Völker, 1980.

Soest, George von. *Zigeuner zwischen Verfolgung und Integration. Geschichte, Lebensbedingungen und Eingliederungsversuche* [Gypsies between Persecution and Integration. History, Living Conditions and Attempts at Integration]. Weinheim: Beltz, 1979.

Spira, Elisabeth T., and Miriam Wiegele. "Das Getto von Oberwart" [Ghetto Oberwart]. *Extrablatt*, Ser. 1, No. 1. (Sept. 1977): 23–26.

Spritzer, Jenny. *Ich war Nr. 10291* [I was No. 10291]. Tatsachenbericht einer Schreiberin der politischen Abteilung aus dem KL Auschwitz. Zürich: 1947.

Stadler, Karl. *Österreich 1938–1945.* Im Spiegel der NS-Akten. Slg. *Das Einsame Gewissen,* Bd. III. Vienna: 1966.

Staff, Ilse, ed. *Justiz im Dritten Reich. Eine Dokumentation* [Justice in the Third Reich. A Documentation]. Frankfurt: 1978.

Steinmetz, Selma. "Die 'deutsche Rassenforschung' ist mitverantwortlich für die NS-Zigeunerverfolgung" [German 'Racial Research' Is Coresponsible for National Socialist Gypsy Persecution]. *Mitteilungen zur Zigeunerkunde,* No. 9. Alzenau: 1978, 2–4.

———. "Zur Geschichte der Zigeunerdiskriminierung" [(Contribution to the) History of Gypsy Discrimination]. *Das Menschenrecht,* Ser. 27, Vol. 148, No. 1. Vienna: 1972, 16.

———. "Die NS-Zigeunerverfolgung im Licht der Gegenwart" [National Socialist Gypsy Persecution Seen against the Present]. *Das Menschenrecht,* Ser. 32, Vol. 171, No. 4. Vienna: 1977, 9–11.

———. "Österreichs Zigeuner. Eine Minderheit besonderer Art" [Austrian Gypsies. A Minority of a Special Kind]. *Arbeit und Wirtschaft,* No. 2. Vienna: 1972, 20–25.

———. *Österreichs Zigeuner im NS-Staat* [Austria's Gypsies in the National Socialist State]. Monogaphien zur Zeitgeschichte. Vienna: 1966.

———. "Die Problematik der Zigeunerintegration am Wiener Stadtrand" [The Problem of Gypsy Integration at the Outskirts of Vienna]. *Das Menschenrecht,* Ser. 24, Vol. 137, No. 2. Vienna: 1969, 7–10.

Strafgesetzbuch mit den wichtigsten Nebengesetzen [Penal Code Book with the Most Important Secondary Laws]. 6th edition. Munich: 1939.

Streck, Bernhard. "Die 'Bekämpfung' des Zigeunerunwesens" [The 'Fight against' the Gypsy Vermin]. In Tilman Zülch, ed., *In Auschwitz vergast, bis heute verfolgt* [Gassed in Auschwitz, Still Persecuted Today]. Reinbek bei Hamburg: Gesellschaft für bedrohte Völker, 1979, 64–87.

———. "Zigeuner unter dem Nationalsozialismus" [Gypsies during National Socialism]. In Edith Gerth, Reimer Gronemeyer, Mark Münzel, and Bernhard Streck, *Projekt Tsiganologie.* Gießen: 1978, 16–28.

Stuckart, Wilhelm, and Hans Globke. *Kommentare zur deutschen Rassengesetzgebung* [Commentaries on German Racial Laws], Vol. 1. Munich: 1936.

Szymanski, Tadeusz, Danuta Szymanski, and Tadeusz Sniezzko. "Über den 'Krankenbau' im Zigeuner-Familienlager in Auschwitz-Birkenau" [On the 'Hospital Wing' in the Gypsy Family Camp Auschwitz-Birkenau]. *'Auschwitz'-Anthologie,,* Vol. 2, Pt. 2. Warsaw: 1970, 1–43.

Tenenbaum, Joseph L. *Race and Reich. The Story of an Epoch.* New York: 1956.

Thiel, Helga. "Die Zigeuner in Neustift an der Lafnitz" [Neustift on Lafnitz Gypsies]. *Österreichische Zeitschrift für Volkskunde,* Vol. 28. Vienna: 1974, 269–80.

Thurner, Erika. *Kurzgeschichte des Nationalsozialistischen Zigeunerlagers in Lackenbach 1940 bis 1945* [Short History of the National Socialist Gypsy Camp in Lackenbach 1940–1945]. Eisenstadt: Amt der Bgld. Landesregierung, Sozialabteilung: Landesfonds für die Opfer des Krieges und Faschimus, 1984.

———. "Ortsfremde, asoziale Gemeinschaftsschädlinge"—die Konsequenzen des 'Anschlusses' für Sinti und Roma (Zigeuner) ["Alien, Asocial Community Enemies"—the Consequences of the *Anschluß* for Sinti and Roma]. In Rudolf G. Ardelt and Hans Hautmann, eds., *Arbeiterschaft und Nationalsozialismus in Österreich.* Vienna: 1990.

————. *Sinti- und Romafrauen: Die Ambivalenz des Ethnischen* [Sinti and Roma Women: The Ambivalence of the Ethnic]. *Nahe Fremde, fremde Nähe.* Frauen forschen zu Ethnos, Kultur, Geschlecht, Reihe Frauenforschung, Band 24. Vienna: WIDEE (Wissenschafterinnen in der Europäischen Ethnologie), 1993.

————. "Die Verfolgung von Minderheiten-Zigeuner" [The Persecution of Minorities—Gypsies]. *Widerstand und Verfolgung in Salzburg 1934–1945*, Vol. 2. Vienna: Dokumentationsarchiv des österreichischen Widerstandes, 1991.

Tyrnauer, Gabrielle. *The Fate of the Gypsies during the Holocaust.* Washington, D.C.: U.S. Holocaust Memorial Council, 1985.

————. *Gypsies and the Holocaust. A Bibliography and Introductory Essay.* Montreal: Interuniversity Center for European Studies [and] Montreal Institute for Genocide Studies, 1989.

Veiter, Theodor. *Das Recht der Volksgruppen und Sprachminderheiten in Österreich* [The Rights of Nationality Groups and Linguistic Minorities in Austria]. Vienna: 1970.

————. "Die Zigeuner in Österreich" [The Gypsies in Austria]. *Berichte und Informationen,* Ser. 18, No. 901. Salzburg: 1963, 13–14.

Vermehren, Isa. *Reise durch den letzten Akt* [Journey through the Final Act]. Hamburg: 1947.

Vinnai, Gerhard. "Der Führer war an allem schuld. Zur Sozialpsychologie des 'Dritten Reiches' " [It Was All the Führer's Fault. On the Social Psychology of the Third Reich]. *Terror und Hoffnung in Deutschland 1933–1945.* Leben im Faschismus. Reinbek bei Hamburg: Beck, Johannes, et al., 1980, 458–75.

von zur Mühlen, Patrik. *Rassenideologien. Geschichte und Hintergründe* [Racial Ideologies. History and Reasons]. Berlin: 1977.

Vossen, Rüdiger. *Zigeuner: Roma, Sinti, Gitanos, Gypsies. Zwischen Verfolgung und Romantisierung* [Gypsies: Roma, Sinti, Gitano, Gypsies. Between Persecution and Romantization]. Frankfurt: 1983.

Weiler, Margret. *Zur Frage der Integration der Zigeuner in der Bundesrepublik Deutschland* [On the Question of Integration of the Gypsies in the Federal Republic of Germany]. Cologne: 1979.

Whitacker, Ben. "Zur sozialpsychologischen Analyse von Minderheitenkonflikten" [On the Social Psychological Analysis of Minority Conflicts]. In Ruprecht Kurzrock, ed., *Minderheiten, Vol. 17: Forschung und Information.* Berlin: 1974.

Widerstand und Verfolgung Im Burgenland 1934–1945 [Resistance and Persecution in Burgenland 1934–1945]. Eine Dokumentation. Vienna: Dokumentationsarchiv des österreichischen Widerstandes, 1975/1979.

Widerstand und Verfolgung in Wien 1934–1945. Vol. 3. Vienna: 1975, 357.

Wiegele, Miriam. "Die Zigeuner in Österreich" [The Gypsies in Austria]. In Tilman Zülch, ed., *In Auschwitz vergast, bis heute verfolgt.* Reinbek bei Hamburg: 1979, 261–72.

Wiesenthal, Simon. *Doch die Mörder leben.* München: 1967.

———. The Murderers among Us. New York: McGraw Hill, 1967.

Wilms, Anno. *Zigeuner* [Gypsics]. Texte von Mirella Karpati und Sergius Golowin. Zürich: 1972.

Wippermann, Wolfgang. *Das Leben in Frankfurt zur NS-Zeit* [Life in Frankfurt during the Nazi Period]. Vol. 2. Die nationalsozialistische Zigeunerverfolgung. Frankfurt: 1986.

Wulf, Josef. "Lodz—Das letzte Ghetto auf polnischem Boden" [Lodz—The Last Ghetto on Polish Soil]. *Schriftenreihe der Bundeszentrale für Heimatdienst,* No. 59, 1st edition. Bonn: 1962.

Würth, A. "Bemerkungen zur Zigeunerfrage und Zigeunerforschung in Deutschland" [Comments Regarding the Gypsy Question and Gypsy Scholarship in Germany]. *Anthropologischer Anzeiger,* Ser. 9. Stuttgart: 1938, 95–98.

Yates, Dora. *My Gypsy Days. Recollections of a Romani Rawnie.* London: Phoenix House, 1953.

Zimmermann, Michael. "Die nationalsozialistische Vernichtungspolitik gegen Sinti und Roma" [National Socialist Politics of Destruction of Sinti and Roma]. *Politik und Zeitgeschichte.* Supplement to weekly *Das Parlament.* Bonn, 1987, pp. B 16–17.

———. *Verfolgt, vertrieben, vernichtet. Die nationalsozialistische Vernichtungspolitik gegen Sinti und Roma* [Persecuted, Exiled, Murdered. National Socialist Extermination Politics against Sinti and Roma]. Essen: 1989.

Zmarzlik, Hans-Günter. "Der Sozialdarwinismus in Deutschland als geschichtliches Problem" [Social Darwinism in Germany as a Historical Problem]. *VfZG* 11. Stuttgart: 1963, 246–73.

Zülch, Tilman, ed. *In Auschwitz vergast, bis heute verfolgt* [Gassed in Auschwitz, Still Persecuted Today]. Reinbek bei Hamburg: 1979.

Unpublished Sources: Files, Archives, Other

Aktenvermerk des Landesgendarmerie-Kommando, Salzburg, zum Gespräch mit Ernst Pilz. Salzburg, February 1980.

Banny, Leopold. Das Anhaltelager für Zigeuner in Lackenbach [The Collection Camp for Gypsies in Lackenbach], 8 Seiten Typoskript. Lackenbach o.J.

Bundesministerium für Inneres, Wien (BMI). Aktenzahl: 84.426-4/48, 47.558-2/52, 68.538-2/52, 65.304-2/52, 99.851-2/53, 119.843-2/53, 55.390-13/54, 58.636-2/54, 79.899-2/56, 178.401-2/56, 95.353-2/57, 55.626-18/68.

Burggasser, Herbert Michael. Die Zigeunerverfolgungen in Österreich. Dokumentation des Zigeuneranhaltelagers Lackenbach. Seminararbeit am Zeitgesch.-Inst. d. Univ. Wien, Vienna, 1977.

Dokumentationsarchiv des österreichischen Widerstandes, Wien (DÖW). Aktenbestände: 333, 668, 696, 1212, 1371, 1978, 2527, 2528, 2570, 2573, 2589, 2606, 4969, 9626, 10501 a, b, c; 11278, 11291, 11293, 11340, 11477, 12232, 12486, 12543.

Duna, W. *Gypsies a Persecuted Race*. See USHMM Library Archives Holdings.

Eidesstattliche Erklärung Julius Brunner an die Entschädigungsbehörde, Köln, March 23, 1957.

Ficowski, Jerzy. "Vernichtung" [Destruction]. *Polnische Zigeuner*. Historische und Sittenskizzen. Warsaw: 1953. Übersetzung von einem Warschauer Juristen (IfZ Munich).

Gendarmerieberichte der Salzburger Rayonsposten, 1937–1940.

Hohmann, Joachim S. "Versagen der deutschen (Zigeuner-) Wissenschaft." Vortrag anläßlich des 3. Internationalen Roma-Kongresses in Göttingen, May 20, 1981 (12 Seiten MS).

Institut für Zeitgeschichte, München (IfZ): verschiedene Nürnberger Dokumente; Bestände—Stichwort Zigeuner: MA 438, 145/1, 1159, 446, 423, Z 1047, Fa-199/51; Erlaßsammlung 'vorbeugende Verbrechensbekämpfung,' Schriftenreihe des RKPA, Nr. 15. Berlin 1941: Dc-1702.

Interview mit Julius Hodosi, Wien. Geführt von Emmi Moravitz, im Sept. 1957.

Mayerhofer, Claudia. Die Zigeuner im Burgenland. Hausarbeit (Völkerkunde) Univ. Wien, Vienna, 1977.

Österreichisches Staatsarchiv, Abt. Allgemeines Verwaltungsarchiv Wien (AVA). Bürckel-Akten: 1360, 1756, 2000 und 2473; Bka-33/1-1930; Bka-Präs. 551 o.Z.; AVA-Unterricht: 2a-41906-a, 2a-313.026-a/39, IV-3a-327.994/39, VI-9b-606-VII/39.

Parcer, Jan. *Das Schicksal der Sinti und Roma im KL Auschwitz-Birkenau*, 1994, See USHMM Library Archives Holdings.

Piper, Franciszek. *How Many Perished Jews, Poles, Gypsies . . .*, 1992. See USHMM Library Archives Holdings.

Postenchronik Schwarzach. Abschriften vom 25.10.39 und 13.8.1940 zum LGK-Befehl, E.No. 2106/1-36/80 vom 8.1.1940.

Staatsarchiv Nürnberg. Nürnberger Kriegsverbrecherprozesse: Fall 1 bis 12, bes. Fall 1-Ärzteprozeß und Fall 4-Pohlprozeß. Fall 1: B 1, 11-4, 12-5, 13-6, 19-12/ C 1/ D 10, C + D/ D 11-2 G E 6 +9/Q 5/ T 10, A-G/ X 6 +7/ Y 5. Fall 4: B 8 IV, VI/ B 9/ B 41/ P 6 +7, alles Rep. 501. Verschiedene Nürnberger Dokumente, Rep. 502 I.

Teleobjektiv-Sendung vom 23.5.1979. Interview mit Herrn Weinrich. Manuskript: 9/122/223.

Totenbuch (Totenbeschauprotokoll) des Lackenbacher Gemeindearztes, ab 1939 fortlfd.

Vermerk aus dem Verfahren der Staatsanwaltschaft Köln (Az: 24 Js 429/61). Zentrale Stelle der Landesjustizverwaltung, Ludwigsburg.

Zentrales Staatsarchiv, Potsdam. Reichsjustizministerium (RJM), 20 Bl.; Reichslandbund/Pressearchiv (RlB/Press), Zigeunerproblem 1936-44, 45 Bl.;

Deutsche Arbeitsfront/Arbeitswissenschaftl. Inst. (DAP/AWJ), Zeitungs-
ausschnitte 1936–1941, 8 Bl.

Newspapers and Journals

Arbeiter-Zeitung, February 12, 1933 (Ein anderes Lied von den Zigeunern.)
Arbeiter-Zeitung, February 16, 1933 (Die 'zahmen' Zigeuner von Sulzriegel.)
Burgenländische Heimat, 10. Jg., 1930-17. Jg., 1937.
Burgenlandwacht, 1. Jg., 1930.
Der freie Burgenländer, 1. Jg., 1921-14. Jg., 1934.
Der Spiegel, Nr. 43, 1979 (Bei Hitler waren wir wenigstens Deutsche).
Die Neue Polizei, 5. Jg., Nr. 3 und 4; 11. Jg., Nr. 1 und 2. München 1951 bzw.
    1957.
Freies Burgenland, Nr. 40., Oct. 3, 1954, und Nr. 41, Oct. 10, 1954.
Gendarmerie-Rundschau, 1. Jg., Heft 4. Wien 1934.
Grenzmark Burgenland, Juli 17, 1938 und Sept. 4, 1938.
Journal of the Gypsy Lore Society (JGLS). Edinburgh: New Series (2), Volumes 1–8
    (1907–1916); Third Series, Volumes 1–3 (1922–1973), and Fourth Series,
    Volume 1, 1974.
Ödenburger Zeitung, 28. Jg., 1926.
Österreichische Neue Tageszeitung, Aug. 9, 1959 (Zigeuner: Von der Romantik
    blieb nur die Musik).
Vierte Welt aktuell. Hrsg. von der Gesellschaft für bedrohte Völker, No. 6, Aug.
    1979.
Volkstum im Südosten. Politische Monatsschrift. Wien, 1. Jg., 1939-19. Jg., 1942.
Volk und Rasse. Illustrierte Monatsschrift für deutsches Volkstum, 9. bis 13. Jg.
    München 1934–1938.

Eyewitness Reports by Sinti and Roma (Austria)

Stojka, Ceija. *Reisende auf dieser Welt.* Aus dem Leben einer Rom-Zigeunerin,
    hrsg. von Karin Berger [Travelers in this World]. Wien 1991.
Stojka, Ceija. *Wir leben im Verborgenen.* Erinnerungen einer Rom-Zigeunerin
    [We Live in Secret]. Hrsg. von Karin Berger. Wien 1988.
Stojka, Karl, and Reinhard Pohanka. *Auf der ganzen Welt zu Hause.* Das Leben
    und Wandern des Zigeuners Karl Stojka [At Home in the Entire World].
    Wien 1984.
Winter, Rosa. "Soviel wie eine Asche" [As Much as Ashes]. Karin Berger, Elisa-
    beth Holzinger, Lotte Podgornik, and Lisbeth N. Trallori. *Ich geb Dir einen
    Mantel, daß Du ihn noch in Freiheit tragen kannst.* Widerstehen im KZ. Öster-
    reichische Frauen erzählen. Wien 1987.

Videos

Genocide. "World at War" series, BBC. Sir Laurence Olivier, narrator.

Gladitz, Nina. "Zeit des Schweigens und der Dunkelheit." WDR 1983.

Huber, Norbert, Hermann Peseckas, and Erika Thurner. "Die Zeit heilt keine Wunden." Begegnung mit Zigeunern in Österreich. Österreich 1984/85.

Seybold, Katrin, and Melanie Spitta. "Wiedergutmachung—Das falsche Wort." ZDF 1989.

Index

Erika Thurner, Ph.D., is University Lecturer for Modern and Contemporary History at the University of Linz, Austria. Currently she is a Visiting Professor at the Institute for Political Science, University Innsbruck/Austria. Publications and research interests include the political and social history of Austria in the twentieth century, and minority, identity, ethnic, and gender studies.

Gilya Gerda Schmidt, Ph.D., is Associate Professor of Religious Studies and Chair of the Fern and Manfred Steinfeld Program in Judaic Studies, the University of Tennessee, Knoxville. She has previously published *Martin Buber's Formative Years: From German Culture to Jewish Renewal, 1897–1909* (University of Alabama Press, 1995).

DATE LOANED

38207800